P9-BZI-068

 **WHY HE DIDN'T CALL YOU BACK**

Also by Rachel Greenwald

*Find a Husband After 35: Using What
I Learned at Harvard Business School*

WHY HE DIDN'T CALL YOU BACK

1,000 Guys Reveal What They *Really*
Thought About You After Your Date

Rachel Greenwald

CROWN PUBLISHERS
NEW YORK

Library of Congress Cataloging-in-Publication Data
Greenwald, Rachel.
    Why he didn't call you back / Rachel Greenwald.—1st ed.
        p. cm.
    1. Single women—Psychology. 2. Men—Psychology. 3. Dating (Social
customs) I. Title. II. Title: Why he did not call you back.
    HQ800.2.G74 2009
    646.7'7—dc22   2008050509

ISBN 978-0-307-40653-8

Printed in the United States of America

Design by Cindy LaBreacht

10 9 8 7 6 5 4 3 2 1

First Edition

The definition of insanity
is doing the same thing over
and over again and expecting
different results.

—ALBERT EINSTEIN

Contents

 **WHY HE DIDN'T CALL YOU BACK**

 **CHAPTER 1**

Everyone Else
Is Into You—
So Why Not Him?

Why, Why, Why . . . ?

It's the new riddle of the Sphinx: "Why didn't he call me back?" You have a great date with a promising guy. You think it went well and expect to see him again . . . but then *poof!* He vanishes inexplicably. You sit around with your girlfriends and debate why he didn't call you back. What happened in between "I'll pick you up at eight PM" and *"poof"?* You speculate, you obsess, you rationalize, you justify. You want to know *why*. When your friends tell you, "It's not you, it's him," you want to know if they're trying to be nice or telling you the truth.

Guess what? There is someone who does know the truth about what really happened on your date. But it's not you. It's not your friends. And it's certainly not your mother. It's the guy you went out with. Which means you'll never know what really happened, right? Wrong. Of course, you'd never dream of asking him yourself because . . . well, who would do *that*? How embarrassing. So I decided to ask him for you! In fact, I asked a thousand hims. I interviewed one thousand guys to find out why you never heard from him again after the first date, or the first few dates. And I got some real answers. It turns out there are clear, consistent reasons why men don't call women back. Sure, sometimes the issue is all his—who hasn't gone out occasionally with a real jerk? But it turns out that many times we're sending out signals we might not be aware of. And the good news is that most of these signals are easy to fine-tune.

Think about this. What if you learned that three out of the last four guys who didn't call you back after a date had the same reason? And that it was something fixable? It might initially hurt your feelings, but it's important to find out the real issue. Especially if it's something that is not an accurate reflection of who you really are. In the early stage of dating, perception is reality. So when the right guy comes along in the future and there's no room for error, you want to be ready.

The Goal of a First Date

Here's a little multiple-choice quiz: What's the goal of a first date?

A) To allow a man to discover the real you, or
B) To get him to want a second date with you?

The answer, in my opinion, is B. If your first instinct was to say A, stop and consider something for a moment. No one can accurately assess a person on a first date, no matter how astute they think their instincts are. People behave abnormally (either a little or a lot) on first dates because they're either nervous, cynical, overeager, shy, keeping their guard up, having a bad day, or drinking too much. How many times have you jumped to negative conclusions about somebody new (a coworker or neighbor, for example), only to end up liking that person later? A man cannot really determine on a first date that you are warm, kind, brilliant, interesting, and great at math. What a man *can* determine on a first date is whether he is attracted to you and intrigued enough by you to want to know the real you. The problem is that he won't meet the real you (and you won't meet the real *him*) if he doesn't want a second date.

Let me be very clear: the goal here is not to change who you are or to pretend to be someone you're not. If you're a person with friends, interests, a career, you're obviously doing well. The point is not to change any of the qualities that make you *you*, but rather to keep the ball in your court. If more men call you for a second date, you increase your options and your opportunities to choose the man you prefer. If *you* don't want a second date with *him*, that's fine—you can politely decline when asked.

The New Dating World

So how easy is it to have a successful first date? Unfortunately, it's not easy at all. During the past ten years, I've observed a shocking trend from my vantage point in the dating business: there are more failed first dates today than ever before. If the upsurge in the dating industry is any proof, people are going on more and more first dates. But these connections aren't working because the number of single people is at an all-time high.[1] It's important to understand this current landscape, especially if you're newly single after a long relationship. The new dating world reflects three major challenges: the fallout from online dating, more sophisticated singles, and easier-to-obtain sex.

1) THE FALLOUT FROM ONLINE DATING[2]

MORE OPTIONS: The question for most singles is no longer *if* they're dating online, but *how many* sites they're using. Singles typically have dating profiles on two or three sites now. And they're open for romantic connections through their social networking sites too (e.g.,

---

[1]Source: *New York Times*, "Why Are There So Many Single Americans?" January 21, 2007, Kate Zernike.
[2]Source: *Unhooked Generation: The Truth About Why We're Still Single*, 2006, Jillian Straus.

Facebook, MySpace, Hi5, Bebo, even blogs). What's important here is the sociological implications of single men (and women) increasingly believing they have infinite first-date possibilities through the Internet. If a potentially better match is only a mouse-click away, why call someone back after a good-but-not-100-percent-perfect first date? Today dating reflects breadth, not depth.

HIGHER EXPECTATIONS: With so many options, singles evaluate more critically. This is very time-consuming, so they try to "surf and sort" as quickly as possible. The initial process becomes all about elimination: screening out rather than screening in. Ultimately, they're screening for perfection instead of potential.

EASIER REJECTION: Because online dates exist primarily behind a computer screen, they are less personal and therefore easier to reject. Dating is no longer about calling someone (or not) on the telephone, it's about hitting the send and reply buttons (or not). It's painless and nonconfrontational to delete the ones you don't want, just like spam.

2) DATERS ARE MORE SOPHISTICATED

MORE RELATIONSHIPS: Men and women come to the dating table today with more relationship experience. People typically begin dating at younger ages now than in past generations, and they stay single longer. The U.S. Census reports that the average age of marriage has risen from approximately 23.5 in 1980 to 26.5 in 2006. Think about what this means: if a thirty-five-year-old woman today had her first boyfriend in her early teens, she has been dating for more than twenty years. Depending on the longevity and number of her boyfriends, she could have, let's say, twenty significant relationships or more under her belt.

DEEPER RELATIONSHIPS: Relationships are not only more numerous, but they are often *deeper*, because now many couples live together (either in or out of marriage). You've seen up close how your partner acts under stress, while he's traveling, and when he's hungry or irritable. Whether you're divorced, widowed, or recently out of a long relationship, you've experienced former partners in much deeper ways, resulting in longer checklists for the next partner. More relationships also mean more breakups, making it harder for people to put their trust into new people they've only just met— and easier to cross someone off the list when they aren't sure.

GREATER SELF-AWARENESS: Intensifying the impact of more and deeper past relationships is the new "self-awareness industry." This includes the rise and acceptance of couples therapy (both for married and unmarried couples), more people in solo therapy, the proliferation of popular self-help books, and more coverage of relationship analysis on popular TV shows. Singles show up to the first-date table with their analyzed experiences under the umbrella of "I won't make *that* mistake again!"

With so much history, men and women are predisposed to quickly project their past onto somebody new and feel confident those quick judgments are accurate. What's the result? The average single person is now more sophisticated and confident than ever about what they are and aren't looking for . . . making the first date an unprecedented minefield.

3) THE SEX FACTOR

Today, sex is easier to obtain without committed dating (via "hookups" or "friends with benefits"), and couples are now more sexually active early in courtship. Consequently, there is not the same pressure for single people to go on multiple dates to get to "the sex part." Simply put, there is no longer the same urgency or physical incentive to pursue a commitment to one person.

Increasingly, everyone is window shopping but few are buying.

> There are more failed first dates today than ever before . . . everyone is window shopping but few are buying.

In the Blink of an Eye

But the biggest challenge for singles isn't anything new at all—it's a long-standing reality. Men and women use snap judgments on first dates to determine whether to go on second dates. People process information quickly and make instant decisions—basically "trusting their gut." They draw conclusions from whatever information they have. Words, behaviors, sounds, and appearances trigger instinctual reactions in all of us. But those reactions come from our biased, preconceived notions about something (e.g., an accent, a clothing style, etc.) and can be misleading filters.

In the book *Why Men Marry Some Women and Not Others* (2003), John Molloy specifically explored faulty first-date impressions. For example, he polled brides coming out of marriage license bureaus and found that over 20 percent of them said they didn't even *like* their husbands when they first met! Luckily, those couples got a second chance—and that's the objective here.

Given the phenomena of snap judgments and faulty first impressions, it's not rocket science to understand that you want a man to have the most favorable information about you on a first date so he wants to spend more time with you. My aim is to help you get past superficial first dates into territory where you and Mr. Potential can *really* get to know each other.

Take Charge

Tradition has dictated that men get to ask out a woman initially, and now, thanks to online dating, men have even more women to choose from. In light of this reality and all the other challenges I've just described, what does it take for women to change the balance of power and be in the driver's seat? I want *you* to be in control of your dating life by being in a position to accept or decline second-date invitations.

You've probably heard that dating is a numbers game. I absolutely believe that's true. Most dates will not, and should not, grow into relationships. Dating is a filtering process for a good reason: so that you don't end up with the wrong person. But if you have to go out with a hundred guys to find only one with whom you want to spend your life, then you shouldn't risk even one guy not calling back—because what if he turns out to be that "one"? I don't want you to ever *wonder* why one man didn't call you back. I want you to *know* why and leverage that information to guarantee every callback from now on. In my perfect world, no woman would ever be left sitting by the phone wondering why a man didn't call again. Scratch that. In a really perfect world, you'll be out on a second date with some cute guy while your home phone rings all night with a bunch of other guys calling to ask if they can see you again.

The Kitchen Colander

To be able to date whom you want, it's important to understand the way a man dates and then falls in love with someone, especially in this new dating world. (Women, of course, go through the same process.) In my experience as a professional dating coach and matchmaker, I've seen men date and fall in love in three stages. First, **the filtering stage,** during which most women are sifted out—it's as if he's using a kitchen colander. During the first few dates, he's filtering out anyone with qualities he personally finds undesirable, even if those qualities aren't "real" but rather perceived by observing trivial things and jumping to conclusions. He shakes the colander hard because he's looking to rule out, not rule in. Next is **the evaluation stage**, where he focuses on one woman who remains inside the colander. He makes a mental list of her pros and cons, which reflect real qualities as he gets to know her better. "Sure," he thinks, "she has certain issues, but there are many fantastic things too." Third is **the acceptance stage.** He decides, "The pros outweigh the cons. I want the whole package." The better he knows her, the easier this acceptance becomes.

The key to understanding this process is realizing that it's *sequential*: first comes filtering, then evaluation, and finally acceptance. I believe that so many first dates are failing not because two people aren't a good match, but rather because one person often gets filtered out too soon before the other one can make an accurate determination of future potential.

Information Is Power

If second dates have become more elusive than ever, what is the solution? How do you avoid getting filtered out? Perhaps it's useful to step back and examine how you'd approach a similar issue in a different area of your life. First dates are actually a lot like job interviews. In a short period of time, you try to make a favorable connection with the person across the table while you are being skeptically reviewed. You are trying to avoid being eliminated so you'll advance to a second round of interviews. You're not exactly sure what the recruiter is looking for, and it's inappropriate to ask. With interviewing (just like dating), it's all about the three P's: preparation, presentation, and perception. If you're prepared for the interview, you can emphasize your strengths, minimize your weaknesses, and ask relevant questions. But what if you're not prepared going in? What if you don't know the hiring criteria? With a few wrong moves, you could be stamped "Not what we're looking for." Next thing you know, you're reading that dreaded letter: "Thanks for coming in . . . we'll call you if anything opens up."

Most career counselors advise job seekers to "do their homework." That is, to get a job, you want to come prepared for the first interview by knowing as much as you can about what a company is looking for. You can study the company's website, ask any friends inside the company about corporate values, and network with contacts to learn current industry trends. You might discover, for example, that one company likes hard workers with a lot of creativity. And in particular, they don't like people who prefer to work alone; the culture is all about being a team player. That due diligence could help you get the job because you'd emphasize your work ethic, creativity, and team orientation above your other skills during the interview. Of course, it's a two-way street—you have to want the job you're interviewing for—but what you should want most is for *them* to want *you*. Get the job offer first, and then decide if you want it. You should have *options*.

Now imagine going on a first date if you knew in advance exactly what most guys are looking for. And more specifically, what men tend to like or dislike after meeting you personally. If only there was such a way to "do your homework" before a date, you'd really have a leg up in the game. Sure, if you and your prospective date have a mutual friend, you can ask a few questions about him in advance. You can Google him, read his Match.com profile, or check out his Facebook page. But sometimes those avenues aren't available, and they usually yield only surface information anyway. Finding out he's a nice guy, thirty-one years old, likes to ski, and doesn't have a criminal record is handy, but it doesn't exactly tell you what he's looking for—or what his deal-breakers are—on a first date. While it's impractical to obtain details about what each guy likes or doesn't like before every date, better information about what *most* men respond to will increase your chances that a guy will ask you out again, ultimately placing the ball in your court. Information is power in both the business and dating worlds. The tricky part is finding that information.

Exit Interviews

During my MBA training at Harvard Business School, I studied a useful management tactic called "Exit Interviews." When an employee is leaving his job, a human resources manager often conducts an Exit Interview to ask his opinions about the company, his boss, and his coworkers. Because the employee is on his way out the door, he tends to express himself candidly. This candor, in turn, allows the company to learn specific and useful information in order to improve its business and better retain good employees in the future. Smart managers will react constructively to the feedback, especially if they hear the same thing over and over again from several exiting employees.

When I became a professional dating coach, I wanted to understand why my clients' first (or first few) dates failed and how I could unmask typical deal-breakers (or "date-breakers," as I call them). So I pioneered using the Exit Interview technique in the dating world. It began in 1998 when Sophie, one of my clients in New York City, complained to me on the phone about James, a twenty-seven-year-old investment banker. They had had a great first date, she said, but two weeks passed without a word from him. She said to me, "Rachel, why didn't he call me back?" Well, I had absolutely no idea—how could I? I'm not a psychic and I hadn't gone on the date with them. But I did have a radical thought: why not call James myself and ask him?

With Sophie's permission, I called James. He was surprisingly willing to talk about their date. Sure, I had to use my charm to get past his initial "there was just no chemistry" answer, but he opened up after a few gentle, probing questions. I had expected that my phone-call attempt would simply become an unreturned voice mail message, but it actually turned into a thirty-minute discussion with this guy. I learned that while he thought Sophie was attractive and the date was fun, she had made several references to being deeply rooted in New York. This had concerned him. According to James, one of the things she said was, "I love New York—I'd never leave the city. My job and my whole family are here." James was originally from the West Coast and hoped to move back there after working a few years on Wall Street. He concluded that Sophie was geographically inflexible and didn't think it was worth pursuing a relationship with her. He admitted shyly that he used to enjoy dating a cute girl without thinking about the future, but he was ready to settle down soon and only wanted to date women with long-term potential.

When I relayed this feedback to Sophie, at first she was surprised—then even a little angry at the wasted opportunity. She remarked, "Well, I do love New York, but for the right guy, and especially if we were married, I might be willing to move." But of course that's not what she had conveyed to him. And because they'd only known each other for two hours, he never probed further about her long-term geographic intentions. She didn't have the option of finding out if James could have been her "right guy." She made The Never-Ever[3] mistake on the first date.

After I hung up from that first phone call with James, I sat there in stunned silence. This Exit Interview idea was so simple, yet so powerful. If I could find out from more men about typical first- or second-date fumbles, I could really help my clients improve their odds of finding the right mate. So I began offering my Exit Interview service to other clients and I called more men. Through trial and error over the next ten years, I fine-tuned my script.

When I called men for an Exit Interview, I initially asked them for only five minutes of their time. But the average number of minutes I spent conducting each interview was forty-three minutes! Importantly, I immediately offered these single guys an incentive to speak openly with me: I told them that if I better understood what they were looking for, I might know someone great to fix them up with (which is true: I know a lot of *fabulous* single women). Then I made small talk, I made sure they felt comfortable, and I offered anonymity in my book and through "aggregated data."[4] We spoke about particular women they had dated and their views on dating in general. While many men started our conversation by giving me glib lines such as "I didn't feel a spark" or "I started dating someone else," I learned to hear those excuses as secret code for "I have a real reason but you'll have to work to get it out of me." And I worked hard. If a man attempted to gloss over a failed first date with the no-chemistry line, I replied, "Can you tell me about another woman with whom you *did* feel chemistry and what she did differently?" Or if he said, "I just got busy at work," I would say, "Well, what could she have done more of, or less of, to make you stop working so hard and ask her for a second date?" Those tactics worked great for extracting concrete answers.

The honest responses I collected proved invaluable to my

---

[3]The Never-Ever mistake is discussed in chapter 3.
[4]Responses from the men I called specifically on behalf of a client or friend were aggregated into feedback "themes" so the woman didn't know which man said what, though some men said it was fine for me to relay individual comments if they could be helpful to someone.

> **Ninety percent of women guessed *incorrectly* why men didn't call them back.**

clients. As a neutral third party investigating date-breakers, I was able to gain candid feedback from the men who usually disappeared into a black hole. And by calling five or six men whom *one woman* had dated unsuccessfully, I usually found a pattern or theme of which the woman was completely unaware. And this is what gets me: women really don't know what happened on unsuccessful dates. I always asked my female clients in advance of my Exit Interviews to predict what they *thought* men would confess as the primary reason things went wrong. The shocker? Ninety percent of women guessed *incorrectly*!

Sometimes ignorance is bliss. But my Exit Interview data finally provides single women with clear and constructive insights about the most common date-breakers today. These answers not only shed light on what might have happened in your past, but more important, they will help you better prepare for a first date going forward and ultimately improve your dating results. I've seen Exit Interviews directly lead to women finding their mate again and again, and you'll read about some of these success stories later in chapter 9.

Dating Smart

Okay, I can already hear you saying, "Are you implying that I should change my behavior to attract a man? If he's the right guy for me, he should like me for who I am!" Absolutely, he should like you for who you are. Just like your friends do, your colleagues do, and your neighbors do. But he can't like you for who you *really* are until he gets to know you. And he can't begin getting to know you *unless you go on a second date*. Smart daters are like chess players: they're always thinking several moves ahead.

This all goes back to the goal of a first date (i.e., being asked for a second). Editing your actions and words according to what men are looking for *in the beginning stages of dating* will allow both of you to let chemistry happen first and then focus later on the inevitable give-and-take. Over time, the things you don't like about each other will be balanced by what you do like and seen through a different lens, if you're both in love. For example, you can imagine rejecting a man after a first date if he had serious halitosis. But if you discovered foul breath on a fifth date, after you'd discovered a hundred wonderful things about him, you'd start to evaluate it a little differently. You might think, "He's really a great guy, so how do I deal with this one issue? Maybe I'll give him breath mints, or I'll buy him one of those tongue cleaner contraptions, or I'll suggest he go to a doctor in case there are any medical reasons . . ." You approach the problem very differently at that point. Rather than a "No, thanks!" knee-jerk reaction, it's all about finding solutions. But first, that guy better pop a breath mint fast so you'll want a second date with him to discover he's worth getting to know!

Smart dating isn't about altering your values or your identity. It's not about being artificial or putting on a show. It's certainly not about settling. It's about gathering information and using it to your advantage. Suppose you find out that the cute guy who asked you out at your friend's party is a chocolate lover. If you're on a date with him at a restaurant and you both decide to share a dessert, wouldn't it be smart to suggest the chocolate brownies instead of the peach cobbler? Similarly, if a guy avoided the sushi restaurant because he knows you're allergic to seafood, I'm sure you'd appreciate it. Perhaps you'd start thinking he's someone you'd like to get to know better. Tweaking your behavior really boils down to being thoughtful and wanting to make someone happy. I'm not suggesting you turn into whatever a guy wants (he'd grow bored with that anyway), but rather that small adjustments in your actions and words will get him to the place—the second date and beyond—where he can see how great you already are.

Look, there's clearly a lot of miscommunication between men and women during early-stage dates, but who's responsible? Some reasons for failed dates are absolutely out of your control, such as when men say, "She was too tall," "My AA sponsor warned me not to date so early in my recovery," or even "My wife doesn't approve

> **Seventy-eight percent of women believed that a man hadn't called them back for reasons *beyond their control*, yet only 15 percent of men agreed with that assertion.**

of my dating"! While I did find some of these cases in my research, it's too easy to say good riddance and blame men for everything. In fact, in my research, 78 percent of women believed that a man hadn't called her back for reasons *beyond her control*, yet only 15 percent of men agreed with that assertion. The remaining 85 percent of the reasons men gave for not calling a woman back involved a negative impression he got after she said or did certain things. And men reported enough women saying or doing the same types of things that significant patterns emerged in the data. You may be surprised to hear how trivial these reasons are, but the good news is that they are usually things that can be avoided.

The Research Process

Interviewing a thousand men means a lot of listening, and it gave me unprecedented insight into how men think. With the help of a few well-trained research assistants, I contacted a wide range of single men through phone interviews, speed-dating events, matchmaking services, online postings, and random intercepts at Starbucks, bookstores, and airport lounges.[5] After asking all these guys, "What was the main reason you didn't call her back?" I got 4,152 reasons[6] that broadly fell into two categories:

1) The date-breakers *during* a first date;
2) The date-breakers *immediately after* a first date.

---

[5] See Notes section at the end of this book for research methodology and data details.
[6] Some men discussed more than one failed date. Some men cited two "primary" reasons for a failed date. (I allowed a maximum of two primary reasons.)

The division of these two categories reflects my finding that sometimes a first or second date actually went very well, but something happened soon afterward to squelch the momentum.

As you'll see throughout this book, these Exit Interviews were shocking, funny, bitter, perplexing, embarrassing, and profound. Encouraging men to confide in me, I finally got the real scoop: what they said you should never do again and what they hoped you'd do more of. But please remember that no one is blaming you here for every failed date or suggesting that you change anything about your core self. You will simply uncover proven data about how men react to women's comments and behaviors of which you may not previously have been aware. Information is power.

Buyer Beware

The majority of men with whom I spoke were genuinely thoughtful and helpful, but some of the stories you're about to read may seem unfair or judgmental (similar to the stories from women you'll read in chapter 7 when I turn the tables). A lot of guys initially didn't want to admit how trivial or shallow their reasons for vanishing were. Most men conceded that it was an *accumulation* of small things that made them stereotype someone negatively and not call her again. Don't expect a collection of all those bad-date stories circulating in urban legends—the ones that have you rolling on the floor with laughter or gasping with horror. Rather, the anecdotes in this book come from everyday dates between two "regular" people (well, mostly!). The stories come straight from the horse's mouth. A few guys do sound like idiots—ones you'd probably never want to date anyway—but I included them if I thought their sentiments could just as easily come from a different guy you *would* want to date one day. While I certainly received an enormous amount of insightful, actionable comments during all my interviews, and those comprise the bulk of this book, be prepared for some ridiculous, gross, and painful quotes—especially in chapter 5, where you'll read a list of amusing outtakes.

How to Make This Book Work for You

My intent throughout this book is to illuminate simple things that fabulous women do every day on dates with Mr. Potential without realizing how his perspective differs from theirs. First you'll find the most frequent reasons men cited as their date-breakers, with detailed explanations and examples. After each reason is described, you can take a quick self-assessment quiz to help you decide whether you fit that particular stereotype. If the shoe fits, you can read what to do about it in the subsequent advice section. As you peruse this research, I'm confident you'll discover at least one major stereotype that you resemble on your dates, and perhaps a few minor ones as well. Be honest with yourself if you relate to certain signals you may be sending unknowingly. Most important, try to be open to the possibility that the stereotype men might attach to you could be something you'll be surprised about.

If you see something that absolutely doesn't apply to you, simply slow down as you drive by the accident scene, glimpse the car wreckage, and be glad it's not you in that twisted metal heap.

And finally, if you want to take this research to the next level, chapter 8 will show you how to enlist a friend (or a professional resource listed on my website) to conduct your *personalized* Exit Interviews. By having a third party call a few of your former dates, you will definitively identify your individual dating patterns. It takes guts to do that, so before I tell you more about that process, let's start by reviewing what men said about other women with whom you might identify.

The Bottom Line

The bottom line is this: you get that he's just not that into you, but *why?* The revelations in this research are raw, candid, and direct from the source. They offer the best insights I have seen throughout my ten years in the dating business. I guarantee that by understanding what men out there are really thinking, and by following my tips, you can attract and retain the right man when he finally comes along. After reading this book, you will be able to confidently answer the frustrating, obsessive, puzzling, universal question, "Why didn't he call me back?"

And then you can do something about it.

CHAPTER 2

What You Said

Questions Single Women Always Ask Me

When you're a dating coach, everybody has a question for you. When they find out that you've interviewed over one thousand men about dating, they suddenly have a million questions. It's a little like being a doctor. I'll be at a party, minding my own business, and suddenly everyone wants to show me their relationship scars. I don't mind. I've learned just as much from these conversations as I have from my official interviews.

These are the top five questions single women ask me about why men don't call back—and what I tell them.

1) A lot of guys call me back, but they're not always the ones I like the most. What does that mean?

If you're getting loads of invitations for second dates, even if they're not necessarily from the guys you hoped would call, you know how to make a good first impression . . . but not consistently. There are two issues to consider here. One, if you're not attracting the men you like the most, maybe you're acting differently around those men. You might not understand the vibes you give off when you're nervous. Two, if you conclude that your first impressions are strong because you usually get callbacks, this is dangerous logic. Because when you're only in the market to find *one* soul mate, it actually matters if even *one* guy you really like doesn't call you back. It is so rare to meet someone you feel genuinely excited about that you have to be prepared to make the most of *every* opportunity. When ninety-nine losers do call and only one Mr. Potential doesn't, there's a problem. If you followed football in 2007, you'll remember that the New England Patriots had a similar problem: eighteen wins throughout the season but one giant loss when it mattered most—in the Super Bowl!

Why let a minor glitch get in the way of a major romance? The issues could be trivial, but they're impacting your scorecard. Whatever is going on, you should find out why your retention stats aren't 100 percent and do something about it. That's what this book is all about.

2) I'm not worried about getting called back for a second date because I just don't meet that many interesting men who ask me for a first date! What can I do?

If you feel like you are simply not meeting the right guys in the first place, I would venture to say that you are actually meeting potentially "right" guys all the time in your daily life but there's a reason you aren't prompting invitations from them. Technically you don't label these guys as "dates who didn't call you back" because they're the male coworkers in your office, your clients through work, guys next to you at the gym, people next to you at the dry cleaner's, or male friends of your girlfriends. They include viewers of your online profile who checked you out but didn't send an e-mail or respond to your "wink." They include the guy you met at a party recently with whom you spoke for fifteen minutes: he had some initial interest, but ultimately he walked away without asking for your phone number. In the male mind, you didn't live up to whatever brief expectations he had. So for him, the getting-to-know-you stage was completed. No date required. These misfires—i.e., frustrating platonic friendships, brief conversations, flirtatious glances, online profile disconnects, or lack of fix-up offers from friends—all essentially represent cases of no callbacks. You can use this book to identify how men are stereotyping you from their first impressions, both in your daily life as well as on an official date.

3) Why aren't you writing a book for men about why women don't call *them* back?

Believe me, if more than seven men in the whole universe bought dating self-help books, I would have written my entire book about all the mistakes men make on dates! Of course my research shows that there are just as many women as men doing the rejecting . . . after all, the whole idea behind this book is to put the ball in your court, allowing you to date the dreamboats and decline the duds. But the reality is that men don't buy the books they probably need the most.

4) How much do looks matter when it comes to guys calling women back?

Looks matter, and that isn't news. The reality is we live in a very visual world. Over the course of a thousand conversations with men, I absolutely had my share of negative and rude remarks about a woman's appearance. From blunt descriptions of pockmarked faces to "elephant ankles," sometimes I feel as though I've lived a lifetime in a guys' locker room. Because looks are obviously important in attracting a man, you should always try to look your personal best. You already know that.

Here's the good news that I verified in my research: it is not *only* about looks. Do men *only* call women back who they think are beautiful? Absolutely not. The majority of reasons men declared for not wanting a second or third date had little to do with a woman's outer appearance. Why? Because men had already factored her looks into their decision to ask her out the first time. In fact, about 80 percent of my Exit Interview subjects had initially either met the woman in person before their first date (i.e., at a party, in the office, at the gym) or had seen her photo online. Having already screened women for appearance before the *first* date, it was usually something else besides looks that precluded a *second* date (one exception being misleading online photos). Further evidence that looks don't always determine second dates comes from the statistic that 68 percent of the men I interviewed told me that the woman they hadn't called back was indeed "good-looking."

Yes, physical appearance is a big part of a man's attraction to a woman, but the point is that men often ask a woman whom they consider good-looking for a first date, but not always for a second date. The equation is not as simple as Pretty Face + Good Body = Callback. The real question is: given a general level of physical attraction, why do men call some women back and not others? Or, put another way, what makes a woman both physically *and* emotionally attractive?

I spoke with numerous "highly sought-after" men who date beautiful women (including models) each week. I even spoke to one of New York's "Most Eligible Bachelors" (as voted by *Gotham* magazine). What prompts those guys to call back one hottie over another hottie (when they are interested in a relationship)? The answer of course has to do with personality, not looks. I also spoke with sought-after "regular guys" who are not looking for Malibu Barbie. Many told me they deliberately target "7s" on the looks scale because those women are sweeter, less arrogant, and have more pleasant personalities than "the 9s or 10s" they believe they could date.

These two quotes best capture the predominant sentiment from the men I spoke with:

> A 6 on the looks scale can become an 8 with a great
> personality. —Brian, age 28, New York, NY

> The really hot women—the ones with the best faces
> and bodies—are usually the most insecure or the
> most selfish. That's not what I want in a long-term
> partner. —Daniel, age 34, Indianapolis, IN

So do looks really matter? Sure, but they definitely aren't everything.

5) Why do you believe the reasons men gave you about why they didn't call again are actually true?

Sometimes my female clients, after hearing the responses from their personalized Exit Interviews, recognize themselves in the answers immediately. Other times, it isn't that simple. Surprise or denial is a common response to hearing that other people don't always see you the way you see yourself. "Why should I believe what he says?" is a common question I get—and it may be one that you have too. Men can lie or lack self-awareness—we've all experienced that before—so it's certainly reasonable to wonder how honest or valid their feedback was. Here's how I know that their answers (especially on an overall basis) are both true and, more important, relevant.

A) I DIDN'T ACCEPT THE EASY ONE-LINERS: As mentioned in chapter 1, I never accepted the pat answers when I spoke to men about the reasons for their failed dates. I probed and listened for their honest responses, and I had a whole bag of tricks I used when they tried to gloss over a touchy topic. I've been conducting Exit Interviews for a long time, so my crap-o-meter is very sensitive! Also, my undergraduate degree in psychology, combined with four years working as a professional interviewer in graduate school admissions, definitely served me well here. When a man tried to stonewall me, I could see right through him.

B) CONSISTENT RESULTS: In conducting the Exit Interviews for this book, I deliberately sought large samples of men of all regions, ages, and ethnicities (see notes section). And I used a range of research methods, including telephone, in-person, and online interviews with men who were either ex-dates of my coaching clients or random subjects (i.e., men approached anonymously in public venues). I also used a male researcher to conduct some of the interviews, thus reducing any potential "female bias" that may have prevented men from being candid with a female interviewer. The consistency of the answers across this range of backgrounds, research methods, and sources helped convince me that the men were being truthful—and that their reasons were real.

C) INCENTIVES: I'm a careful gal, so just to be doubly sure I got real answers in these interviews, I offered men a good old-fashioned bribe. I said, "If you can tell me what you're *really* looking for"—i.e., what this particular woman you didn't call back lacked—"then I might have someone else to fix you up with who meets your criteria." Most men I spoke to were still unattached, and they really liked this idea. While ultimately I didn't have a great single woman in mind for each and every one of them (nor were some of them worthy of my clients or friends!), I have introduced more than one hundred women to my Exit Interviewees over the years.

D) A SOUNDING BOARD: Men are only human! After a date, especially the older they get, they don't just head to the locker room for a bragging session—they actually have feelings about the date (good or bad) and enjoy some debriefing. But they don't have that same post-date gossip posse available to them like women do. So I became their sounding board. Not only did they want to talk about what went wrong (and right) on their dates, but I think my interview request sometimes flattered them or bolstered their self-confidence. Fine by me. I was getting helpful answers from them regardless of any benefits they picked up along the way.

E) SOME IS BETTER THAN NOTHING: It's better to listen to what men *do* say than not ask them at all. Certainly there were some men with deep psychological issues that they wouldn't or couldn't share with me in an Exit Interview. But what those men *did* share was still useful and interesting, especially when I heard the same things again and again from different men. The issues reported—even if incomplete in some cases—can still provide actionable insights to improve your next date.

F) IT WORKS! The bottom line is: Exit Interviews work! My clients who took this feedback to heart reported significant improvements in their dating lives. Many are now engaged or married to wonderful men. They made simple adjustments—that did *not* involve changing their personalities—and soon had more second- and third-date offers pouring in. More follow-up dates meant more opportunities to really get to know someone better, as second dates led to third and fourth dates, and beyond. In my experience, women who opened themselves to the Exit Interview process quickly found The One (or more potential Ones).

Top Three Reasons Women *Think* He's Not Calling Back

Before I called a man for an Exit Interview on behalf of one of my female clients, I always asked her to guess what *she* thought his primary reason was for not calling again. As I've mentioned, the women were wrong *90 percent* of the time. Their guesses usually fell into three categories:

#1: TIMING

Forty-four percent of women guessed that timing was the culprit for their date's disappearance. This encompassed several excuses: "He wasn't ready for a commitment at that time" (because he was newly single, playing the field, still hung up on his ex, or immature), "He was busy with work [or traveling]," or "He had another priority in his life" (training for a marathon, being a single dad, etc.).

#2: FEAR

Twenty-one percent of women guessed that fear was preventing his callback. This encompassed several excuses: "He was afraid of intimacy," "He was scared of being hurt again," or "He was intimidated by my success [or lifestyle]."

#3: WHY BOTHER?

Thirteen percent of women guessed that because *she* was not interested in a second date with *him*, he picked up on her vibe during the date and decided to cut his losses rather than pursue a lost cause.

OTHER

The remaining 22 percent of women made miscellaneous statements such as "Maybe he was seeing someone else," "The age difference was too great," "He thought I was too fat," "He didn't want to date a single mom," or "I'm shocked; I definitely thought he would ask me out again."

One woman guessed her guy who didn't call back was secretly gay, but when I spoke with him he exclaimed, "She was a dog freak! She talked about her dog too much, she had dog hairs on her jacket, she showed me a photo of the dog on her iPhone, and she was planning a birthday party for her dog." (Of course, it's possible this guy was gay *in addition* to her being a dog freak—I have no idea!)

Another example was the woman who asked me to call her best friend—a guy—to ask why he frequently fixed up other female friends with his male friends but never offered to fix *her* up. She reluctantly guessed that his reason was that he was secretly in love with her, even though she only had platonic feelings for him. When I called him, he revealed that she always talked about "hot, gorgeous men" she wanted to meet, and while he had many great male friends, none of them would qualify for the cover of *GQ* magazine. So he assumed she wouldn't be interested in meeting them and thus never tried to play matchmaker on her behalf.

Overall, I found two interesting threads through the majority of women's guesses about why they weren't called back. First, their guesses often sounded as vague as those I heard initially from men. Women didn't, or couldn't, pinpoint specific occurrences during their dates that may have precipitated a man's disinterest. Of course, in the beginning some of the reasons men cited *did* refer to timing, fear, or a feeling of "why bother," but when I peeled back the layers of the onion, this was rarely the real issue. Second, most women's guesses reflected reasons *beyond their control*. Yes, sometimes that was true: remember that 15 percent of men said their no-callback reasons were due to things beyond the woman's control, but *85 percent* said their reasons were directly related to a negative impression they got after she said or did a few things they didn't like. The good news is that I found those things were often very much under a woman's control, which is empowering. By knowing how men perceive seemingly innocuous comments or actions, women will be able to connect with the right mate when he finally comes along.

 **CHAPTER 3**

What He Said

Top Ten Date-Breakers
During a First Date

This chapter reveals the most common date-breakers men described that occurred during a first date and what you should do about them.

As you read the reasons why men didn't call women back, keep in mind that the goal here is *not* to scare you away from dating, give you a litany of regrets about the past, or make you feel bad. At all. The goal is to figure out what *illusionary* triggers are keeping the men you'd like to see again from getting to know the real you.

One of the key insights I gleaned from my one thousand interviews is that if a man doesn't call a woman back, it's because by the end of the first date he perceives her as fitting an unflattering female stereotype. A woman says or does a few small things (the date-breakers) that lead to this stereotype. Even though we all know what the word "stereotype" means, pause for a moment to really absorb this definition: *a stereotype is an oversimplified, exaggerated image of a group* (such as "Football players are stupid" or "French people are unfriendly to tourists"). People use stereotypes to quickly catalog the world around them in the absence of in-depth knowledge. In the dating world, men use stereotypes to efficiently evaluate women given the limited information they can glean during their first date. You know what I'm talking about because women equally stereotype men on first dates. What's crucial here is for you to recognize the most common stereotypes men attach to *you* based on seemingly trivial date-breakers—so that you can avoid them next time.

And what's important to remember is that because of the reasons described in chapter 1 in the New Dating World section (e.g., a better match being only a mouse-click away), men are trying to rule out—not in. So they are overly focused on determining if you fit a *negative* female stereotype, rather than a positive one. I've chosen the most vivid examples from my Exit Interviews to illustrate each stereotype, but use these examples to extrapolate what *you* might be doing, even if in less pronounced ways. If you don't recognize yourself in the preliminary description of each section, I encourage you to keep reading to the end, because familiar behavior may become apparent. The "Sound Familiar?" questions at the end are designed as a final checkpoint for accurate self-assessment.

While I've numbered the reasons men gave according to frequency, the importance of each reason is not inherently reflected by its ranking but rather by whether or not it describes *you*. If a reason at the bottom of this list seems more relevant to your dating style, that's actually the *most* important item you should focus on.

The notes section at the back of this book provides the raw figures of the 4,152 reasons given by the one thousand men about why they didn't call a woman back.

#1 REASON HE DIDN'T CALL BACK
The Boss Lady

It felt more like a business dinner than a date.
—Carl, age 28, Philadelphia, PA

I get enough aggression at work all day. When I come home, I want to be with someone softer, more nurturing. —Jacob, age 31, New York, NY

Her attitude was like, "This is how it's going to be" instead of "This is what I'm thinking but I'd like to hear your thoughts too." —Kiran, 52, Seattle, WA

The top reason that I heard from men about why they didn't call a woman back came down to one thing: dominant behavior. Many men basically said the date failed because they'd rather hire her than date her. They may respect her intelligence and admire her capabilities, but that doesn't necessarily mean they're attracted to her. They weren't saying they wanted someone simple, needy, or uncomplicated, but they didn't want to feel tense, belittled, or neglected in their personal relationships.

The term "boss" here reflects men's attitudes that certain women seem *argumentative, competitive, controlling, not feminine, too independent, not nurturing,* or some combination of the above. In other words, some women give off a "masculine" vibe. Of course, women don't use the same terminology to describe this behavior. Instead, women might rightfully identify themselves as *persuasive, capable, street-smart, organized, modern, confident,* or *forthright.* You say "potato"; he says "potahto."

This is a tough spot for contemporary women, particularly those who have successful careers. It has roots in behavioral science: in the end, men and women are all a lot like Pavlov's dog. We behave according to the ways we're rewarded. If Pavlov's dog learned that he got a doggie treat every time he barked, then he'd eventually start barking a lot. In the workplace, women (like men) are rewarded with promotions, bonuses, praise, and respect for taking charge and being capable. As women have risen up the corporate ladder, they have adopted many traditionally male characteristics to succeed, whether they work in finance, law, retail sales, or party planning. It's not easy to just switch off this alpha personality after you leave the office. But that comes at a cost.

One man told me that most women he meets today would prefer he "admire their accomplishments rather than their butts." Welcome to Dating 101. If you'd take professional respect over lust, you might have just lost that second date. I call these Boss Ladies part of "The Cinderella Generation": they broke the glass ceiling but broke their glass slipper along with it. Of course it's unfair. Luckily I don't believe your only choice is between a big promotion and a date with a guy you're crazy about. Landing both can be as simple as gaining awareness of the issues and making a few easy adjustments.

While it's hard to transition from taking charge, focusing on the bottom line, and organizing schedules, it's imperative to grasp that men say the "image" of the woman they want at 8:00 PM isn't the same image of the woman they want at 8:00 AM. He's not buying red roses for his fabulous female colleague with whom he works side by side during the day—the one with whom he debates a client strategy and who he thinks would do a damn good job running the company. He says he's not intimidated by her (though perhaps he is). He really does respect her. Many men just don't picture coming home to her (or, more precisely, the *stereotype* of her) after a long day. In fact, as far as professions go, 44 percent of the men I polled in a separate online survey responded that their first-choice profession for a woman they'd like to marry is "schoolteacher."[1] And this poll was conducted in 2008, not 1950!

Throughout my interviews, most men clearly told me they wanted an intelligent, accomplished woman with whom they could share stimulating conversation. It wasn't really her job title that

---

[1] See notes section about Craigslist survey.

tipped the scale as they debated calling her back, but
whether or not she seemed
to have a *soft demeanor*—as
far as they could tell during
a one- or two-hour first
date. This time frame is
crucial because ultimately

> **The issue is not what you are or aren't at your core, but rather that trivial comments or actions are screening you out before he can really get to know and appreciate you.**

the issue is not what you are or aren't at your core, but rather that
trivial comments or actions are screening you out before he can really get to know and appreciate you.

Are You The Boss Lady?

The Boss Lady encompassed six categories of behavior, as shown
below. Although some of these overlap, each comes with subtle dis-
tinctions. Do any of these descriptions ring true for you . . . even a
little piece of them?

ARGUMENTATIVE

Paul, a twenty-eight-year-old art dealer from Miami, FL, told me,
"I think women feel they have to *prove* they're smarter than me if
they want to be taken seriously." Several men expressed frustration
that they couldn't find a woman who challenged them intellectually
but didn't bulldoze them at the same time. The sentiments I heard
repeatedly were that men *do* want to hear what their date thinks, yet
they want the discussion to be a fun, intellectual exchange of
ideas—not a heated argument.

Scott, a forty-one-year-old doctor from St. Louis, MO, griped
about being on one date when he felt "like the whole evening she
was practicing for the final exam of a debate class. It was point-
counterpoint all night." He described one example about reading
the menu at a restaurant to select an appetizer to share. He mentioned that he didn't like curry. His date shot back, "Who doesn't
like curry? How can you not like curry?"

Scott said the issue about him not liking curry was argued for a couple minutes, and no matter what he said, she had a "challenging retort." She quoted facts about everything from nutrition content to parents who don't push their children to try new foods. It's not that she delivered her comments in a mean voice, he explained, it's just that the whole thing got exasperating. "Jeez," he sighed to me, "all she had to do was say, 'Okay, you don't like curry, then do you want to share the artichoke dip?' You know, [it] wasn't that big a deal, but I had gone out with another woman that week who was more easygoing, so when the curry thing started things off on the wrong foot, I began to tune out."

I bet Scott's date thought she was being playful or that she was simply "sparring" with him to prove she was up to the challenge she thinks men want. But surprisingly trivial or mundane verbal exchanges like these can build up in the male mind as symptoms of a larger issue. Scott told me about two other small examples from that date similar to the curry issue and ultimately admitted he had labeled her "an argumentative person."

Bart, a twenty-eight-year-old political speechwriter from Washington, DC, described his recent date with Holly, one of my clients. He said she was everything he was looking for . . . until their date vibe plummeted. He explained how they had been joking around about their parents when he mentioned that his mom was a housewife. According to him, Holly's smile faded as she said, "Careful now . . . you're treading on a touchy subject. I hope this doesn't mean you expect *your* wife to stay home with the kids. Personally, I love my job and expect to keep working after I start a family." Bart said the discussion turned serious as they espoused their views about women, work, and family. He told her he's open to whatever his future wife wants to do. She asserted that he might say that *now*, but later he'd probably fall back on the traditional housewife model he saw growing up. They debated this thorny issue, and Bart concluded Holly was "sort of combative." He said he's not attracted to that type of girl. When I gave Holly this feedback, her response was a curt "Well, he just has a fragile ego." Yet she had earlier told me she hoped to see him again. My observation is that it was too early to know whether he had a fragile ego or not. If they'd gotten to know each other better on subsequent dates, they would have been able to more accurately evaluate each other's views and *then* make an informed decision about any future potential.

COMPETITIVE

Some of the dating stories I heard about The Boss Lady had a competitive vibe. The women in this category were slightly different from the argumentative ones (who seemed to argue for the sake of proving their knowledge or intelligence), because these women wanted to "win." Whether they were trying to win an unspoken contest of name-dropping about who knew more important people in Manhattan, or who knew more about wine, or who got fewer hours of sleep after a late-night party, it didn't matter. This type was a "one-upper." Men told me that when a woman tried to "trump" their comments or stories, it sparked a competitive instinct rather than a romantic feeling. Guys didn't think "How impressive!" Nor did they say "Oh, how cute, she crushed me at bowling!" Sure, I heard a few expected stories about dates where the man didn't like losing on the tennis court, golf course, or even with an Xbox. But that's an old lesson most of us know: let him win a little to soothe his ego.

On a basic level, competitive women were described as being focused on *winning* the point, rather than being accommodating and gracious (which was considered more ideal for a long-term partner). This type of competitiveness emerged in subtle ways. SekouWrites (his real name, which he gave me permission to use, and yes, it's all one word) is a thirty-six-year-old writer from New York, NY, who told me a story about a woman he perceived as competitive when they were simply trying to figure out where to rendezvous. He met Alma at his book signing party in Brooklyn and was very attracted to her. When SekouWrites called her to confirm the time and place for their first date, Alma told him she had a meeting that day starting at 5:00 PM that would last two hours and asked if he could please come to her office lobby at 7:00 PM. He said, "Oh, sometimes meetings run late, so why don't you just call me when it's over and I'll come pick you up? I'm only ten minutes away." She replied, "What's wrong with *my* plan? I think it's better if you just come at seven PM. I'll be ready."

He told me it wasn't that he didn't like her plan—he was just trying to strategize about the best possible way to organize the evening. But they sparred back and forth for several minutes discussing the logistics of where and when to meet. While his description certainly contained shades of the "argumentative" woman, SekouWrites emphasized that it felt like "all she cared about was whether her plan 'won.'" He said she tried to act "jokey" but her voice sounded to him like a kid chanting on the school playground, "My plan's better than your plan!" Ultimately they met at 7:00 PM in her lobby, but the rest of the evening he was overly sensitive to certain comments. When she said, "Let's walk instead of taking a taxi," he heard, "I know what's best!" He admitted he was probably too judgmental, but regardless, he didn't want a second date.

I repeatedly saw throughout my interviews that once a guy had a whiff of something he didn't like, he started to look for other evidence to back up his initial hypothesis. Sure enough, he always found stuff. I suppose when someone looks hard enough, he can find just about anything.

Jake, a twenty-six-year-old mechanical engineer from Sacramento, CA, had another story that illustrated a similar competitive streak. He recounted an evening with a woman named Carla whom he never called back. They were introduced through a mutual friend hosting a dinner party who had hinted separately to Jake and Carla in advance that they might like each other. Jake considered this dinner party their first date, and he was eager to meet Carla since his friend had described her as beautiful, petite, and sassy. When they met in person that night, they chatted casually before sitting down at the group table. "This woman has potential," he thought. Because the party was small, most of the conversation tended to include the whole group. At one point the topic turned to global warming, and things got dicey as one guy stated he didn't believe there was even much of a crisis. "Didn't you see the Al Gore film?" asked Carla. "Of course," replied the other guy, "and it was ridiculous." "Well," said Carla, "I saw the film three times and one of the scientists whom Gore quoted was a professor of mine at Yale. I can tell you his data is rock-solid, backed by Nobel Prize–winning scientists." "It's all political propaganda!" claimed the other guy across the table.

The barbs flew between them for several minutes. Watching Carla spar at the table that night with her "adversary," Jake felt like she cared less about sharing her point of view and more about who knew more facts and "winning the round." He admitted that he thought the other guy was making inflammatory remarks, but it was Carla he was watching closely. He said he wants a woman who can share her ideas but still knows how to handle herself gracefully when confronted by a jerk. He said her style made him "cringe in his chair" and he told me, "She was competitive . . . aggressive . . . always trying to one-up the other guy. I can see how that approach goes a long way if she's your divorce attorney, but who wants that in a girlfriend?"

CONTROLLING

The Boss Lady who's successful in her job usually likes to be in control. She is used to taking the reins. But when this quality overflows into a date with a new man, it can be a turnoff—at least in the beginning. Later, when two people get to know each other better, they tend to adapt to a rhythm where one person makes more of the decisions, or at least certain types of decisions, so that day-to-day choices as a couple don't turn into power struggles. But because most guys are used to their own way of doing things (whether they are twenty-two or seventy-two), they bristle at women whom they perceive as too controlling on a first date.

I want to reiterate something important here: it doesn't matter on the first date whether deep down you really *are* or *aren't* a "controlling" person—or whether you have any other negative traits, for that matter (we all do). And no, I'm not suggesting you trick him into thinking you're someone you're not. But if he *perceives* you as controlling on a first date, my research indicates that he's not going to ask you for a second date. Case closed. But that doesn't mean a relationship with the "real you" wouldn't make him (and you) happy, even if you are indeed "controlling."

When a man gets to know you better later on, there's a good chance that the very style he might have labeled "controlling" on date number one will be viewed as "organized" or "forthright" when balanced by all the other wonderful qualities he comes to appreciate in you. With the advantage of time, he looks at you through different glasses. As you date and get to know each other, you will learn whether your styles mesh or not. Perhaps your controlling nature will be a problem in your dynamic as a couple, perhaps not. The object early on is to prevent his knee-jerk reaction to a negative stereotype from ruining a potentially fabulous relationship that could develop.

The cues reported to me that signaled a woman as controlling often revolved around surprisingly mundane events during a date, such as opening an umbrella or even loading the dishwasher. Ryan, age twenty-six, a hedge fund manager from Newark, NJ, told me that it was raining the night he met Tina for their first date. They met at her apartment and planned to walk to a nearby café for a drink. He had forgotten to bring an umbrella, but luckily Tina had an extra one. During the elevator ride down, Tina offered a litany of comments: "Here's an umbrella . . . No, don't open it now . . . Just put it in your jacket pocket . . ." Ryan laughed when he recalled the story. "I didn't even know her for five minutes, and already she was telling me what to do and when to do it!" He said that he takes instructions all day long from his boss, so he isn't looking for that on weekends. When I sounded surprised that a few words in an elevator determined the outcome of the evening, he said, "Look, by itself it wasn't a big deal, but it made me aware of the issue, and after a couple other similar things she said during the rest of the date . . . well, I meet a lot of great girls, so I just moved on."

Another man I interviewed, John, a thirty-seven-year-old advertising executive from Berkeley, CA, told me a story about

Shauna. He had liked her initially—she seemed warm and bright, and they shared a unique passion for playing marathon sessions of Scrabble. The momentum was growing between them, and at the end of their first date, she volunteered to cook him dinner next time at her apartment. The second date at her place started off well, except he noticed she was very particular about certain things. Minor stuff didn't really bother him right away, but it started to build up. He remembered that she asked him to take his shoes off at the door, reminded him to put her CD back in the right sleeve when he turned on the music, and suggested (twice) he let the red wine breathe before he poured it. After dinner they played Scrabble and then kissed passionately on her couch until 1:00 AM. Finally she said it was getting late. He still planned to ask her out again at that point and offered to help her load her dishwasher before he left. She grinned and said, "Thanks, I'd love that."

But within two minutes the mood changed. Shauna told him he had incorrectly loaded a heavy iron pot on the top rack next to the wineglasses and that they might break. She jumped in and placed it "correctly" herself. He felt that "only a control freak would care about how a dishwasher was loaded . . . [instead] she should have cared more that I was helping in the first place." Although he smiled in the kitchen at her and muttered, "Oh, sure, sorry," her dishwasher comment reinforced a "controlling" stereotype that had started to form in his mind earlier. He said to me, "I don't need that for the next fifty years."

When Shauna and her friends later dissected why she never heard from John again, I'm sure the dishwasher never came up in their post-date analysis!

NOT FEMININE

Heterosexual men are, by definition, attracted to women, not men. That may sound obvious, but today the line is often blurred between what's masculine and what's feminine. Some men told me that women made little comments or gestures that reminded them of being at work or with their buddies. Harlan, a twenty-nine-year-old lawyer in Hanover, NH, mentioned a woman he once chatted with at a young-alumni happy hour event. Toward the end of the evening, she asked him for his e-mail address and suggested they stay in touch through her LinkedIn network. He said LinkedIn is a business network—not a social network like Facebook—and it made him feel like their connection was more professional than flirtatious. When I pressed him further ("Was that the *only* reason you weren't attracted to her?"), he recalled that the LinkedIn remark was consistent with some other observations he made about her: she was wearing a business suit, she didn't wear any jewelry, and she had a short haircut. He said he thought she was smart but wasn't attracted to her masculine vibe.

Owen, a thirty-two-year-old management consultant from Charlotte, NC, recalled asking a woman for her number and she handed him a business card. He assumed that meant she wasn't interested in anything personal, so he later tossed the card in his desk drawer and didn't ask her out. Though he did say one day he might call to use her services (she's a Realtor). He said it seemed "more feminine" when a woman wrote her number on a napkin or piece of scrap paper in "girly handwriting" and even cuter when she reached for his cell phone and typed it in. That's when he knew the connection was personal, not professional.

Other men described "masculine" women who had a brisk power stride when they walked across a restaurant or down the sidewalk, or women who tried to hail a taxi instead of letting the man do it, or women who used phrases such as "The bottom line is . . ." Business lingo especially sounded masculine to many men and doused a flirtatious vibe. Carl, a twenty-eight-year-old architect from Philadelphia, PA, said, "We talked too much about our jobs, which were in the same industry . . . The conversation seemed transactional. It felt more like a business dinner than a date."

Cameron, a fifty-one-year-old banker from Minneapolis, MN, initially told me he didn't know why he didn't call Carol back for a second date. He sighed: "The chemical attraction just wasn't there." I probed, "When did you decide you weren't attracted to her? Do you remember your initial reaction when you saw her?" He finally remembered that when he arrived at Starbucks for their date, Carol was already seated and talking on her cell phone. She gave him a half smile to acknowledge him and mouthed, "Gimme a sec." She quickly returned to her phone call and proceeded to give instructions, presumably to her assistant, about wiring money to a client's account. Her formal business tone during her call made him feel like he was back at the office. He couldn't shake the business vibe after she hung up. He never quite felt a spark ignite between them. Physical attraction is so ephemeral—a few little gestures or work-themed comments can extinguish a romantic mood.

Date wardrobe also played a role here. Perhaps not surprisingly, most men are still old-fashioned in feeling a positive initial response to feminine clothing. I'm not suggesting women wear a hoop skirt and carry a parasol, but the reality is that we're dealing with quick, instinctual reactions—think cavemen! If a man shared an anecdote about The Boss Lady during my phone interviews, I asked if he remembered what his date wore. As you'd expect, many had no clue, but they remembered if they were attracted to her or not. Her clothes were likely part of that memory, whether the men noted them consciously or not. So I followed up with my online survey and I asked more specifically, "What would you really like to see a woman wear on a first date, if she's someone with long-term potential?" A whopping 68 percent of the answers involved a skirt or dress. Noticeably absent were corporate pantsuits (and military uniforms!). Comments about "hot jeans" only accounted for 17 percent. One man summed it up, "If you're a girl, dress like a girl!"

Certainly what constituted feminine or sexy was individual and varied by age group, but the themes of "looking like a girl" and avoiding businesslike vibes cut across the board.

TOO INDEPENDENT

Here's a popular mantra I hear from many single women: "This is who I am. I'm not going to pretend to be someone I'm not. I want a man, but I don't *need* one." My reaction is always, "Of course!" But with that mantra comes a prickly attitude. And how do men respond to that, whether the mantra is verbalized or only intuited? Do they fall all over themselves trying to pursue her, romance her, and prove they want her just the way she is? Umm, not exactly. What men told me is that this attitude is a turnoff, and they can spot it right away. Mateo, age forty-five, a lawyer from New York, NY, said, "I don't want a damsel in distress—I'm not looking to rescue anyone—but it'd be nice to feel needed sometimes." Another man, Jay, a twenty-three-year-old film production assistant from Los Angeles, CA, told me how he went to pick up a date one night and when she got into his car, she didn't buckle her seat belt. He suggested she strap in and tried to make a little joke out of it by saying, "Buckle up for safety!" She turned to him and said in a breezy tone, "I can decide whether to buckle my own seat belt or not." He quipped to me, "Yeah, so that just made me want to lean over and smother her in kisses, right?"

Garrett, a thirty-nine-year-old venture capitalist from Atlanta, GA, was one of five men I called for a series of Exit Interviews for one of my private clients, Claire. As standard protocol prior to starting my process, I asked Claire to guess why each of the men had not called her back. She speculated that Garrett in particular was turned off by her Bible study references, since he told her he wasn't very religious. But instead Garrett told me "the calamari story." He took Claire to his favorite seafood restaurant and suggested they order calamari to start. Claire frowned. So Garrett said, "Oh, you don't like calamari?" She replied, "I do, actually, I just prefer to make my own choices." A week later when I gave Claire her cumulative feedback from all five interviews, I reported that four of her ex-dates essentially said she came across as too independent and having hard edges. I recounted some examples, including the calamari story (with Garrett's permission). She claimed that what Garrett told me wasn't even true. She remembered that exchange but said she told him, "I like calamari, but the shrimp sounds good too." Who knows what was actually said. It doesn't matter. The fact is that Garrett built a case in his mind from an accumulation of her "vibes" and seemingly insignificant dialogue. In his words, "She was too independent and probably some big feminist." He lost interest in pursuing her.

By the way, during the in-depth hour I spent on the phone with Garrett, he only once mentioned religion (referring to his observation that her Bible study showed she had passion for something), as one of the things he *liked* about Claire.

NOT NURTURING

A common impression about The Boss Lady is that she's not the nurturing type. And ultimately, if a man is thinking about long-term potential with someone, he might evaluate what kind of mother she'd be to his kids. Most guys don't come out and say this explicitly, but after all my interviews, it's clear to me from the stories they tell that this evaluation (fair or not) happens more than you'd think. An example from Mitch, a thirty-eight-year-old medical supplies salesman in Boston, MA, is typical.

Mitch was tired of dating and wanted to find a relationship that could lead to marriage. One night he had a great date with a woman named Audrey, and they ended up in her apartment at the end of the evening with a bottle of wine. As they chatted, he noticed a puppy roaming around, which he said Audrey ignored after a brief introduction ("Oh, that's my dog, Rex . . ."). As he sat there observing her during the next hour, he couldn't help thinking to himself, "If this is how she treats her pet—totally ignoring the poor puppy, his water bowl is empty, she's not playing with him—imagine how she'd treat her children!" He never called her again. My guess is that Audrey loves her puppy and, if she's anything like most dog owners I know, dotes on him all the time. She was probably trying to give Mitch her full attention that night. This sounded unfair to me, but that's what made up his mind. After hearing enough variations on Mitch's perception during my research with other men, the message came across loud and clear: if a guy is in a serious dating mode, he is often monitoring little things about you to predict what kind of mother you'll be to his future children.

Zachary, a thirty-four-year-old doctor from Irvine, CA, lamented the fantastic woman he dated once who conveyed she wasn't the nurturing type. In the context of a discussion they had about a 2002 documentary film they had both seen, *Searching for Debra Winger*, she said, "I love my career and I don't want kids anytime soon." He left wondering when "anytime soon" was (two years? ten years?) and if she would *ever* want kids. He admitted maybe she didn't want him to feel pressure to fast-track their relationship and might have been saying that for *his* benefit. But if that was true, it backfired. Maybe she genuinely didn't want kids anytime soon, so they weren't a match. But Zachary wanted to find a woman whom he could eventually marry and start a family with, so he backed off after she emphasized her career.

It's not only whether your behavior or your words seem nurturing or not, but also what you do for a living that factored into men's first-date impressions. After my online survey revealed "schoolteacher" as the most preferred job for someone with future-wife potential, the next-most-popular preferences were "nurse" and "chef." The top three roles all reflect nurturing stereotypes. Also, a few men specifically mentioned in my phone interviews "I'd never date a lawyer" or "I don't want anyone with an MBA, thanks!" Andy, a thirty-six-year-old stockbroker from Dallas, TX, told me about one woman he dated: "She was a career woman, but I'm looking for a woman who just happens to have a career."

Yeah, all that irritates me too (especially the MBA part!). But reading between the lines, I didn't conclude that men were interested in only dating women with certain professions. Of course a female corporate lawyer, for example, can have a marriage that is as wonderful as that of a schoolteacher. I don't think these men literally meant they wanted or didn't want specific careers, but rather they wanted the initial stereotype of someone nurturing, caring, giving, and patient.

SOUND FAMILIAR?

You may not have noted similarities to yourself among The Boss Lady anecdotes thus far, as it's not always easy to recognize yourself through other people's stories. So you can use the self-assessment questions below to verify whether men might be stereotyping you as The Boss Lady before they get to know the real you.

AT WORK . . .

❏ Do you command attention when you walk into a room?

❏ Would you describe your job environment as follows: the harder you push for something and the tougher you are, the more you will succeed?

❏ In past performance reviews or casual feedback from coworkers, have you ever heard any of these comments:

"I admire how you stand up for what you believe in!"

"I'm just glad you're on *my* team; I'd hate to be on the other side!"

"We love your persistence!"

"Were you on the debate team in high school?"

WITH YOUR FRIENDS AND FAMILY . . .

❏ Has anyone ever told you "You'd make a great lawyer!"?

❏ Are you the one who always organizes the plans for a group outing?

❏ Do you ever use the phrase "Wanna bet?"

ON A DATE OR WITH A PAST BOYFRIEND . . .

❏ Do you sometimes meet a guy after work before going home to change your clothes?

❏ Has a guy ever described you as "challenging" or "tough"?

❏ Has a guy ever told you, "Jeez, don't be so defensive! That's not what I meant . . ."

YOUR PERSONAL PHILOSOPHY . . .

❏ Do you believe you're usually right?

❏ Are you proud that you don't let anyone take advantage of you?

❏ Do you think, "I'm very independent—I'd like a boyfriend, but I don't need one!"

If you answered yes to more than five questions above, you may be perceived (or misperceived) as The Boss Lady. There's no doubt you're smart, successful, and admired, and of course you shouldn't change who you are deep down. But you may consider tweaking some of the things you do and say on a first or second date. Men who don't know yet how fabulous you are may think you're The Boss Lady and miss the chance to get to know you better on the next few dates.

So, What Should You Do?

Throughout my research, many anecdotes initially made me wonder whether some guys were better off knowing early on that a woman—a nameless, faceless woman (certainly not you or me!)—was argumentative, controlling, or competitive, in order not to waste time in a doomed relationship with her. But suddenly I realized that I'm The Boss Lady too! I hope my marriage isn't doomed. I'm controlling and argumentative, just to name a few of my lovely qualities. Guilty as charged. Yet my husband seems happily married. And I certainly haven't hidden my personality 24/7 for sixteen years. So I asked him one night about it, and the conversation went something like this:

ME: I'm kinda controlling and argumentative, huh?

HIM: (*laughing*) Is this a test?

ME: No, no . . . really. I'm curious.

HIM: Then, yeah, *obviously* you are . . . why?

ME: You're happy being married to me though, right?

HIM: Definitely.

ME: So, what's wrong with you? I mean, how can you be happy if I'm not a rosy ball of sunshine? [*Not my best metaphor, but that's what popped out of my mouth.*]

HIM: Because I know you so well. [*He was quiet for a few moments and then smiled at me.*] I take the good with the bad . . . I guess overall there's more good than bad.

No one's perfect. That's why I believe so strongly that the goal of the first date should be simply to encourage a man (assuming he's not an ogre) to ask you out again: so he can get to know you better, you can get to know him better, and both of you can start to see the whole package. This package deal is probably why people are asked in marriage vows whether they take their mate "for better or worse."

If you have tendencies that might cause you to be perceived as The Boss Lady, here are six suggestions to help you soften your image and allow *you* to choose whether a second date happens or not.

1) CHANGE THE DELIVERY

Some of the negative perceptions that a man has about The Boss Lady are reactions to how she speaks and acts, not necessarily to her inherent personality. This is key because there's something you can do about it (and will *want* to do about it one day with a guy you're really interested in). The distinction lies in delivering your comments with a softer approach rather than combative assertions, with witty banter rather than dry job-speak. The "good type" of Boss Lady appears straightforward, real, and confident, while the "bad type" seems demanding, harsh, and self-righteous. It's not easy to strike the right balance. He says he doesn't want someone too independent, but he doesn't want someone needy or clingy either. He doesn't want someone argumentative, but if you agree with everything he says, he'll think you're boring.

Take an example from the dinner party mentioned earlier when Jake watched Carla aggressively argue about global warming. Since men said they want a woman who sparks interesting conversation but doesn't draw a line in the sand, how could she have delivered her opinions differently? Carla could have gracefully told the other guest, "All I know, whoever's right, is that it's great to see an issue like this get so much discussion . . . ," and then bridged to a different topic. With a comment like that, there are no winners or losers in the debate. Carla hasn't forsaken her identity to get a man. Rather, this comment makes Carla look like the bigger person.

Toning down your conversation style from combative and defensive to gracious and even a little flirtatious goes a long way. Try sprinkling qualifying or humbling words into your dialogue, such as "I think" or "maybe" or "sometimes," which allow for disagreement and aren't adversarial. Rick, a forty-seven-year-old marketing manager from Newport Beach, CA, put it this way: "I want my future wife to have her own mind but still be on my side. It's not that I want her to agree with everything I say, but if she takes the contrary stance all the time, it makes me feel like we're adversaries instead of partners." I guess a little nuance goes a long way.

2) PLAY GAMES

A different challenge is warding off the "business dinner ambience." This can permeate a date with a simple question like "So, what do you do for a living?" Sharing your current and past work history is common getting-to-know-you conversation, but next time try something new. Instead of dutifully providing your job title and a résumé summary, try answering that dry question with a playful or flirty guessing game, or even adding a funny story about something that happened to you once at work. Obviously try to read the guy while you're doing this to make sure you don't become annoying, but you can respond something like this (in person or via e-mail):

HIM: So, what do you do for a living?

HER: Well, here's how I spend my days. See if you can guess what I do. My office always smells great. When clients walk in, they usually have problems or pain. I'm not a doctor, but I use sterilized tools. My clients include stressed-out professionals and women who can't get pregnant. By the time they leave, they're usually happier and hopeful.

HIM: (*smiling*) Hmmmm . . . Are you a really nice human resource lady with a bottle of Valium?

HER: Nope. Guess again.

HIM: I was thinking maybe a masseuse, but then you wouldn't exactly use sterilized tools, would you?

HER: Nope.

HIM: Maybe a therapist, like a shrink? But again, I can't imagine what the tools are.

HER: Okay, you're getting closer. I'm a type of therapist: I'm an acupuncturist!

HIM: Wow, that's interesting!

HER: Yeah, and you wouldn't believe what happened one day when . . .

This guessing-game format sparks more intriguing banter than the typical what-I-do-for-a-living spiel that you hear on most first dates. But think it through in advance, as clever clues can be elusive on the spot. And by the way, it's not that *every* piece of background data should be turned into a guessing game or riddle (how annoying would *that* be?!), but simply realize how exchanging demographic data points can feel like filling out a census form. The Boss Lady needs to mix it up, steer clear of business vibes, and sometimes turn factual into flirty.

3) PLAY BALL

For The Boss Lady with a competitive edge, I want to recommend something about different types of games: bowling, golf, Scrabble, etc. While a few men mentioned they didn't like losing a game, I don't want you to conclude that it might be better to avoid games altogether on first dates. It's fine to play sports or board games, and you don't always have to let him win, but remember what your parents and coaches told you when you were younger: "It's not whether you win or lose; it's *how* you play the game." Exhibiting nonaggressive, playful mannerisms is crucial during any game. So rather than betting who wins the next round of golf, pumping your fist in the air after a great putt, and shouting "Who's your daddy!" you can compliment one great stroke he takes, ask for pointers on something that's not your best skill, joke about the movie *Caddyshack*, or take a break midgame to rest and observe the beauty of the course.

Realize that if you really like the guy, you might be channeling all your nervous energy into overfocusing on the game rather than relaxing and having fun. Regardless of why your competitive streak emerges, save the victory dance for later when he knows you better. Later he'll see that you both have different areas of excellence, that you both can thrive on competition by challenging one another to do better, and that your common interests are something to enjoy as a couple. But none of that will be evident on the first date if you tend toward The Boss Lady profile, because he might want a re-match but not a second date.

4) PULL A JUNE CLEAVER

Do something that is deliberately an anti–Boss Lady thing. If you're the hard-nosed career type with the power briefcase, why not offer, for example, to cook him a homemade meal on the second or third date? Play the part with flair: wear a cute apron, se-lect a girly cocktail to serve (think Cosmopolitan versus whiskey on the rocks), maybe bake a pie. If you don't know how to do any of this (like me), enlist a friend to help you (your date doesn't have to see your accomplice in this caper). And of course, if he offers to load your dishwasher later, whatever you do, don't criticize his technique! Constructive criticism doesn't belong anywhere on the first few dates. Save it for your employee performance reviews at work (and your husband!).

I'm clearly not suggesting you revert permanently to the image of an old-fashioned housewife. I'm only talking about a few ges-tures early in the relationship. This kind of tactic can help offset any perceptions he might harbor if you tend toward The Boss Lady pro-file.

I remember when I was growing up, my mother used to greet my father when he came home from work every night with a little bowl of peanuts. Believe me, she was no June Cleaver, but she claimed that "men love peanuts!" and it made him look forward to coming home and relaxing. I have no idea whether her peanut theory is true, and he probably just liked the attention. But as a joke once, I decided to test her approach. On the fourth date with my then-future husband, I greeted him at the door of my apartment with a little bowl of peanuts in hand and explained my mom's theory. What can I say? He loved it. I never did this again, but I'd like to think that night he started envisioning what it would be like coming home to me in the future.

5) LOOK LIKE A WOMAN

It's easy to peg an all-work-and-no-play gal in a cocktail party crowd simply from her attire. She wears the same professional outfit from work to the after-hours event. It's a suit jacket with a structured, tailored fit. It's probably expensive and it's definitely black. It probably covers a stiff blouse. At work, conservative clothes allow you to be taken seriously, but they're not exactly alluring by candlelight (except maybe in some kind of boss-secretary sex fantasy, but save that for much later . . .).

Whenever I start working with a new client, one of the first things we do is review her dating clothes. My clients usually have impressive wardrobes. They tell me, "Oh, let's not waste time going through my closet; if there's one thing I know, it's that my clothes are fabulous!" They reassure me that their labels are Armani, Donna Karan, whatever, and how their friends always compliment them on what they're wearing. But that's my first red flag: when I hear that the compliments are coming from female friends, I push even harder to review their clothes. Because what impresses a woman is not necessarily what creates physical attraction in a heterosexual man. Women tend to be wowed by fashion, which is great, but be sure the outfit looks feminine and flattering on you. Upon close inspection, most of my clients are not dressing *femininely*, no matter how much status their labels have.

Of course, I'm not suggesting that "feminine clothing" translates as Laura Ashley lacy dresses. But, for example, you could wear a skirt (not too tight, not too short) and a vibrant or soft-hued top that shows your curves, revealing a little bit—yet not too much—cleavage. Avoid tight jeans and low-cut blouses on a first date even though you might think (or might be told by friends) you look "hot." Looking hot reflects a certain type of goal on a first date—it signals a hookup goal, not a find-my-mate goal. Also, men repeatedly told me that longer hair is more appealing (longish layers, shoulder-length or below).

6) LOOSEN THE KNOT

Like the Rolling Stones say, "You can't always get what you want . . . but you just might find you get what you need." I think this is one of the most essential truths in a happy marriage. While I watch women parade by on dates night after night, year after year, with their mental checklists of what they *want*, they rarely seem to focus on what they *need* in order to make themselves happy. One friend of mine, happily married, confided in me once that she chose her husband "because he took the knot out of [her] stomach." At first I thought that sounded really unromantic, but then I realized she has a very uptight and nervous personality, and that's exactly what she needed. I think a calming influence made her happier through the years than what fell off her checklist when she met him: height and hair.

So consider treating the cause, not just the symptom. In addition to focusing on softening your approach, think hard about the men you're selecting. For The Boss Lady, a nurturing type of guy can be optimal (e.g., the male versions of teachers, nurses, chefs). Yet that profile is the opposite of what most successful career women are looking for. They typically want the high-powered types who have equal or higher professional wattage. But we all know those types: they are usually domineering, self-centered, and workaholics. Your best match is probably a man who balances you emotionally. Rather than seeking someone similar to you, consider the men with more traditionally "female" energy, i.e., nurturing, sweet, surrendering, patient. Really ask yourself this question: Could you be happy in a marriage where you're The Aggressive One and he's The Gentle One? Where you're The Breadwinner and he's The Stay-at-Home Dad? Most women initially reject this marriage model, but I encourage the hard-core Boss Lady to sit with this portrait for a minute. The next time you're on a date with a sweet guy who you think is "not your type," please consider that he might be just what you need.

If You're The Boss Lady . . .

WHAT'S HOT:	WHAT'S NOT:
1. Feminine skirts	1. Professional pantsuits
2. Flirtatious banter	2. Shop talk
3. "Thanks for helping me!"	3. "Do it this way!"
4. "What do you think?"	4. "When I want your opinion, I'll tell you what it is."
5. Rhett Butler and Scarlett O'Hara	5. Bill and Hillary Clinton

#2 REASON HE DIDN'T CALL BACK
The Blahs

It's not like we didn't have a good time.
It was just uneventful.
—Noah, age 44, Ridgewood, NJ

She was nice. Really.
—Patrick, age 28, San Diego, CA

It was like watching grass grow.
—Randall, age 36, New York, NY

It's not bad, it's not good . . . it's just nothing special. The Blahs seep into dates everywhere, and it's no surprise. With our organized dating culture on steroids today from so many connections—Internet dating, speed dating, matchmakers, and more—first dates are a dime a dozen. It's too easy for single men and women to find themselves dating on autopilot, strangers exchanging vital statistics across a table instead of two people really getting to know each other. Everyone is looking for the "wow" and bored by the "nice." When men described a woman as "perfectly nice!" or "very pleasant!" they ultimately didn't feel that elusive spark. Nothing motivated them to call for a second date.

I encountered several men in my research whom I dubbed "The Kings of First Dates." Their dating calendars were beyond full with women they described to me as "very nice" but didn't make it over their first-date hurdle. You probably know some Kings yourself. They're the ones who go on a million dates—but usually only *first* dates. They're reliable for their perpetual willingness to meet someone new. Everyone wants to fix them up. They are either good guys, great guys, or the only bachelor left in your circle. There's just one teensy problem: they don't really click with anyone. I thought if there was any hope for deciphering why "nice" didn't make it to date number two, these high-volume date guys were it. I couldn't wait to get them under my microscope!

Jonas, a twenty-eight-year-old merchant banker from New York, NY, was a King of First Dates. We spent over an hour on the phone one night as I poked and prodded his dating outlook. He said, "I meet fantastic women every week . . . I'm really lucky. I rarely have a bad date because I usually meet [them] through friends of friends . . . Most of these women are pretty, sexy, smart, accomplished . . . they're all great. I guess I'm just looking for someone to tip the scale." It's good to be the king.

Kevin, a forty-seven-year-old corporate attorney from Seattle, WA, said that dating in recent years has become "like watching cable TV. There are five hundred channels to flip through now—it's not like back when there were four major network channels to choose from. It's hard to just pick a show and put the clicker down."

It seemed as though the Kings were numb from too many dates and just wanted someone to wake them up. "Nice" wasn't going to do it . . . how about "perfect"? I spoke several times to another King of First Dates: Cole, a forty-five-year-old corporate relations VP in Washington, DC. He regularly dates "perfect" women who have it all: brains, beauty, and charisma. He meets most of these women through his network on Facebook, and over the course of my six-month correspondence with him, he sent me several updates and photos of himself with his "new new thing." These women looked like they belonged on the runway of a fashion show. In one e-mail to me, he described a woman he'd just met at a party who was gorgeous, a former competitive gymnast, his same religion, from a good family, and graduated from an Ivy League college. He was so excited; their first date was planned for the coming weekend. I typed back, "C'mon, there's got to be a red flag—no one's that perfect." He responded, "She's that perfect. I'm so pumped for this date. It's hers to lose, baby!"

While I normally don't like guys calling me "baby," and I was a little annoyed by his arrogance, I nevertheless liked Cole. I can't explain it, but his self-assurance was endearing. You had to be there. Anyway, I made a note in my calendar to follow up with him to see how his "perfect" date played out. Two weeks later I e-mailed him again, "So, Cole, how's the 'It's hers to lose' girl? Did she live up to your dreams?" He replied, "Which one?" I dug up his old e-mail from my inbox and forwarded it to him: "You know, *this* girl here!" I wrote. "Oh, yeah," he typed back, "there was nothing wrong with her, I guess. Just not enough spunk. I thought you meant one of the other girls I went out with last week . . ."

Some of these guys have so many dates they can't even remember who's who. Even when they were "pumped" for a date! The take-away for me was not that Cole is a player—though he may be—but rather that he's a kid in a candy store. And if you're the next strawberry gumdrop, it's just not enough to be sweet. "Nice" and "perfect" have become euphemisms for "nothing's wrong . . . but nothing's *compelling*." It seemed to be all about standing out in the crowd. It's not that men in my research were saying they didn't want someone nice or perfect, but rather that those traits are generic. Finding that elusive chemistry with a woman begins with her energy level, a feisty attitude, and sensuality.

Do You Have The Blahs?

The Blahs encompassed five categories of behavior in my research.[2] Do any of these ring true for you?

LACK OF ENTHUSIASM

If you've been single for a while, sometimes it's hard to find the energy for a fix-up with your second cousin's high school friend or another Internet date. It's also hard after a bad breakup or after a long day at work. It's *especially* hard when you answer the door and he doesn't look like Prince Charming . . . but you're still going to try, you tell yourself. You sigh, grab your purse, and try to recall whether you TiVo'd *Dancing with the Stars*. At least you'll have something to look forward to when you're back home in ninety minutes.

---

[2]Men aged fifty-plus were 63 percent less likely to cite The Blahs than younger men as their primary no-callback reason.

But are you really trying? A lack of enthusiasm can become a self-fulfilling prophecy, and your date will pick up on that vibe. And what if your first impression of him turns out to be misleading? What if you end up really liking him—it just wasn't evident in the first fifteen minutes? If your big inner sigh just set the evening off on the wrong foot, you might never get to find out.

Of course, you may not even *realize* you seem unenthusiastic. Men reported lots of small cues that sounded benign but emitted low energy. Ron, a thirty-year-old executive recruiter from Phoenix, AZ, tried to describe why his date had The Blahs. He just couldn't put his finger on it. Finally he said, "I guess one example was the way she dressed. She wore this plain sweater and jeans. It was like she made no effort to dress up for me." Ron explained that her clothes signaled to him "This date is no big deal." I probed to find out what he would have preferred she wore. He said, "I don't know, I guess something fun . . . a little provocative or flirty . . . I don't mean she should have worn a short skirt, but, you know, just something with flair!"

Joel, a thirty-eight-year-old associate dean at a college in Amherst, MA, commented that his date had "the lean-back slump." For Joel, it was his date's body language that was a giveaway. She leaned back in her chair and kept her distance. She didn't lean forward when she spoke. "I got the sense that she wouldn't be disappointed if I didn't call her back," said Joel. So of course he didn't. Beck, a thirty-one-year-old landscape architect from Philadelphia, PA, explained that when he feels chemistry with a woman "she laughs at my jokes, she leans in closer to hear my stories, and she can poke fun at me in a good-natured way."

Walter, a fifty-one-year-old store owner from Trenton, NJ, recalled being on a date with a woman at a restaurant. He said, "She stared at the menu for a few minutes, sighed, and said, 'I guess I'll have the chicken.' I thought to myself, 'Don't do me any favors.'" Instead, he likes it when a woman looks at the menu and says enthusiastically, "Oooh, I know what I'm having!" or "The cherry-glazed chicken looks delicious!" He said it's those little things that set the energy level for the evening.

> "She stared at the menu for a few minutes, sighed, and said, 'I guess I'll have the chicken.' I thought to myself, 'Don't do me any favors.'"

A different attitude about the enthusiasm topic came from Tom, a forty-five-year-old investor from Wilton, CT. He says he's looking for a (woman who expresses intense passion about something she does—anything at all.)But it's not simply because it makes her livelier. He explained candidly that he's a workaholic who loves his job. He wants someone who truly understands what it's like to be completely absorbed by a passion. He doesn't want her to complain to him one day, "You spend too much time at work . . . is your job more important than I am?" He wants her to relate firsthand to being swept up by something all-consuming so she won't take his long hours personally.

JUST PLAIN BORING

Marcus, a thirty-four-year-old lawyer from Indianapolis, IN, complained about a woman who was bland. He said, "She was polite and pleasant, but . . . *boring*. She didn't contribute any new ideas to our conversation." Alex, a twenty-six-year-old MBA student from Ann Arbor, MI, replied, "Our date was a long series of small talk with smiles pasted on our faces." Kyle, a thirty-nine-year-old business owner in Orlando, FL, said, "She watched a lot of TV . . . she made a lot of references to her favorite shows, like, 'That guy resembles Jack on *Lost*' or 'I can loan you my season one DVD set of *The Office* since you've never seen it.'" He said he perceives people who watch too much TV as unoriginal.

When I asked Jerry, a twenty-four-year-old salesman from Minneapolis, MN, why he dubbed his date boring, he recited some of their conversation topics as "work, siblings, current events, blah, blah, blah." Then he gave me this example: "She said her iPod is always on the 'repeat' setting: she listens to the same song over and over . . . boring! My parents are kinda like that. They have their comfortable routines; they only like what's familiar. I want more variety and adventure in my life."

NO OPINION

While men appreciate a woman who's flexible, they don't want a Stepford wife. Several men described dates with "nonengaging women" who had "lots of yes-or-no, dull answers." They reassured me that "she was fine!" and "there were no red flags!" as they tried to defend why a "perfectly good first date" didn't turn into a second date. Eventually they might concede, "She never called me out on anything" or "She told me 'either way is fine.'" This syndrome was the opposite extreme from The Boss Lady, who had too many opinions and wasn't afraid to bulldoze anyone who disagreed. It's definitely not easy finding the right balance.

Robert, a thirty-six-year-old conference organizer from Albany, NY, remarked that a woman he dated once was "Oprahized." He said, "She was the type who did everything Oprah told her. The whole night it was 'Oprah says this' or 'Oprah knows one thing for sure . . .' This woman had no opinions of her own!"

I learned that reading a restaurant menu could be a Rorschach test. Asher, a thirty-one-year-old insurance claim investigator from Columbia, MO, says he has few second dates because of his "menu pet peeve." Whenever a woman orders the same thing he does, it's an immediate date-breaker. He says it shows a lack of imagination. On a recent brunch date, one woman made the fatal mistake of ordering the same thing as Asher: the French toast. He explained to me that after a "mirror order" occurs, he makes polite conversation for the duration of the date, but he does not intend to see the woman again.

I'd venture to say that mirror orders are not the only reason why Asher has few second dates. . . .

FAILING THE TESTER KISS

Many of my female clients are perplexed by a man who kisses them passionately at the end of the night but then tells me later during an Exit Interview that the evening had The Blahs stamped all over it. If a guy labels the date only "so-so," isn't that a disconnect with a serious kiss? Samuel, a sixty-one-year-old hospital administrator from Portland, ME, explained it this way: "Helen was a nice woman but I didn't feel any sparks during the evening. I wanted to give things one last try, because if I could be attracted to her, she's just the kind of person I'd like to be with. I reached out and embraced her . . . tried to stir up some passion . . . but in the end, it just wasn't there."

In fact, I repeatedly heard about "tester kisses" in other categories outside The Blahs. Men were echoing Samuel's comments that despite some red flags on the date, they believed if the goodnight kiss was spectacular, then the other issues might pale compared to sizzling physical chemistry. Sometimes chemistry is just not there, and you move on, but I think eliminating red flags earlier during a date can certainly help someone be more receptive to "sizzle" at the end of the night.

SPORTY GIRL

A subset of The Blahs is a type I call "Sporty Girl." She's the one who has lots of guy friends but few who lust for her. It's not that she's dull—in fact, she's quite interesting. She runs marathons, or goes heli-skiing, or maybe hikes Kilimanjaro. But she has The *Sensual* Blahs. She is viewed as a guy's buddy rather than his lover. More on this later in Madison's case study (chapter 9).

SOUND FAMILIAR?

You may not have noted similarities to yourself among The Blahs anecdotes thus far, as it's not always easy to recognize yourself through other people's stories. So you can use the self-assessment questions below to verify whether men might be stereotyping you as The Blahs before they get to know the real you.

AT WORK . . .

❏ In your job environment, is it best to keep your head down, stay neutral, and not stir things up?

❏ Has your boss ever said to you, "Drink a lot of caffeine before your presentation!"?

❏ In past performance reviews or casual feedback from coworkers, have you ever been told:
"Try to take more initiative . . ."
"Don't be afraid to tell me if you disagree with my ideas . . ."
"Think outside the box!"

WITH YOUR FRIENDS AND FAMILY . . .

❏ Have you ever been told fondly, "You're such a *nice person!* Someday the right guy will appreciate that!"

❏ Has anyone ever seen your outfit for a date and said, "Don't be afraid to show a little skin!"

❏ Has someone recommended that *you* in particular should read the book *Why Men Love Bitches?*

ON A DATE OR WITH A PAST BOYFRIEND . . .

❏ Do your dates tend to initiate over 75 percent of the conversation topics?

❏ Have you ever heard "You don't sound too excited about that, would you like to do something else?"

❏ Has a guy ever told you, "I bet you're from the Midwest, right?"

YOUR PERSONAL PHILOSOPHY:

❏ Do you think it's smart to keep your opinions to yourself when you're with people you don't know very well?

❏ In general, do you like to "play it safe"?

❏ At an ice cream shop, do you choose vanilla ice cream over more exotic flavors?

If you answered yes to more than five questions above, you may be perceived (or misperceived) as having The Blahs. There's no doubt you're a nice, well-mannered person with many assets; of course you shouldn't change who you are. But you may consider tweaking some of the things you do and say on a first or second date. Men who don't know yet how fabulous you are may dismiss you as The Blahs and miss the chance to get to know you better on the next few dates.

So, What Should You Do?

The Blahs often come disguised as "no chemistry," but this kind of experiment sometimes just needs a change in formula. In the right light, under certain circumstances, these misfires have a better chance than most for a real connection. Obviously I'm not suggesting that you should be with someone if you don't feel a romantic spark, but the theory here is that if two wonderful people go on a date, and if a certain set of events occurs, they might spark. Contrary to the fairy-tale notion that the magic is either there or it's not, sometimes making an effort to light the fire can pay off. If you suspect you have The Blahs, here are six things you can do to spice up your next date.

1) DO YOUR HOMEWORK

Instead of leaving witty conversations to chance, it really helps if you spend one hour prior to your date mentally preparing interesting conversation starters. It's the same thing you'd do to prepare for a job interview. Think of creative questions to ask that differ from the standard get-to-know-you questions (see next page for suggestions). *Be sure not to ask these questions out of the blue, or they'll seem awkward.* Focus on how you phrase and pace your questions so he doesn't feel badgered. Be on the lookout through the evening for a logical bridge to nudge a particular conversation topic around to some of your creative questions. When you're prepared, you can be proactive in sparking fun conversations.

Also, read any current *New York Times* bestselling book to prompt upbeat, intriguing banter on first dates and at cocktail parties.

Twenty Creative Questions to Ask Your Date (That Won't Make Him Yawn)

What's your best secret skill?

What was your favorite toy as a kid?

What's the best gift you ever gave someone?

What's the most embarrassing thing that happened to you in grade school?

If your house was on fire, what's the first thing you'd grab on your way out?

What's the one place you've never been but really want to go?

When you were young, what did you want to be when you grew up?

What's one of your all-time favorite books [or movies]?

What's the worst job you ever had?

Tell me about a funny practical joke you've played on someone.

What's the best advice anyone ever gave you?

What's your favorite board game?

If you could live outside the U.S., where would you live?

What's the best birthday you ever had?

If you could have any animal in the world as a pet, what would it be?

How do you wish your parents were different?

What was your best Halloween costume?

What's the bravest thing you've done?

What's the most fun family vacation you've had?

What's the luckiest thing that ever happened to you?

Pop culture nonfiction books play especially well, such as *Stumbling on Happiness* by Daniel Gilbert, *The Geography of Bliss* by Eric Weiner, or *Blink* by Malcolm Gladwell. These books are easy to summarize for anyone who hasn't read them and can be great sources for thoughtful or quirky questions. Stay away from books on women's issues, religion, and politics—they're usually too controversial for a first date.

Be careful here to avoid the "intelligent yet boring" trap. I had a client who dated an orthopedic surgeon once, and prior to their first date she researched his field of medicine on the Internet. She thought she was cleverly doing her homework. He later told me that while he was impressed with her intelligent questions, their evening was boring because they spoke too much about his work.

2) GET EXCITED

As you saw from the many anecdotes earlier in this chapter, men are going to get a dull vibe if you're not enthusiastic during a date. Now, don't go overboard and turn into an eager beaver, but within the realm of cool, find two excuses to show off your positive energy in the first half hour of your date. It might be in the form of a personal compliment ("Wow, what a great jacket!"), a comment about a choice he made for your evening ("Oh, I've been dying to try this new restaurant, I'm so glad you chose it!"), or a comment about something exciting you're planning ("I can't wait to go . . . "). If he asks a mundane question, such as "How was your day?" you might energetically reply, "Great! And our date gave me something to look forward to." If he says, "Tell me about your job?" you can either play the guessing game suggested earlier, or try this: "There's a funny story about what happened last year when I interviewed for my job . . ." or "You meet the most interesting people in my line of work. For example . . ."

3) GIVE HIM A LITTLE BACK TALK

Avoiding The Blahs is about creating conversational banter—not just exchanging facts. Men were telling me that a woman's sassy attitude is definitely alluring. It's that good-natured teasing they like, the kind that says "I'm on to you, mister. Those glib lines don't work with me . . . try again." Remember in grade school when you got in trouble for giving your parents back talk? When you're on a date, that impertinence can spark good chemistry.

For example, Julian, a fifty-five-year-old dentist from Providence, RI, said he had a boring date. I kept asking him for examples: What did she do? What did she say? What didn't she say? Finally he remembered one thing that reflected her overall demeanor. He complimented her eyeglasses and then asked her, "Do you always wear glasses, or do you sometimes wear contacts?" Her reply was, "I usually wear contacts, but my eyes were tired tonight, so I put on my frames." He said it was just a boring response. I pointed out to him it was a boring question. Then I said, "Okay, let's set aside your less-than-electrifying question for a moment. What might have been a better reply from her in your example?" Julian suggested, "She could have said, 'Don't worry, I'll take them off later if we kiss.' Or she could have said, 'Someone at work told me these frames make me look like a sexy librarian—what do you think?' To me, those flirtatious comments would have made me sit up and pay attention!"

Let's say a guy inquires whether you have any siblings. Don't provide a fact sheet about how many, where they live, and how many nieces or nephews you have. Try to answer with the angle most people wouldn't. For example, tell him a funny story about a family trip gone awry or the embarrassing trick your older brother played on you in third grade. Or describe the label you held among your siblings: were you the smart one, the wisecracker, or the one who always got in trouble? These twists on answering standard questions can start a chain reaction leading to more intriguing and less superficial dialogue.

4) GET SCARED

Your first date doesn't have to be confined to coffeehouses or restaurants. Scary activities that get your adrenaline pumping (such as riding roller coasters, watching a horror film, or going to unique venues for trapeze lessons or indoor skydiving) are recommended for The Blahs. Sharing a scary experience prompts your adrenaline to spike and your pulse to quicken, simulating a sexual response.[3] According to David Givens, PhD, an anthropologist at the Center for Nonverbal Studies, "The mind mistakes any sort of arousal for sexual attraction, and will attribute this excitement to whomever you're with."

5) TELL A GOOD JOKE

Everyone loves a good joke. If you know a funny one, fantastic. If not, ask some friends in advance for ideas. Obviously select a joke in good taste that best reflects your personal sense of humor. This is a quick way to liven things up and break through any fog that may be hovering over your date.

6) READ BETWEEN THE LINES

What if you think your date is going well, but suddenly he asks an out-of-the-blue question that seems a bit odd? Maybe he says randomly, "Tell me something you're passionate about." Sure, this could be an innocent, rehearsed query he asks every woman, but more likely it's a red flag. His train of thought might have gone something like this: "She's kinda dull . . . I wonder if *anything* gets this girl fired up. Hmm, how to find out? Hey, I know! I'll ask her what she's passionate about . . ." That's a wake-up call saying your date energy is lagging. Sit up straight, answer his question with gusto, remember your homework, and order a double espresso!

---

[3]Source: MSN.com article "First Dates: Dos and Don'ts to Create Chemistry" by Matt Schneiderman, February 2008.

If You Have The Blahs . . .

WHAT'S HOT:	WHAT'S NOT:
1. "I just read a fun book about what makes people happy. I was surprised that . . ."	1. "I hear it's supposed to warm up later this week."
2. "Instead of dinner, would you be up for trying indoor skydiving?"	2. "Dinner and a movie sounds fine."
3. Putting a sassy spin on mundane questions	3. Reciting facts
4. Stylish high heels or boots	4. Comfortable flats or sneakers
5. A passionate good-night kiss	5. A peck on the lips

#3 REASON HE DIDN'T CALL BACK
The Bait & Switcher

Just once I wish I could have a date with a woman who *exceeded* my expectations. —Josh, age 42, Dallas, TX

I'd guess only 20 percent of women represent themselves accurately online.
—Dillon, age 26, New York, NY

Hope is everyone's mirage. —Source unknown

"Bait and switch" is a business term used to describe deceptive advertising. A customer is tempted by an advertised bargain (the "bait") and lured to the store. But when he arrives to make the purchase, a salesman might tell him there's a hidden charge, tell him they're out of stock, or persuade him to buy a different item—usually something more expensive and therefore not the bargain he expected (the "switch"). In dating, this practice is used by women who create false expectations of themselves (both physical and otherwise) to encourage a man to ask them out, hoping he'll overlook something less than desirable when they meet in person or when she better explains a negative situation. This was the number-three date-breaker men cited overall (and among men who described online dates only, it was the number-one date-breaker). Men felt duped and let down. It seems obvious, right? Based on faulty or insufficient information, he expected her to be one thing, but she was something else.

Yet it's not so simple. Sure, there are the trite scenarios from online dating horror stories where he discovers she lied outright about something (her age, her body type, a misleading photo). But this section is not only about couples who had never met prior to their first date (remember that I've been collecting this data since 1998, long before Internet dating became fashionable). Consider these two statistics:

→ Thirty-five percent of the men who cited The Bait & Switcher were not on a blind date (i.e., they had already met their date at least once in person—at a function or with friends—before their first date). The "switch" was based on something misleading she had initially said, not based on a different physical appearance than he anticipated.

→ Forty-two percent of the men who *did* meet a woman through the Internet and then cited The Bait & Switcher agreed with the statement "She represented herself fairly online." In other words, she didn't lie or post a misleading photo, but he jumped to incorrect conclusions from statements she made that were too vague or expectations that he imposed upon her.

What's going on? Basically it's this: You hear what you want to hear. You see what you want to see. The tide of dating is such that hopes and dreams swell prematurely, leaving a disappointing reality in their wake. This is human nature. But there is something you can do to improve your dating retention rate: sell, but don't oversell yourself up front. Regardless of your looks or personality, you'll have a greater chance for a second date if you are a little better, rather than a little worse, than what he expected.

Are you The Bait & Switcher?

The Bait & Switcher encompassed four categories of behavior in my research. Do any of these ring true for you?

LIES AND LACK OF SELF-AWARENESS

Sometimes it was simple: she lied. Of course men lie all the time too, so this is by no means gender-specific. The physical examples I heard from men dating online ranged from the benign to the outrageous. The most popular deception, as you might expect, involved body type. Kevin, a thirty-four-year-old commercial Realtor from Austin, TX, developed incredible e-mail and telephone chemistry with a Miami woman he met through Perfectmatch.com. He felt so compelled to meet her that he flew to Miami for their first date. But when he saw her, he said, "She easily weighed over two hundred pounds." Then he added dryly, "Even without her tool belt." She had sent him photos of herself in which she looked slender. "Maybe it was her sister in the photo, or maybe her face had been Photoshopped on a different body," he speculated. He was on the next flight home (and immediately canceled his Perfectmatch subscription).

I heard anecdotes about women who posted photos of themselves taken too many years ago and women whose photos used lighting that can best be described as overly generous. Whether they encountered facial acne or shorter hair than appeared in the photo, men just didn't like the unexpected. I also noted a subgroup of replies in this body category: the unexpected size or shape of one specific body part. Craig, a forty-five-year-old lawyer from Atlanta, GA, said, "She was seated when I arrived at the table . . . later, when I saw the size of her caboose, I almost choked on my own saliva." Nice guy, that Craig.

There were outright lies about nonphysical problems too, both from online and offline encounters. These included lying about being a model, where she went to college, and her real age. I learned that men expect a little fudging of the truth about age: they conceded it was not a big deal if her age was one or two years different than she initially claimed but were turned off abruptly if they found out her real age differed significantly. I also learned how easy it is to get caught. With sites ranging from MySpace to Google to Date-Detectives, it's easier than ever to verify the details of someone's life.

Third-party intermediaries (well-meaning, matchmaking friends) can sometimes be the culprits behind exaggerations or lack of awareness. Ed, a thirty-six-year-old photographer from Salt Lake City, UT, was fixed up by his coworker. His date was oversold as "utterly fabulous." When he finally met her in person, he was disappointed that she was "utterly average."

Honestly, *I was bored* by these surface responses coming from certain men. I wanted to dig deeper into this bait-and-switch problem.

UNMET EXPECTATIONS

In what initially seemed to be a giant contradiction, about a third of the men who claimed to be victims of The Bait & Switcher (i.e., the woman was worse than he expected on the date), later admitted these same women had "technically" represented themselves accurately before their date. Now this was interesting.

Travis, a twenty-five-year-old fitness instructor in New York, NY, says his number one must-have is a physically fit partner who is dedicated to exercise (the foundation of his job). He recalled a woman named Shelly he met on Chemistry.com who had written in her profile that she "exercised regularly." Her photo was gorgeous and she seemed to fit many other criteria he wanted. He couldn't wait to meet her. When they eventually met in person, he asked her what she liked to do for exercise. She replied, "I love to walk to work! It's great to start the day with a brisk fifteen-minute walk." Travis said he could never fall for someone whose idea of exercise was walking to work in Manhattan. He asked her several more questions to gauge her interest in athletic activity but felt disappointed by her responses. Now Travis limits his dating pool to women he meets in the cardio-kickboxing classes he teaches. You might think this dating pool is more of a puddle, but he says it serves as a better fitness screen for him.

Travis admits that Shelly had been honest "technically": she hadn't lied or exaggerated. Shelly does exercise regularly—just not in the way that met Travis's expectations. His hopes about her colored what he expected to find, and once he discovered those hopes were built on a faulty premise, he dismissed her as a potential mate before really getting to know her—and worse, wasted her valuable time.

Shawn, a forty-one-year-old Realtor in Newport, RI, revealed another nuance in this arena. I had personally fixed him up with my client Ruth. Though he's Catholic and she's Jewish, both had told me they were "spiritual but not religious" and were open-minded about meeting each other. But Shawn later told me that by the end of their date, he got the distinct impression Ruth was more religious than he had expected. "She made a point of emphasizing Judaism throughout the night," Shawn lamented. "She told a funny story about a Passover dinner; she used a bunch of Hebrew words I didn't really understand; and she told me how important it was for her to raise her kids Jewish." Shawn continued, "Though Catholicism has been a big influence in my life, I might be open to raising my kids in another religion if they have good values and faith in God. But it seemed like our backgrounds would be more of a problem for *her* down the road, so I didn't ask her out again." A week later when I shared this Exit Interview recap with Ruth (with Shawn's permission), she exclaimed, "That's ridiculous! Wow, I had really liked him. He was *so* cute and had a lot of qualities I'm looking for! I was receptive to dating a non-Jew. . . . maybe subconsciously I wanted to test his attitudes about religion before deciding if he had long-term potential."

But Ruth's "test" was premature, and frankly she sabotaged her own self-proclaimed open-mindedness. By not-so-subtly raising a big topic like religious differences on a first date, she forced him to make a hasty decision before getting to know whether the rest of a relationship with him could be really compelling. Instead, Shawn left the date feeling misled by what he expected versus what he encountered, and neither of them had a chance to learn more about each other.

I'm not trivializing the impact of religious differences in a marriage or any other major difference between husband and wife. Yet I'm illustrating here how two wonderful people, who were self-described as open-minded, got off on the wrong foot by not allowing chemistry to happen first and some inevitable give-and-take to happen later.

THE CYRANO DE BERGERAC

In today's dating culture, so heavily dominated by the Internet, there is another subcategory that stands alone under The Bait & Switcher umbrella. It is the disconnect between someone's vibrant electronic personality (i.e., writing skills combined with lack of inhibition) and an initially dull face-to-face personality (i.e., shyness or quiet demeanor). While this topic overlaps with both "lacking self-awareness" and "unmet expectations," this specific dynamic was so prevalent that it requires its own spotlight.

Online dating has actually reversed the process of finding chemistry between two people. It used to be that two people met face-to-face (in a classroom, at a party, etc.), and if they felt a spark, they went on a date to discover whether they had anything in common. Now two people first assess online whether they have common ground and *then* meet to assess chemistry. It's a system guaranteed to produce a lot of failed first dates.

Caleb, a twenty-nine-year-old chemist from Madison, WI, admitted he's shy. He said he is looking for his opposite and became enamored once with a vibrant, clever, "electronic woman." She later showed up in person as awkward and introverted. She didn't make eye contact and gave one-word answers. He also noted that she was dressed in all-black clothing "like a widow in mourning," which he couldn't reconcile with the colorful personality he met through his computer screen.

Charlie, a thirty-two-year-old film animator from Los Angeles, CA, said his date "pulled a Houdini . . . she seemed self-assured on her keyboard but then showed up and told me things like, 'You're so good-looking that I find it hard to talk to you' and 'Guys like you usually don't ask me out.'" He also said she fidgeted with her hands most of the night and generally came across as insecure. This was a disconnect between his anticipation and his experience.

BEER GOGGLES

Full disclosure: you can't do much about the situations described in this section. However, I wanted to include them because they do reflect some of The Bait & Switcher examples men described to me. While most men in my research revealed "actionable stories" for women, certainly some did not. But I think even when you can't do anything about his reason, it can still give you closure to understand what happened.

A guy's memory, or getting swept up in a unique time and place, sometimes created The Bait & Switcher. As some men explained, it was like the euphemism "beer goggles," where a woman looks better and better as a man drinks more and more. Karl, age twenty-four, from Orange County, CA, said, "She looked better to me at two AM in a dark bar."

But it goes farther than beer goggles. For some guys, it's "nostalgia goggles." Bob, a twenty-three-year-old psychology graduate student from Omaha, NE, ran into Marla at a party, someone he had known in high school but hadn't seen in five years. She looked great, so he asked her out. He soon realized that they had nothing in common anymore. His initial interest was based on his perception of her in high school (spontaneous, creative), which he realized did not reflect who she had become in recent years (uptight, conservative). At least, that was his first impression during their date. I wondered if Marla had really changed or if she was simply nervous about being on an official date with a friend from high school. We'll never know.

Sometimes you change, or he does, or lighting doesn't work in your favor, or unfortunately you don't have a connection anymore in a different time period or setting. Sometimes the reasons men don't call back can be illuminating, though not always fixable (nor would you want them to be).

SOUND FAMILIAR?

You may not have noted similarities to yourself among The Bait & Switcher anecdotes thus far, as it's not always easy to recognize yourself through other people's stories. So you can use the self-assessment questions below to verify whether men might be stereotyping you as The Bait & Switcher before they get to know the real you.

AT WORK . . .

❑ Do you work in any type of sales position? And if so, did your training teach you certain "tricks" to grab the customer's interest?

❑ In past performance reviews or casual feedback from coworkers, have you ever been told, "You'd be great in the PR department; you really know how to put a spin on something!"?

❑ Has a colleague ever said, "I saw your photo on Facebook [or Match.com] . . . wow, I didn't even recognize you!"

WITH YOUR FRIENDS AND FAMILY . . .

❑ Have you ever been referred to fondly as The Exaggerator?

❑ Has anyone ever told you, "You'd do well in politics!" or "You'd make a great poker player!"?

❑ Do you sometimes defend yourself by saying, "A *white* lie is not a lie!"?

ON A DATE OR WITH A PAST BOYFRIEND . . .

❑ Has a guy you met online ever said, "You're different than I expected . . .," or "Oh, so *that's* what you meant in your profile . . ."?

❑ Has a blind date ever told you, "Your friend spoke *so* highly of you—I almost couldn't believe someone that perfect existed!"?

❑ When you really like a guy, do you tend to stretch the truth about something—maybe because you think he wouldn't be interested if he saw the real you?

YOUR PERSONAL PHILOSOPHY:

❑ Do you believe that if only you can get your foot in the door, you can make almost anything happen?

❑ Do you think, "What he doesn't know won't hurt him . . ."?

❑ Do you secretly admire how Bill Clinton phrased his famous comment "I did *not* have sex with that woman"?

If you answered yes to more than five questions above, you may be perceived (or misperceived) as The Bait & Switcher. There's no doubt you're strategic, clever, and a positive person; of course you shouldn't change who you are deep down. But you may consider tweaking some of the things you do and say on a first or second date. Men who don't know yet how fabulous you are may perceive you as The Bait & Switcher and miss the chance to get to know you better on the next few dates.

So, What Should You Do?

If you can relate to The Bait & Switcher, consider whether you are being efficient with the hours you spend dating. Bait-and-switch methods lead to many failed first dates, which can be emotionally damaging to you over time. Putting your best foot forward is different from wasting your time and energy by creating false expectations. Here are six suggestions to help you date productively.

1) SELL, BUT DON'T OVERSELL

If you've fallen into The Bait & Switcher trap, the most important thing you can do is figure out the difficult balance between promoting your assets and not overpromising. Try to be honest and self-aware without prematurely dousing his interest. I know this is easier said than done, but the greatest enemy of the first date is unmet expectations. You have to be confident, but not so much that he's expecting a combination of Elle Macpherson's looks, Ellen DeGeneres's wit, and Madeleine Albright's intelligence to walk through the door. You should select some of your best traits, along with a few of your relative weaknesses, and then sprinkle references about both sides into pre-date interaction.

As a guideline during an e-mail, phone call, or online profile description, use a 3:1 ratio rule. For every three mentions about your positive traits, refer to one of your "lighter" drawbacks (e.g., "I'm a bad cook" rather than "I have herpes"). Use a self-deprecating, not insecure, tone. In an online profile, use this 3:1 ratio by displaying three great photos of yourself next to one "average" photo. Net-net you want him to be "moderately hopeful" about meeting you. He shouldn't put your date super high on the anticipation scale because then there's nowhere left to go but down.

2) BE MORE PRECISE

Online, you will be more efficient with your time if you can be more precise in your dating profile by giving detailed examples rather than writing vague generalities. Using broad statements is not necessarily widening your audience; it often allows men to create fantasies in their mind that usually build, then crash. That's not to say that you should provide every last detail about yourself—it's good to maintain a little mystery—but remember this adage from the advertising world: if you try to be all things to all people, you end up being nothing to everyone.

Pick just a few areas about yourself to give some flavor. For example, when you say "I love to read," do you mean celebrity magazines, historical fiction, or computer trade journals? Provide some specific titles as your favorites. If you say, "I am comfortable in either jeans or a ball gown," clarify whether you're a fashion magazine editor who goes camping once a year or you're a forest ranger who owns a fancy dress on the off chance she's invited to a Bar Mitzvah. Offline, if you're chatting with someone at a party, make an effort to provide similar examples. Not only be precise, but be honest about what you say and write, because it has to hold up later if the relationship progresses. Simple details go a long way toward setting expectations accurately and not wasting your time with the wrong guys.

3) PUT A POSITIVE SPIN ON IT

Sometimes there is something about yourself that needs an initial positive spin to avoid inviting a negative stereotype. I believe in the distinction between lying and spinning something to your advantage (maybe I have a bright future in politics). For example, many women have jobs that provoke less-than-desirable assumptions by men. Maybe your job title is "CEO of the Realty Corporation," which can sound intimidating, or your title is "tax accountant," which can make you sound dull. If so, don't reveal your title right away. You can initially say that you "work in real estate" or liven up your title a bit by smiling and saying, "I'm a math magician!"

I had a client once who was a psychotherapist. As soon as she told men her profession, many of them withdrew. Perhaps they felt uncomfortable with the idea that she might analyze everything they did or said. So I advised her not to use the label "psychotherapist" initially, but rather describe her job (vaguely but truthfully) as a "private coach"—someone who helps clients figure out how they can best achieve their goals. If her date pressed for details, she could select "light" examples about how she helped her clients overcome a fear of flying or become more assertive in a job search. When men came to know her better and trust she wouldn't evaluate them as if they were her patients, they'd probably feel more comfortable with her real job title.

If you have a physical feature that might be a strike against you, use online photos to *balance* it, not hide it. For example, I know one woman who has a very, very large derrière, but she also has a sexy hourglass shape (small waist, C-cup breasts, great legs). Rather than try to hide her bottom in her online dating profile, she posted full-body photos taken from a side angle that showed both her front and back. Her wonderfully proportioned figure was attractive to some men and not to others. By "putting her best butt forward," she accurately set expectations for her dates and filtered out men who would waste her time and deflate her confidence.

Sometimes the spin might involve something trickier, such as an age difference. I work with many women who are single in their forties and don't want to reveal their age right away. They worry that men will rule them out over fertility concerns. I think they should never lie, but if asked directly about their age at a social function or on a first date, I think it's okay to reply with something flirty, like "Let's just say I'm old enough to know better than to answer that question . . . but young enough to put a smile on your face." Maybe that's too Mae West? But you get the idea. However, for an online dating profile, I believe you should reveal your real age because the only way to fill in that two-digit blank space on a website is with the truth or a lie. Ultimately, the truth is the only foundation for a healthy relationship, and when a guy finds out that you lied about your age (and he always will), he'll think, "If she lied about one thing, what else did/could she lie about?" This is how *your* mind works too when you catch a guy telling any lie. So, yeah, you've gotta come clean about your real age. But . . . okay, you caught me in a good mood today: I'll give you a thirty-day leeway to round down if your birthday just passed!

4) TEMPER THE SHOCK

Sometimes spinning the issue is not an option for you if you have one specific physical issue that stands out prominently. If you've never met the guy before, it might be better to address it head-on with him in advance. Your issue might include anything from un-usual and visible scars, to abnormally bad teeth, to a lazy eye. I'm sure you are self-aware enough to know your own blatant issues, but if you're genuinely unsure, immediately ask a few friends who are the type to provide honest feedback. It's important to find out first whether the issue is real or something classifiable as you being hard on yourself. If it's the latter, forget this advice: no need to call atten-tion to something he probably won't notice. But if it's the former, try to lower his expectations just enough so that he'll still meet you but isn't hoping for the moon and the stars. Then there's only one place the date energy can go when he sees you: *up*.

Here's an example from my personal travel escapades to illus-trate my point. Two years ago I booked a trip to be a guest speaker at a conference in Washington, DC. Using recommendations from my trusty Frommer's guide, I reserved a room at a small hotel that I'll call the Adams Court Hotel. The following week a friend told me about TripAdvisor, the online site where customers post candid reviews of their travel experiences. So I looked up the Adams Court Hotel on TripAdvisor and saw both good and bad reviews. A few of the bad reviews were *really* bad, including comments about moldy shower curtains and dingy carpeting. Tragically, my deposit was nonrefundable at that point. With a heavy heart two days later, I ar-rived at the hotel. And guess what? It wasn't as bad as I had feared. I was actually delighted! I enjoyed my stay and would return again to the Adams Court Hotel.

In the dating world, I want you to create a nonrefundable-deposit approach with anyone you've never met in person. Whether you meet online or through a fix-up, try to develop a rapport via e-mail and phone before mentioning any physical issue you might have. Let him get to know how funny, kind, and smart you are before meeting face-to-face. Let the e-mails and phone calls go on a bit longer than usual (in this case about two or three weeks with regular contact) before agreeing to a live date. Set the time and place, but just prior to the meeting (within four hours), call him to confirm the location. This is an excuse: what you're really going to do is set realistic expectations by preparing him for your issue without leaving him time to politely back out of your date. Unless he's an utter cad (whom you don't want to date anyway), most nice guys will still show up if they've committed the time to you.

As an example, let's say you have a bad scar on your neck and you're self-conscious about it. Maybe in the past, others have registered "controlled surprise" when they've seen it, and you've endured some awkward moments. You don't need that interfering with an otherwise great first impression you make. So casually mention in a last-minute pre-date call or e-mail a brief story about how you got the scar. No need for details, but depending on what really happened, you might say something like, "Oh, by the way, I have a bad scar on my neck—you'll see it when we meet—it's no big deal, but I didn't want you to be surprised by it. I had an accident when I was younger—but I'll save that story for another time! See you soon!" Alerting him in advance allows his reaction to shift from "I was so surprised when I saw that terrible scar" to "Oh, the scar wasn't as bad as I expected . . . in fact, she's a great girl—I'd like to get to know her better."

What if your little shock is more like an earthquake? For example, what if you are severely overweight? If so, you're not alone. Approximately 127 million adults in the U.S. are plus-sized. You can find your target audience with preset expectations on dating websites such as www.BBWPersonalsPlus.com, www.largeandlovely.com, www.BBWcupid.com, and www.largefriends.com. There are clearly men out there who accept and want overweight women. Dozens of websites advertise successful connections between big, beautiful women (BBW) and their admirers. Offline, you can focus on meeting men through affinity groups: like-minded settings where you can bond over something more significant than appearance (such as your church or synagogue). There are many niche affinity groups in local cities now that connect singles through the Internet, for everyone from people who speak French, to people who love pug dogs, to fans of the Dennis Prager radio show. Look at www.meetup.com for hundreds of groups near you that might be appealing.

Don't waste your time trying to hide a severely overweight body (or something equally distinct) on dating websites. He'll find out eventually, and no, his untempered shock when he sees how different you look from what he expected will not be overshadowed by your sparkling personality. Instead, use the truth to screen men early on who might be drawn to you. You should still highlight, for example, your pretty face, but don't show a photo that's clearly misleading about your body type (or check off the "slender" box).

5) TAKE THE REINS

There is a study that claims 50 percent of couples married or living together were introduced by good friends or family members.[4] Networking through friends is essential when you're single, as you already know. But take the reins of your would-be matchmakers and make sure they don't oversell you during a fix-up. Remember that unmet expectations are the enemy. If you find yourself fortunate enough to be fixed up by a friend (and I use the word "fortunate" because I think singles sometimes can be very ungrateful when a person goes out of their way to broker an introduction), be sure to tell him or her politely but clearly, "Please try not to oversell me." Blame it on my "sell but don't oversell" advice. Then give your friend some examples of what to say about you that's positive yet tempered. In my experience, friends don't perceive these suggestions as pushy, but rather they genuinely want a little help when it comes to "marketing" someone they care about.

6) MAKE THE BEST OF IT

There's only one guarantee in dating: you're going to have some bad dates. Sometimes one or both of you will experience the bait-and-

---

[4]University of Chicago, Edward Laumann, PhD.

switch factor despite your best pre-date screening efforts. You might find yourself surprised to be sitting across from a complete jerk or a complete bore. Perhaps he's equally disinterested in you. Now you're both stuck for at least an hour together until one of you politely yawns and says it's getting late, or until you fake some kind of emergency and run out. Rather than write off this date as a total loss and allow your energy level to deflate, recognize that you can mine for gold here.

One of my Chicago-based clients once found herself on an excruciating blind date arranged by her sister. Instead of shutting down at dinner and not making any real effort at conversation, she decided to make the best of it. She casually quizzed the guy, "So, how do you typically meet single women in Chicago?" He mentioned that he'd had some good experiences with speed dating through Hurry Date. She'd never considered speed dating as an option for herself in the past, but after he recommended it so highly, she signed up for one session the following month. There she met a man she later married. When someone asks her now how she met her husband, she smiles and says "Through a blind date." What she means is that she leveraged the situation with a terrible blind date who led her down a path to meet the right guy later.

Also, try to *enjoy* your dates for what they are—a chance to meet someone new—rather than being laser-focused on meeting The One. It's just an hour or two! Everyone has something interesting to say if you're patient enough to ask good questions and really listen. Even if there's absolutely zero romantic chemistry, find something he knows about that you don't. If he's a sports fanatic and you know nothing about sports, ask him, "What's the most exciting play you've ever seen in baseball?" You'll probably enjoy his story, and I promise these tidbits will come in handy one day with a guy you actually want to impress.

You can also find yourself across the table from someone completely mismatched for you, but he might be perfect for another single friend. In that case, wait a few weeks after the date and then e-mail him to offer an introduction to your friend. You can write something like this:

Hi Jim!

It was great meeting you a few weeks ago. I know we didn't have a lot in common, but I think you're a great guy and wondered if you'd be interested in meeting a friend of mine. I think the two of you might really hit it off. If you're open to this, let me know and I'll send you more details about her. Hope you're doing well!

All the best, Jane.

Not only is this good karma, but down the road perhaps your friend or your failed-date guy will return the favor. Always remember that even the worst cases of bait-and-switch dating—the ones that can't be cured—can still lead to something positive.

If You're The Bait & Switcher . . .

WHAT'S HOT:	WHAT'S NOT:
1. Revealing some of your assets	1. Overselling your stock
2. Spinning a potential negative	2. Out-and-out lying
3. Tempering the shock in advance	3. Hoping the shock will dissolve when you dazzle him with your personality
4. Being set up with a guy because you're "a great girl"	4. Being set up with a guy because you're "a great girl who's prettier than a model and smarter than Einstein"
5. Setting expectations	5. Setting expectations you can't meet

#4 REASON HE DIDN'T CALL BACK
The Park Avenue Princess

> She was looking for a "perfect 10": the guy who's a 5
> on the looks scale with $5 million in the bank.
> —David, age 37, Long Island, NY

> It was all about "Buy me, take me, give me."
> —Mark, age 52, Los Angeles, CA

> Her definition of tragedy was her cleaning lady not
> showing up for work. —Jared, age 28, Atlanta, GA

Men don't call back The Park Avenue Princess for several reasons. Often she's very high-maintenance or she's picky about her discerning tastes, from sushi to handbags. She can appear very interested in money. Sometimes she is perceived as fake or superficial. She expects a man to take care of her, financially and emotionally. Whether she's a daddy's girl, a successful professional, or just a girl with aspirations, she is looking to marry a lifestyle along with her man.

It's no surprise that men are wary of The Park Avenue Princess. She conjures up nightmares for him of Paris Hilton or Zsa Zsa Gabor. Men—both rich and poor—know that money is a factor on the dating circuit. But like a bad country-western song, they just want to be loved for who they are. They don't want to be taken advantage of financially or wonder if her feelings are genuine. And they especially want to feel appreciated.

Are You The Park Avenue Princess?

The Park Avenue Princess encompassed five categories of behavior in my research. Do any of these ring true for you?

THE MONEY DETECTIVE

Just as men sometimes screen women for beauty, women sometimes screen men for money, or the potential for money. This dynamic is nothing new, but today the Internet facilitates and validates these connections (e.g., www.richorbeautiful.com and www.millionaire match.com). Outside these sites, however, women have a money-screening handicap because net worth is less transparent in the real world now than ever before. Gone are the good old days when class structure and blue blood were the telltale signs of wealth. Financial security isn't obvious anymore.

If a man says he's unemployed, does that mean he's a retired Internet millionaire, has a trust fund, or can't keep a job? What if he's a partner in a law firm? You might assume he's making a great salary, but perhaps the bulk of his paycheck goes to alimony, goes to graduate school loans, or sits in the bank because he's such a cheapskate. What if he mentions his "ski house in Colorado"? Does this mean ultra-rich or average Joe? You have no idea if he has a mansion in Aspen or a shared backcountry yurt in the middle of nowhere. Thus, when The Park Avenue Princess wants to assess whether a guy is wealthy enough for her, her only option is to play detective.

What seemed to amuse the men I spoke with was how transparent women are at the detective game, even when they think they're being subtle. Gordon, a thirty-six-year-old entrepreneur from New York, NY, claims to know every trick question in the book: "Women hear that I'm an entrepreneur, and they don't know how to evaluate my financial situation. So they slip in these proxy questions throughout the date, like 'Is your apartment a one-bedroom or two? Do you have a car in the city? Does your company give you stock options?' They think they're so subtle." Other proxy questions that made men smirk included "What kind of car do you drive?" "What neighborhood do you live in?" "What does your dad do?" "Which hotel did you stay at on your trip?" "How many does your boat sleep?" For divorced men: "Do you pay alimony?" And then my personal favorite: "Do you fly commercial?"

Dale, a thirty-seven-year-old investment banker in Denver, CO, said, "I lived in Manhattan for a while and noticed how women there ask more up-front questions about what you do for a living, while Colorado women ask about your outdoor activities. Yet underneath it feels the same. Whether their questions are about my job title or what type of sports equipment I have, I still think they're trying to calculate my income. I thought I would get away from that when I moved here. But my 'managing director' title and Orbea-brand mountain bike have the same effect on their bottom line. The only difference now is my zip code."

George, a forty-eight-year-old software engineer from Los Angeles, CA, says it's very hard to find sincere women in LA: "I actually own two cars—a Prius and a Corvette—but I purposely drive my Prius on a first date to fend off the gold diggers." And Gerry, a sixty-four-year-old insurance broker from Hartford, CT, says, "I know what women really want to hear, but I like to mess with them. Sometimes I'll let it slip (falsely) that I owe five months of back rent or I maxed out my credit cards, just to test how fast they'll look at their watches and calculate when they can politely go home."

SekouWrites, the thirty-six-year-old writer from New York, NY, recalled a conversation when he discovered he wasn't rich enough for his date, Elizabeth. Like himself, she had just moved into a new apartment. The two of them were having fun comparing stories about trying to decorate their new digs. But suddenly he felt things going downhill. Elizabeth was referencing her Ralph Lauren paint colors and Italian leather sofas, while he was thinking, "I can barely buy Ikea furniture, and I didn't even *know* paint had designer labels." He quipped, "When she mentioned her new Egyptian-cotton sheets with five hundred thread count, I knew I'd be sleeping alone that night in my own cotton-jersey sheets."

> "[Women ask me] 'Does your company give you stock options?' They think they're so subtle."

HIGH MAINTENANCE

Men also complained about women who seemed high maintenance or spoiled. Nick, a twenty-two-year-old fireman from Ft. Collins, CO, remembered asking his date, "How was your day?" She replied, "Oh, it was hard . . . I couldn't get my nails done because I had to write a paper . . . I didn't get a long enough nap . . ." Nick figured if that was a "hard day" for her, she was too spoiled for his taste. Malcolm, a sixty-six-year-old book publisher in San Diego, CA, said a woman remarked at one point during their date, "My favorite time of day is coming home after my maid has finished the housework. Everything is so clean and organized." Malcolm said the word "maid" sounded snobby and the whole comment rubbed him the wrong way. She later made a few other mentions of her high-end taste, which made him conclude that he could never maintain her lifestyle on his salary. Assuming they wouldn't be compatible (without knowing whether she cared about or needed his income), he never called her again.

High maintenance wasn't defined only by talk of manicures and maids. Being picky, fastidious, or delicate played a role in this category too. Wayne, a thirty-seven-year-old computer consultant in Raleigh, NC, told me he dated a woman once who mentioned that she traveled with her own hypoallergenic pillow and later said, "I only go to doctors at the Mayo Clinic" and "I'm sensitive to noise: I need my soundwave machine to fall asleep." Wayne surmised, "She didn't exactly seem like the type who could handle anything life throws at you, which I think is an important quality in a mate." Barry, a twenty-six-year-old magazine editor in New York, NY, gave me one example about ordering water at restaurants: "The waiter asked whether we wanted tap or bottled, and [my date] said bottled, but only if they had Evian . . . it wasn't bad enough she didn't want tap water, but then she didn't want just *any* bottled water—it had to be a certain brand!" Those are the girls you can never please, he concluded.

SELF-CENTERED

Sometimes men described a princess-like attitude that translated into everything being "all about her." Interestingly, these tended to be guys who felt that everything should be about them! Austin, a twenty-seven-year-old medical resident at a hospital in Staten Island, NY, had been on call the night before his first date with Sasha. He called her at 10:00 AM to decide where they'd have lunch, and he mentioned he was exhausted but was looking forward to meeting her. She suggested they meet at a café near her apartment on the Upper East Side. Austin proceeded to spend about ninety minutes walking to the waterfront, then taking the ferry and the subway to meet her. Before the date even commenced, he was feeling resentful that she'd chosen a convenient location for herself without considering his situation. He remarked that he fully believes in chivalry, but said, "C'mon, suggesting a place closer to a sleep-deprived resident on Staten Island would have gone a long way with me."

During lunch, Austin and Sasha actually had a great conversation and found many things in common. He thought she was cute but ultimately not for him "because she was the type who looked out for number one." As I probed for some examples that led to this stereotype, he remembered two things she said (besides her restaurant location choice). She had told a story about a friend who'd asked her for help on moving day, but Sasha feigned back pain to get out of it. And he said that during lunch an air-conditioning vent was blowing cold air on her, and she asked him if he'd mind switching seats (not thinking the vent would then bother *him*). Did this represent a few random, innocuous comments from Sasha or her real character? We'll never know because Austin never called her again.

Jonathan, a sixty-eight-year-old biology professor from Princeton, New Jersey, recalled asking a woman where she wanted to have dinner. She suggested a restaurant named China Garden, but Jonathan said he had just eaten there a few nights earlier. Her reply was, "Oh, so you're familiar with it? Great, then let's go there." Jonathan had meant to imply that she should pick another place—

that he was tired of it. But he said that didn't even occur to this woman. He told me, "She was very self-centered. She wanted to go to China Garden and didn't care if I'd just been there, whether· I might want something different . . . It's these little things that are a window into someone's personality."

I found myself not liking Jonathan after our interview. I wished I had told him that maybe next time he should speak up when he has a restaurant preference. After all, he had asked her where *she* wanted to go in the first place. So I wondered if Jonathan's response begged a key question in this research: how can you possibly predict the way a man will interpret something you say? The answer, of course, is that you can't predict (or control) the way someone perceives every word you utter. But if you discover a *pattern* through personalized Exit Interviews where several men had similar perceptions about you, this consistent feedback (even from men you don't want to date anyway) might help you recognize what's leading to some no-callbacks. (More about personalized Exit Interviews in chapter 8.)

CAN'T AFFORD YOU

One unfortunate result of The Park Avenue Princess syndrome is that a man can feel like he will never *be* enough or *have* enough for you, even if you genuinely like him and don't care about his bank account. I often hear women inaccurately speculating that a man doesn't call back because he's intimidated by their personality—but according to men in my research, they're more "intimidated" (or put off) by their *things*.

Anna, one of my clients, encountered this problem. After conducting six Exit Interviews for her, I learned that three of her ex-dates worried they couldn't support the lifestyle to which she was accustomed and consequently decided not to pursue her. Paul, a twenty-six-year-old comedy writer in Burbank, CA, was one of them. He lamented that while he was attracted to her, he didn't want to "get in over his head." He described his salary as moderate. One example Paul gave me was that he and Anna had discussed their passion for skiing on their first date. Anna had suggested maybe one day he could ski with her in Vail, where her family had a condo. He knew he wouldn't be able to afford a Vail ski trip anytime soon. He also noted her diamond-stud earrings and the Mercedes she parked at the restaurant. Anna had really liked Paul and wasn't looking for (or in need of) a rich guy. She said, "I can take care of myself financially . . . and besides, who says comedy writers can't hit it big one day?" But the inadvertent impression she gave to her dates was that they needed to "afford" her, or at least afford to keep up with her.

Another time, I conducted an Exit Interview for a friend of mine named Monique. She's a dynamic, beautiful woman with a great job. She's not rich, but she earns a good salary and likes to enjoy what she earns. I called a guy she liked but who hadn't asked her out again. His name is Richard, and he's a thirty-three-year-old computer security specialist in Long Island, NY. Monique had guessed she didn't hear from him again because he was dating someone else, but I learned that wasn't what happened. At first, Richard told me a few vague reasons why they weren't a good match, but after a little pressing on my part, he admitted one restaurant incident stood out in his mind as a turning point during the first fifteen minutes of their date. The waiter came by their table to ask what they wanted to drink. Monique ordered a glass of champagne. Richard immediately thought to himself, "Hmmm. She's used to nice things." He told me, "On the one hand, I think champagne is classy, so that was a positive thing about her . . . but on the other hand, champagne is expensive. It made me a little nervous because I intended to pay for dinner."

Richard went on to clarify that he didn't not call her back because she ordered champagne, nor because he didn't want to pay for it, but rather because her order just got him thinking they were too different. After she ordered champagne, he began scrutinizing her for indicators to see if she was out of his financial league. When she mentioned an upcoming trip to Paris and he noted her diamond-studded watch, he believed he had an accurate assessment of her. Was Richard insecure about his monetary status? Probably. Did his monetary status matter to Monique? No—as long as he had a professional job and seemed intelligent, she considered him someone with potential. Unfortunately, they never had the chance to clarify their attitudes about money because he didn't ask her out again.

One of the things I told Richard was that I found it very interesting how he remembered a glass of champagne a full year after the date had occurred—it had clearly made an impression on him—and asked if he would mind if I shared some of the details from our conversation with Monique. He said that was fine if I thought it could help her; he felt she was a genuinely nice person, even if she was someone he "couldn't afford" and they were "too different." When I told Monique his champagne anecdote, she said, "Why should I order a different drink on a date than I would normally order if I was out with my friends?" She was also unaware that champagne would cost more than an average cocktail and therefore didn't understand why it might signal expensive tastes. Next she laughed off his remarks about her Paris trip and her watch, saying, "Clearly he has issues." She made some good points. However, if she wanted him to call her back, what mattered, frankly, was *his* perception. In Richard's case, he felt uncomfortable with her signs of wealth, and when he added up those few minor pieces of "princess evidence" throughout the evening, he decided not to pursue anything further.

Although Monique had initially liked him, she really wasn't that bothered that they never went out again. But it'd be a shame if these little misperceptions prevented a new guy she really cared about one day from calling her back.

Another element in this Park Avenue Princess category that I heard several times from men was the oh-so-romantic sentiment that they couldn't afford *to divorce her*. Many divorced men described feeling burned by divorce settlements and were particularly wary of dating The Park Avenue Princess. Martin, a forty-nine-year-old hospital administrator in Berkeley, CA, said, "I was one of the lucky ones: she took everything but left me with my self-esteem . . . I actually ask myself after a date now, 'Is she someone I'd want to be divorced from?' I know that may seem cynical, but with marriage failure rates today, this is a valid question. You should marry someone you think wouldn't pillage you under adverse circumstances. Um, do I sound bitter?" (Nah, Martin's not bitter . . . !) But it goes to show that men were particularly sensitive to the money issue if they had experienced a division of assets in the past. The top criteria for their next wife? Someone with low-maintenance attitudes or sufficient income of her own.

LACKING APPRECIATION

Sometimes it's not about dollars and cents but rather your *attitude* toward money that can label you The Park Avenue Princess. For example, the arrival of the dinner check, and how you handle it, turns out to be a moment when he's watching you closely and extrapolating your attitude.

Restaurant checks often bring anxiety for women on a first date. What should you do: Ignore it? Grab it? Offer to pay half? What are the implications of your action? Women ask me about that frequently, so I sought the male opinion. By telephone and online survey I asked how men preferred women respond to a restaurant bill on a first date. Eighty-four percent of men indicated "I expect to pay for the first date."[5] Men elaborated that what they wanted most was to feel *appreciated*. They said they preferred a "fake purse-grab" to a "blind eye" because it signaled she appreciated his gesture. An expectation that he would pay for everything was one of the things that often led to the princess label. And a heartfelt thank-you went a long way.

SOUND FAMILIAR?

You may not have noted similarities to yourself among The Park Avenue Princess anecdotes thus far, as it's not always easy to recognize yourself through other people's stories. So you can use the self-assessment questions here to verify whether men might be

---

[5]Eleven percent of men indicated "I expect to split the check"; 3 percent indicated "The person who asks for the date should pay"; and 2 percent indicated "The person with the higher income should pay."

stereotyping you as The Park Avenue Princess before they get to know the real you.

AT WORK . . .

❑ Do you "dress for success"?

❑ Is your job environment one that rewards the revenue you generate rather than great ideas or hard work?

❑ In past performance reviews or casual feedback from coworkers, have you ever been told, "Try getting along better with the secretaries and administrative staff"?

WITH YOUR FRIENDS AND FAMILY . . .

❑ Is your inner circle composed primarily of wealthy people (such that you may be out of touch with the mind-set of someone who doesn't have a lot of money)?

❑ Have you ever been told fondly, "I hope you get that promotion, win the lottery, or find a man who can afford your tastes!"

❑ If someone wants to fix you up on a blind date, do you ask right away, "What does he do for a living?"

ON A DATE OR WITH A PAST BOYFRIEND . . .

❑ When reading a menu, do you choose what you want without looking at the price?

❑ Has a guy ever pointed to your jewelry and asked, "Is that real?"

❑ Have you ever not been attracted to a guy after a first date because you didn't think he could afford the lifestyle you want?

YOUR PERSONAL PHILOSOPHY:

❑ Do you believe a "real gentleman" should pay for everything on a date?

❑ When traveling, do you expect to feel pampered?

❑ Are you proud of what you've earned and think there's no need to hide it?

If you answered yes to more than five questions above, you may be perceived (or misperceived) as The Park Avenue Princess.

There's no doubt you're savvy, sophisticated, and have high standards; of course you shouldn't change who you are deep down. But you may consider tweaking some of the things you do and say on a first or second date. Men who don't know yet how fabulous you are may think you're The Park Avenue Princess and miss the chance to get to know you better on the next few dates.

So, What Should You Do?

If you can relate to The Park Avenue Princess, here are four suggestions to help you come down to earth so you can learn more about him on a second date.

1) STOP ASKING

The reality? It's almost impossible to accurately gauge a man's financial situation during a first date. So stop trying to find out. Even if you try, your efforts will probably be wasted. If your date *does* have a lot of money, he's probably been around enough gold diggers to know how to spot and avoid them, or he has developed a plan to hide his money (like George driving his Prius instead of his Corvette). A man with a lot of money will always be on the lookout for whether you like him for who he is. If he *doesn't* have money, then he might conceal that fact by borrowing a friend's fancy car, wearing a knock-off Rolex, or charging dinner at an expensive restaurant on a gold card with heavy debt. You simply won't know right away what's real and what's not. The only thing you *will* do is turn him off with your not-so-subtle questions. You will eventually learn about his financial situation if the two of you hit it off.

2) PROMOTE YOUR DOWN-TO-EARTH SIDE

What if you're falsely perceived as a princess? You are genuinely open to dating men with varied economic statuses, but you get a bad rap because you have your own money and enjoy spending it. In that case, you need to actively promote your down-to-earth side with words and actions. On a first date, be careful not to drop any hoity-toity references to your Prada bag or your fractional jet ownership. Don't suggest the fanciest restaurants or order brand liquors. If you're dating online, craft a profile that underscores your low-maintenance personality. One of my friends had a great line she used to accomplish this tactic in her online profile. She wrote, "I'm the kind of girl who takes the middle seat and lets my hair air dry." By saying she was okay with that middle seat in a car or airplane that nobody wants, and she doesn't even need a hair dryer, she accurately portrayed herself as down-to-earth. She attracted boatloads of great guys wanting to meet her, many of whom commented about that one line when they wrote to her.

Another man, Nate, a twenty-six-year-old pet store owner in Cleveland, OH, told me something he loved about a girl he dated named Samantha. He told her he'd pick her up at 8:00 PM, and Samantha replied, "Perfect! I'll get home from the gym around seven thirty, so that'll give me plenty of time to shower and be ready by eight." He couldn't believe it—a girl who could shower and be ready in only thirty minutes? It was a small thing that made a big impression on him.

3) FOCUS ON HIM

Remember that a man interested in a relationship with you wants to know that you'd be a good partner—someone who is not always thinking of herself first. I know it's hard to catch yourself sounding selfish in every little situation that arises. But next time he asks what your preference is (whether to meet closer to his neighborhood or yours; whether to attend the Knicks game or the Celine Dion concert), remember his question is not all about what's best, easiest, and most appealing for *you*. I'm not saying you should make it all about him, or morph into one of those girls with no opinion, but if you mix it up early on (sometimes optimize his needs, sometimes your needs) you'll have won half the battle.

4) SHOW SINCERE APPRECIATION

During the first date, select a few ways to explicitly demonstrate that you appreciate him. Regarding the issue of who pays on a date, you can offer to split the bill (but graciously thank him if he pays the whole tab), or pay for parking or ice cream after dinner, or bring him a small "inside joke" gift (something funny you discussed pre-date). If he asks you out a few more times, you can buy concert tickets or offer to cook him dinner. And always thank him immediately when he pays for something, instead of saving your gratitude for the end of the evening—by then it's too late; he has already formed an opinion of you. Your thanks can be small and demure; you don't need to lavish appreciation every time he whips out his credit card or pays the taxi driver. Excessive gratitude will ring false and spotlight money in an awkward manner.

Also focus on thanking him for the *gestures* he makes, not only what he pays for. If he takes you to a restaurant located in your neighborhood (far from where he lives), thank him early on for being considerate enough to select a location close to you. This type of appreciation will go farther than thanking him only when the dinner check arrives.

A different form of showing appreciation is to focus on who he is as a person. Try telling him directly why you were intrigued enough to go out with him in the first place (assuming the real reason wasn't his yacht). This is a nice way to extend a sincere compliment by noting something specific about his demeanor or something he said that was witty or intelligent—anything not related to shallow signals of monetary status. This demonstrates that you appreciate him for something money can't buy.

If You're The Park Avenue Princess . . .

WHAT'S HOT:	WHAT'S NOT:
1. "What's your favorite thing to do on the weekend?"	1. "What's your favorite hotel in St. Barts?"
2. Asking about his day	2. Asking about his year-end bonus
3. Learning more about his family	3. Learning more about his family's holdings
4. Letting your hair air dry	4. Letting him know you and Paris Hilton share the same hairstylist
5. "Wow, thanks for being so patient with me on the golf course today. You're a great teacher."	5. "Wow, nice golf clubs! Are those Callaway titaniums?"

#5 REASON HE DIDN'T CALL BACK
The Closer

It felt like she was interviewing me to be a sperm donor. —Wade, age 40, St. Louis, MO

I understand a woman's need to clarify whether I'm looking for something serious, but my honest response is always "Yes, if the right person comes along." So how does that help her decide if I'm a good prospect? —Matthew, age 43, Wilmington, DE

I think because our e-mails became so intense so quickly, she thought we were soul mates before we even met in person. —José, age 27, Phoenix, AZ

The Closer is a woman on a mission to get a boyfriend, a husband, a baby, or all of the above.[6] She is focused on using her time efficiently to close the deal. She's not interested in something casual. Whether or not she is trying to be subtle or has decided to lay her cards on the table, she's in interview mode. Her focus, unfortunately, has exactly the opposite effect of the one she's hoping for.

Encountering The Closer, men feel like they're being evaluated as a future husband and father. It's not that they don't want the job—they just don't know if they want the job *yet*. It's premature. They feel deflated about losing spontaneity or guilty about potentially wasting the time of a nice girl like you. Sometimes they feel like they're on a bad episode of *The Bachelor* as they watch overzealous comments or gestures that happen waaaay too soon.

No one likes wasting their time. Efficiency is good. Maybe you've accelerated your search for a mate because the last jerk you dated dragged things out for three years before you realized he was never going to commit. You're not going to make *that* mistake again. Maybe you just turned forty and you have baby fever. Maybe you're lonely, whether you're twenty-two and fresh out of college or fifty-two and recently divorced. It's great to know what you want and go after it, but the trick is not sabotaging yourself in the process.

Are You The Closer?

The Closer encompassed four categories of behavior in my research. Do any of these ring true for you?

INTERVIEW MODE

A woman in interview mode often thinks she's being subtle about evaluating her date's readiness for a relationship. She has read a few dating books, so she knows it's a turnoff to come on too strong. She

---

[6]Men age thirty-six to forty-nine were 91 percent more likely than men in other age groups to cite The Closer as their primary no-callback reason.

knows she can't exactly blurt out on the first date, "Where is this going?" So she tries to get in through the back door. Gary, a thirty-year-old franchise owner from Orlando, FL, told me about a woman who said, two hours into the first date, "I have this quandary. Maybe you can help me. I'm really enjoying our evening, but my friend wanted to set me up on a blind date this weekend. *Now* I'm not sure what to tell her . . ." Gary was taken aback. He thought this woman was terrific, but suddenly her question irritated him. He replied with the first thing that came to mind: "Well, I think it's too soon to be exclusive." You can imagine she didn't take that comment well. Her response was a snippy "I never said we should be exclusive—we just met! I was only . . . wondering . . . well . . . never mind! I'll just tell my friend I'm up for it." Their moods both plummeted downhill afterward and they never saw each other again.

Joshua, a twenty-nine-year-old soccer coach in Santa Fe, NM, recalled a woman on a first date who asked him a few skeptical questions about his readiness to commit, including "How long was your last relationship?" He felt what she really wanted to know was whether he was a "player." He said women assume that because he's good-looking and works in the sports industry, he's not serious about finding someone special. He's sensitive to this type of inquiry, which he frequently encounters. He says he's genuinely trying to connect with someone on a deep level, but when a woman starts doubting him, it's deflating. He complained, "I'm tired of it; it's trite."

Harris, a thirty-year-old investment banker in Seattle, WA, told me the story of a woman with whom he started exchanging messages on Facebook. They had a few mutual friends, and he wanted to ask her out, but the momentum evaporated when she sent him this message: "I looked at your company website and saw how successful you are. But I'm really not into material things. I'm much more down-to-earth. Do you think a relationship could ever work between us?" Harris said he didn't fault her for trying to be practical, but her question rubbed him the wrong way—like skipping ahead to the last page of a mystery novel to see whodunit. How could he speculate so soon on their future?

Men told me frequently about feeling "grilled" to determine whether their intentions were serious. And they weren't talking about a few casual questions from someone who sincerely wanted to learn more about them. These questions were too numerous, too scripted, and sometimes too personal. They progressed throughout the night, from "Do you have siblings, and if so, do they have kids? Are you close to your family?" to "I'm over the whole dating thing, aren't you? Are most of your friends married?" to "Where do you see yourself in five years? Do you own or rent your apartment? Have you ever lived with someone or been engaged?" and sometimes to "Um, you haven't had a vasectomy, right?"

The trouble with this interview process is that even if you get the answers you're looking for, they don't necessarily tell the whole story. You should especially be wary of the false-positive syndrome. Aaron, a forty-two-year-old engineer in Alexandria, VA, told me about a woman he really liked by the end of their first date. She asked him directly whether he was interested in anything serious. Because he wanted to see her again, he offered her this: "I don't know you well enough to guess where we're headed, but in theory, yes, I'm looking for someone long term . . . I'm a person who has staying power in relationships." He gave her some examples by citing a seven-year live-in girlfriend and another three-year relationship. But I wondered if that girl was thinking what I was thinking. Do failed long-term relationships prove commitment or failure to pull the trigger? Either way, romantic history isn't reliable proof of anything. Just like the stock market, past performance does not predict future performance—good or bad.

> "I didn't want to feel guilty if things eventually didn't work out between us, so I erred on the side of letting go rather than risk wasting her time."

Mike, a forty-five-year-old venture capitalist in New York City, gave me a different viewpoint. He admires women who lay their cards on the table. He said, "One woman I met last week came right out and said, 'I'm not looking for a fling. I want to find the right guy and start a family. Are you looking for the same thing?'" His reaction wasn't negative at all—on the contrary, he said he appreciated her candor. He liked her a lot. She was someone who knew what she wanted and wasn't afraid to go after it. But he never called her again. He explained to me that he was newly single after living with someone for four years, and he *just wasn't sure* what his plans for the future included. He clarified that his real problem was guilt: "I didn't want to feel guilty if things eventually didn't work out between us, so I erred on the side of letting go rather than risk wasting her time."

STATIC CLING

Sometimes the desire to close the deal showed up not in the form of interview questions, but rather in needy or clingy comments and behavior. When a woman begins sniffing too early for reassurance that her growing intimate feelings are mutual, The Closer image can emerge. Kent, a twenty-eight-year-old tax accountant from Washington, DC, was kissing a woman good night at the end of their first date, and she whispered, "Can I stay over? Just to hug and fall asleep?" He believed she wasn't intending to have sex with him, but her question sounded so needy. He said it took the thrill out of their kiss. He avoided the question and promised to call her the next day. He never did. He told me he feels bad about that now.

Hayden, a twenty-four-year-old graphic designer from Seattle, WA, described a girl who texted him when he went to the men's room during their date. He actually loved it—no one had ever done that to him before and he thought it was funny. He had excused himself from the table and three minutes later she texted him at the urinal, "Just thinking about you." It was a playful thing to do, he said. He smiled and texted her back, "Can you sneak away from your date—he looks boring—meet me outside?" Flirtatious messages were rapidly exchanged and he finally returned to the table. He said, "I was *digging* this girl."

But then Hayden said she started to get really insecure. Soon she began asking questions that he interpreted as, "She wanted reassurance that I felt the same exhilaration she was feeling." For example, first she asked him if he was having a good time and later asked whether he was dating anyone else. During dessert she asked him what his plans were for the coming weekend, which he thought was a hint he should suggest their next date together. He told her he'd planned a ski trip with friends, and she acted disappointed. He started to pull back a little at that point. When he was walking her home an hour later, it was cold outside and he offered her his gloves. Her reply was, "Oh, that's so sweet, thank you! I'll give them back to you next time I see you." He said her borrow-something-to-return-later ploy was so obvious, and he quickly made up an excuse about needing his gloves for the ski weekend. He ended the evening with the gloves in his pocket and no plan to see her again. I wonder what she thought happened in between "Meet me outside" and "Good-bye."

Andrew, a thirty-one-year-old physical therapist from Philadelphia, PA, responded to the ad I posted on Craigslist in which I was looking for single men to talk about their dating experiences. He shared with me his "seasonal dating" strategy. He says he meets a lot of women online and dates them year-round—except during his dating off-season, which runs from Thanksgiving through Valentine's Day. He explained his schedule is similar to that of athletes who use the off-season to rest, recuperate, and focus on other goals. He said that most women during the holidays tend to get needy in terms of wanting both gifts (Christmas, Valentine's Day) and his time (come to this holiday party, meet my family, go out with me on New Year's Eve). So November to February is a logical time for him to opt out.

Although I found Andrew's strategy ridiculous, I included his point of view because I think it's very interesting sociologically. It's not only that his philosophy underscores The Closer stereotype, but that men are dating so frequently, and expecting the continuation of frequent dating, that they need an *off-season* to rest! This ties in to the changed dating world discussed in chapter 1: online dating provides men with the illusion of infinite options.

WOMAN OVERBOARD!

Some women go overboard thinking a first date is more than it is. They might feel too close, too soon. This can emerge in the smallest of ways. Hugh, a thirty-one-year-old greeting card publisher in Kansas City, KS, mentioned a woman who told him during dinner that his eyeglasses had fingerprints on them. She reached over, took off his glasses, and wiped them clean with her napkin. He remembered this small gesture because "it felt like we were an old married couple. It was kind of weird to have someone wipe my glasses who I'd known for less than an hour." Other men mentioned feeling awkward with pet names: "sweetie" or "baby" on first dates sounded prematurely intimate.

Steven, a forty-two-year-old writer from Honolulu, HI, had an upcoming first date with a woman he met through Chemistry.com. Her profile was interesting and he began corresponding with her. Over the course of two weeks, they exchanged lengthy and personal e-mails. He was excited to meet her, until the day prior to their arranged date. "She started going overboard," he said. "I mean, we'd had some great e-mails, but we'd never met yet, and I felt like some of her comments were too much." When I asked him for details, he actually forwarded one of her old e-mails to me so I could see for myself. She had written: "Did I tell you I really like the name Steven? It sounds good when I say it to myself, and I find myself saying it quietly and with some regularity these days." He went to meet her but said it was a letdown. He explained that her overzealous writing started to sound creepy and predisposed him to start their date with a cynical attitude.

Steven's anecdote is a cautionary tale not only for toning down your e-mails, but also for privacy. Be careful what you write online to a man you barely know. One day he might forward your intimate e-mail to an author writing a book!

Sometimes going overboard simply meant referencing the future before a man expressed wanting another date. Men described women on a first date who offered them tickets for a Celtics game three weeks away or to see *Wicked* on Broadway the following month, volunteered to loan *The Kite Runner* after their next book group meeting, and invited them to join their house-share in the Hamptons next summer. These men said they obviously knew what was really behind those offers: it was the implicit question "Are we going to see each other again?" Faced with making a quick and premature decision in the middle of a date when they hadn't made up their minds yet about wanting a second date, they started to pull back.

Peter, a thirty-two-year-old waiter from Hanover, NH, recalled one woman who had invited him to spend the afternoon at the park while she was babysitting her nephew. He thought it was a little odd for a first date, but she explained it was her only free time that weekend. Peter said it turned out to be fun because he loves kids. However, they only saw each other one more time because "she brought him six stamps on their second date." "Huh?" I asked. Apparently, he had casually mentioned some errands on his to-do list, including needing to buy stamps. When she showed up for the second date, she handed him six stamps and said, "Now you can spend more time with me today instead of doing your errands." He said the first thought that crossed his mind was, "Whoa! Cancel your subscription to *Bride* magazine, honey!"

"Jeez," I thought after hanging up the phone with Peter. Babysitting + stamps = marriage-crazed? Men can be a *bit* too sensitive! Recognize that sometimes an innocent circumstance or a small gesture intended as "thoughtful" may cause him to associate you with all the overzealous women he dated in the past. You're not dating in a vacuum; you're paying the tax on all the overboard behavior that came before you.

> **You're not dating in a vacuum; you're paying the tax on all the overboard behavior that came before you.**

OH, BABY

You may have heard comedians tell that old joke about how to get rid of a single man. How? Just tell him you love him and want to bear his children. Sure, it's just a joke, and you know better than to look him in the eye after the appetizer course and start picking out baby names. But talking about offspring is tricky even for savvy daters. Anil, a forty-three-year-old doctor and single dad from Chicago, said the "kid discussion" on a first date with Jane actually started out well. He has two sons and tells women about them up front. He told Jane a little about each boy's age and personality. She gave a lovely response at first. Instead of interrogating him about his custody situation like most of his dates in the past, she said, "I envy you having two great boys." Just when he was feeling a rush of warmth toward her, she made a few comments about her desire to have her own children. Anil said that he probably wants more children one day, especially with a woman he loves, but her explicit admission made him nervous because he wasn't *exactly sure* what he might want in the future. He felt an internal pressure not to lead her on *just in case* he decided against having more kids. So he never called her back.

Wade, a forty-year-old architect from St. Louis, MO, once met a woman who transitioned rapidly from innocent questions about his family (where he grew up, where his siblings lived, etc.) to a nosy interrogation about his gene pool. "She actually asked me, at different points during the evening, what my SAT scores were and if anyone in my family had a history of alcoholism." He said, "I felt like she was interviewing me to be a sperm donor."

Men are already so sensitive these days about baby fever, especially around women in their thirties and forties, that you don't even have to mention the word "children" to panic them. Rick, a thirty-seven-year-old entrepreneur from Las Vegas, NV, said, "I watched her pet a dog on the sidewalk . . . you should have seen her! She was like, 'Ohh, doggie, you're so beautiful! What a sweet dog.'" Rick's response to her effusive pet affection was, "That girl wanted a baby so bad, I could smell it . . . like I was watching her eggs dry up one by one right there on the sidewalk!"

Hard to believe, but Rick's still on the market, ladies. Anyone who wants his phone number, feel free to e-mail me for it. . . .

TIME OUT

You might be wondering by this point whether a man's likes and dislikes are simply a matter of individual taste. For example, Rick saw a woman pet a dog and concluded she was desperate for a baby, while Mitch (who was quoted in The Boss Lady section) thought his date was ignoring her dog and concluded she wasn't nurturing. I want to take a time-out here and emphasize something important about my Exit Interview research. The seemingly trivial things women said or did—such as petting a dog—seemed to *build up* into a stereotype. Sure, different guys responded either favorably or unfavorably to the same thing. But, with a few exceptions, the date usually didn't hinge on one thing. Rather, an accumulation of "clues" along a similar theme resulted in an unflattering stereotype. In other words, if you asked questions during dinner about his gene pool, and then lamented how all your friends are married, and then murmured terms of endearment like "baby" and "sweetie," and *then* you petted the dog effusively, he probably concluded you're The Closer. It wasn't just about the dog petting.

The key to handling this situation on your next date depends on which stereotype you most resemble. Let's take the dog-petting example. If you think some of your first dates might label you The Boss Lady, you would try to demonstrate *more* affection with the pooch. If, on the other hand, you know that you are kinda-sorta-really fixated on finding a husband and having kids (i.e., The Closer), it's best to *avoid* looking too snuggly with the pooch right away.

SOUND FAMILIAR?

You may not have noted similarities to yourself among The Closer anecdotes thus far, as it's not always easy to recognize yourself through other people's stories. So you can use the self-assessment questions below to verify whether men might be stereotyping you as The Closer before they get to know the real you.

AT WORK . . .

❑ Is your job environment one that rewards "rainmakers" (i.e., people who bring in new business)?

❑ In past performance reviews or casual feedback from coworkers, have you ever been praised for your "killer instinct"?

❑ Are you the person in your department upon whom your boss relies to "get the job done"?

WITH YOUR FRIENDS AND FAMILY . . .

❑ Do you feel pressure to get married, either from nosy relatives or because all your friends are couples?

❑ Do you often confide, "I think he might be The One . . . ," or "I started silently naming our kids during dessert . . ."?

❑ Do you frequently hear (in any context), "Just be patient . . ."

ON A DATE OR WITH A PAST BOYFRIEND . . .

❑ Have you ever accidentally confessed during a first or second date, "I've got a crush on you . . . ," or "It's been a long time since I've felt this way . . ."?

❑ Has a guy ever told you, "Well, that question seems a little premature . . . ," or "Let's not jump the gun . . ."?

❑ Are you prone to use future-tense verbs on a date, perhaps just as a reflex or habit?

YOUR PERSONAL PHILOSOPHY:

❑ Does the phrase "Let's just see what happens" drive you crazy?

❑ Do you want to have lots of kids and feel internal pressure to "get started"?

❑ If you're nervous about something, do you feel a strong need to resolve things quickly—no matter what the outcome?

If you answered yes to more than five questions here, you may be perceived (or misperceived) as The Closer. There's no doubt you're pragmatic, efficient, and family oriented; of course you shouldn't change who you are deep down. But you may consider tweaking some of the things you do and say on a first or second date. Men who don't know yet how fabulous you are may think you're The Closer and miss the chance to get to know you better on the next few dates.

So, What Should You Do?

If you identify with The Closer, here are five suggestions to help you take a deep breath.

1) STRIKE THE RIGHT CHORD

Like most things in life, it's usually good to find the balance. Pet the dog happily, but don't obsess over the dog. Express that you're interested in a committed relationship, but act neither overly focused nor overly breezy. What about when it comes to children? While most women are smart enough not to blurt out their desire to procreate, you have to be sure to balance the topic of children carefully. You don't want to appear overanxious, nor do you want to make the opposite mistake by implying you lack maternal instincts or that you're not a nurturing person (as cautioned for The Boss Lady). Especially when you're in the childbearing years, the best way to handle this predicament is to make a point of mentioning someone else's kids casually—such as your niece or the baby at the next table—with a brief remark. How about something like this: "That reminds me of the Dr. Seuss book I read to my niece last weekend, *Oh, the Places You'll Go!* Do you know it? It's my favorite." Or "That's so funny, that baby looks like he's ready to grab that chocolate cake right off his mother's plate!"

Something nonchalant like that demonstrates that you're not immune to kids; you're the kind of person who finds children endearing. *But*, immediately follow your remark with a definitive statement, such as, "I can't imagine having children right now—but I do think kids are amazing!" That should strike the right chord: you have maternal instincts but you won't be ovulating during dessert.

2) DON'T STEAL HIS LINES

Never reference the future on a first date *no matter what*, unless he does it first. Don't say "When will I see you again?" That's his line. Don't say "What are your plans this weekend?" That's his line. What if you're in a bind because you need a date to the benefit party you're chairing next week . . . but he hasn't mentioned getting together again? Too bad, you can*not* ask him—take your brother instead. What if you have two symphony tickets that will go to waste Saturday night unless you invite him? Bummer! Send them to me, care of my publisher. Be strong in your resolve not to mention the future too soon, because in a guy's mind tickets to something next week might lead to meeting your parents next month, and then *wham!* Suddenly you're The Closer.

3) BE UNIQUE

There are so many women out there who are on a mission, trying to figure out whether their new guy is ready for a serious relationship or whether he's a time waster. So stand out from that crowd and be different. Deliberately ask questions on your first dates that have no reference to his gene pool, his earning potential, his past relationships, or his current attitudes about settling down. Helpful questions to get to know him better as a person, rather than as a future husband or sperm donor, might include "Are you reading any good books right now?" or "What's your favorite thing to do on a Sunday morning?" These topics are wide open: they allow him to tell you what's important to him rather than what's on your agenda. That will set you apart from all the other Closers he has dated.

4) KEEP IT FUN

One of the biggest problems for The Closer is actually the venue where most first dates occur: restaurants. Usually two people sit across from each other at a table and make conversation for two or three hours. That's a lot of talking. If you tend toward Closer behavior, it's easy to lapse into dangerous territory in this venue. So consider suggesting a date plan that is more active—such as bowling or a picnic at the zoo—to avoid the intensity (and temptation) of those first-date Closer traps. If conversation lags, you can focus on the activity rather than filling the silence with nosy questions. Help yourself avoid this pitfall by creating an active environment in which you'll succeed.

5) REMEMBER THE CHOCOLATE BOX

"Life is like a box of chocolates: you never know what you're gonna get," says Forrest Gump. It's the same in dating: you pick a guy and take your chances that if things work out, he'll be ready for a commitment. Sometimes, though, you'll end up with a time waster. Whether he makes noises on the first date about wanting to settle down or wanting to play the field, men said that not only is a woman's interrogation about their commitment attitudes far from subtle, it emits a scent of desperation and is often the very cause of lost relationship potential. In any case, we all know that regardless of what he says, all bets are off when the right woman comes along (whether that's you or the next girl). Sorry, but you just have to invest some time up front, taking a chance that things will progress the way you want.

Did you see that funny episode of *Friends* when one of Ross's girlfriends wanted to send out a joint Christmas card to their family and friends? Ross worried the card would classify their relationship as too serious and told her, "We're not there yet." So his girlfriend asked, "Where *are* we then?" Instead of answering her, he tried to show her increasing signs of commitment. He started with making her a mix tape and ultimately gave her a key to his apartment (then immediately changed his locks).

During or after a great first date, your Mr. Potential (like Ross) is probably closer to making a mix tape than making copies of his apartment key. If you can't live with the ambiguity early on, you might pressure him to quickly demonstrate his feelings outside his comfort zone, only to watch him reverse his hasty gesture later when he realizes he's not ready.

If You're The Closer . . .

WHAT'S HOT:	WHAT'S NOT:
1. "Hi, are you Mike?"	1. "Hi, are you my soul mate?"
2. "It's great to see you."	2. "When will I see you again?"
3. Open-ended questions	3. Questions with right and wrong answers
4. "Cute kid."	4. "I bet we'd have cute kids."
5. "I love frozen yogurt."	5. "Sorry, I can't see you on Tuesday because I'm having my eggs frozen."

#6 REASON HE DIDN'T CALL BACK
The Flasher

> I don't even know what "endometriosis" *means*,
> but it sure didn't sound good!
> —Ted, age 24, Park City, UT

> For me, it's all about how little drama there is. If I
> don't see too much drama, she's got my attention.
> If there's a lot of drama, I'm done.
> —Matt, age 48, Austin, TX

> She immediately told me her dad cheated on her
> mom . . . I could see she had trust issues. And that's
> usually only the tip of the iceberg.
> —Darryl, age 32, Lexington, KY

> I'm usually a lot more forgiving if she's hot. At least in
> the beginning. —Zachary, age 27, Ft. Lauderdale, FL

The Flasher divulges negative personal information about herself on a first date, often without realizing it. This is typically labeled "baggage," and it lands with a thud on the "con" side of the inevitable pro/con list he is tallying for you in his head in real time during your first date. Single women *must* know by now they shouldn't reveal their baggage on a first date, right? So it surprised me how often I heard from men about these slipups. It wasn't only that women talked about their physical and emotional problems, but that most of them had *no idea* the information they were revealing wasn't flattering—and, more important, that it directly resulted in a failed date.

Many men reported that whenever they meet a great girl, there is usually a "but." As in, "She was great! Just the kind of girl I'm looking for—but . . ." They understand no one is perfect. The problem is that they don't know her well enough to gauge whether the baggage she reveals will turn out to be heavy or light. Understandably, men tend to assume the worst: negative issues will turn out to be even more serious than whatever is initially disclosed. Faced with the *uncertainty* of a difficult problem or trait to bear for the next fifty years, most men just take a pass.

I speak to single women all the time, so I know the other side of this story. Usually, it's not that women make the rookie mistake of revealing baggage too soon. What's happening is this: many women view the disclosure of certain facts as "opening up" or "creating a bond" instead of as confessing a dark secret. And some women are merely trying to be efficient: they don't want to waste their time with a guy who can't deal with their issue. Others simply define certain facts as "quirky" or "this is who I am." And sometimes women have a few drinks, feel tipsy, and accidentally confess something they regret the next day.

Are You The Flasher?

The Flasher encompassed four categories in my research. Do any of these ring true for you?

PHYSICAL BAGGAGE

Physical baggage usually fell under the umbrella of medical history. Most often the things I heard about were not externally visible, so women *did* have a choice to reveal or conceal the issue on the first date. Men encountered everything from the serious to the benign to the sexual. The diverse examples they described included diabetes, chronic fatigue syndrome, Reynaud's disease, high cholesterol, surviving childhood incest, having an abortion, tendinitis, not having had sex in several years, lactose intolerance, and herpes.

An issue can be revealed innocently—even if it's nothing too serious—but the guy may not know how to evaluate it. Bryce, a forty-year-old wilderness guide from Jackson, WY, recalled a first and only date with a woman where they were talking about their mutual passion for cycling. She said that she has trouble knowing what to eat before a long ride, and he suggested a brand of energy bars. She remarked, "Oh, I can't eat those because of my blood-sugar problem." Bryce didn't want to pry, but this kernel of infor-mation stuck with him through the evening. He began to watch what she ate (she left more than half her meal untouched on her plate), and when they ordered dessert she said she couldn't eat any-thing with chocolate. He said he was worried she had some kind of weird eating problem, or maybe diabetes. He never called her back to find out. His answer irritated me. First I told him that maybe she wasn't hungry, didn't like her food, was watching her calories, or simply was excited about meeting him and didn't want to pig out in front of him. As for the energy bars, everyone has certain foods that don't agree with them for some reason; no big deal. Then I asked him, "Are you saying if she did have diabetes, for example, that you wouldn't want to see her again because of that?" He answered, "No, no, that's not what I meant . . . never mind." (*Ooops, not the way to draw out your interview subjects, apparently!*) But clearly he couldn't help worrying about her health despite the rational arguments I gave him or the disapproval I inadvertently expressed. Maybe he's a jerk, but other than this example, he didn't seem like one during the hour that I interviewed him. He just felt uncomfortable with the tidbit of information she revealed about her blood sugar and then was turned off when he spied a few other potential clues.

So let's be honest here: if two equally cute guys—total strangers—were lined up in front of you, and you were asked, "Which one would you like to meet: Stranger #1, who has diabetes, or Stranger #2, who doesn't have diabetes?" you'd probably pick Stranger #2. Because you don't know anything else about them, and perhaps you have a limited understanding of diabetes, you'd pick the one who has no known health issue. This doesn't make you a bad person; it just makes you human. But if you get to know those two guys better, and Stranger #1 is smart, funny, and kind, while Stranger #2 is dull and selfish, you'd probably make a dif-ferent choice. My point is that revealing any baggage too soon prevents someone from making a good decision about wanting to know you better.

Paul, a thirty-seven-year-old graphic designer from Toronto, Canada, was on a first date with a girl he met on a ski trip. When the waitress asked for their drink orders, his date asked for sparkling water. She explained a few minutes later that she doesn't drink liquor because her mom is an alcoholic. Paul didn't know much about alcoholism, but he knew one thing: it can be hereditary. I told Paul that I thought life was full of unknowns—maybe the odds that his date or her kids would become alcoholics were no greater than her being hit by a bus crossing the street. He said, "Yeah, I guess . . . I know it sounds a bit irrational, but that's just what went through my mind . . . I guess anything *potentially* negative is 'strike one' on a first date . . . hey, you asked me to be *honest!*"

One of the more emotional interviews I conducted was with Greg, a twenty-five-year-old computer programmer from Knoxville, TN. He reluctantly told me about a situation he still feels guilty about to this day. He went out with a woman who disclosed on their first date that she was diagnosed with Hodgkin's disease at age sixteen. She told him she was fully recovered now and a stronger person for having beat cancer. Greg said to me, "What an impressive thing to beat cancer—I mean, she [seemed like] a brave person . . . I really liked her: she was funny, cute, mature . . . But when I got home I looked up Hodgkin's on the Internet. I learned that radiation and chemo can indirectly affect the reproductive organs. I was really torn. I wanted to be sympathetic, but . . . I don't know, I definitely want kids someday . . ." He postponed his decision whether or not to call her again, and a few weeks later he met someone else. He told me this was one of the more cowardly things he's ever done, and he made me repeat my promise to keep his real name disguised in this book.

It struck me that even nice guys are human. It may be unrealistic to ask them to cope with something too heavy and too uncertain when they barely know a girl. Greg might have evaluated her history (and their future) differently if he had spent more time getting to know her first before she revealed her story. These examples from

Bryce, Paul, and Greg show how men on first dates, when "flashed" with limited or incomplete information, will assume the worst.

EMOTIONAL BAGGAGE

Inside first-date territory, when two people click right away and are getting to know each other, they start to dig deeper. But there are a lot of land mines. One popular disclosure I heard from many men, especially in New York City and Los Angeles, involved seeing a therapist or taking antidepressants. Language such as "shrink" and "meds" was common fodder for first-date banter. Glenn, a thirty-six-year-old photojournalist from New York, NY, remembered a fun date with a woman named Laura where the sparks flew. He was really attracted to her. At one point he remarked to Laura, "I told my shrink I had a date tonight." She laughed and said, "Hey, I told my shrink I had a date tonight too!" They joked about their therapists for a while and later made out passionately in the taxi before he dropped her off. He promised he'd call her, but he never did. He said the more he thought about Laura, he realized he was potentially repeating a pattern of his: getting involved with emotionally unhealthy women. In the past, his therapist had observed that that dynamic never ended well for him. I said, "How do you know she's emotionally unhealthy?" Glenn replied, "Because she told me she's seeing a shrink. Who knows what her issues are, but I have enough issues of my own to deal with."

I thought Glenn's story was particularly interesting—not only because of his unfair double standard, but because *he* had been the first one to mention the word "shrink" during their date. In this case, Glenn set Laura up unintentionally and she took The Flasher bait. He laid an invisible trap for her by dropping the first reference about his shrink, even making it sound kind of cute. He signaled that seeing a shrink was okay, so she felt free to chime in.

> **"Who knows what her issues are, but I have enough issues of my own to deal with."**

But because he didn't know her well enough to ask why she needed or wanted therapy, he jumped to negative conclusions after the date ended. It's not that Laura should have lied about seeing a therapist, but she didn't have to respond with a "me too" comment (especially since Glenn didn't *ask* her). When Glenn said he told his shrink about her, Laura could have tilted her head playfully and said, "Oh . . . did you? And what did you tell her about me—something good, I hope?"

Another Flasher incident involved a woman whose parents were divorced. Chuck, a thirty-year-old paralegal from Iowa City, IA, told me about a great conversation he had with a woman named Rebecca on their first date. He said they really bonded because both of them had divorced parents. They talked about what it's like to grow up with feelings of guilt, anger, and abandonment. He thought she really understood his background. While he enjoyed their date very much, he decided not to call her back. With a hint of Glenn's double standard, he said, "What I really need is someone the opposite of me—someone rock solid . . . a stable influence." Of course, after one date, he had no idea whether Rebecca was "stable" or not. He stereotyped her simply because they had spoken at length about growing up with turbulent feelings.

I also heard about Flasher incidents occurring when a man asked his date, "You seem so great; why are you still single?" This often prompted the woman to launch into confession or self-deprecation mode, revealing some of her less-than-desirable issues or failed relationships. Perhaps she regretted her answer later, but in the heat of the moment she couldn't help the knee-jerk responses: either to downplay how fabulous she is or to admit some deep-seated issue. It's hard to take a compliment, but you should definitely assume every guy who asks that question is trying to flatter you. The only response you need is "Thank you! I just haven't met the right person yet."

ALARM BELLS

Some baggage sounded potentially so serious that men heard clanging alarm bells. They didn't need to go home and contemplate whether or not to call her back: these disclosures were immediate date-breakers. Preston, a forty-nine-year-old bookstore owner from San Francisco, CA, described dating a woman who told him, after three glasses of wine, about her father's prison record for domestic violence. Preston wanted no part of that family drama. Other men told me about women who discussed everything from overcoming drug addiction, to being arrested for shoplifting, to having an eating disorder, to having a child with a handicap. No matter how impressive the stories about overcoming adversity were, or whether they were couched under the "really getting to know each other" or "just being honest" umbrellas, the news was too big. It carried too many stereotypes for the man to question, process, and rationalize on a first date. I believe that none of these stories would be permanent date-breakers for every man later in a relationship. When someone knows you well enough to balance your positive traits with your baggage, it's an entirely different equation. It's really all about timing and presentation. (More about this in the upcoming "So What Should You Do?" section.)

QUIRKS AND CONTROVERSIES

The most interesting stories to me were the ones in which women seemingly had no idea they were revealing controversial information about themselves. For example, I heard stories of dates that failed due to women disclosing that they smoked, were extremely picky eaters, read tarot cards, had had a lesbian encounter, graduated two years late from college, lost their virginity when they were thirteen, were fired from a job, or had three cats. (Note: these were not all about the same woman; I'm talking about eight *different* ladies!) Some women revealed they had never traveled outside the United States, and some admitted they were living at home with their parents. I imagine most of these women thought they were just talking about themselves or making a joke about a few quirky habits or situations. But men were hearing it as a form of baggage. I realized that The Flasher label expands beyond revealing physical and emotional issues. It encompasses *anything unusual* revealed to a stranger who doesn't have a broader context than a first date in which to process it.

During an Exit Interview for one of my thirty-seven-year-old clients, I discovered one example that he dubbed "weird" and she dubbed "admirable." She had divulged during their date that she hadn't had a serious boyfriend in fifteen years. She said she's proud of this fact because it demonstrates that men with whom she *does* get seriously involved are very special. Her date didn't see it that way. He assumed there must be something wrong with her.

Another Exit Interview I conducted revealed a situation where my thirty-year-old client mentioned on the first date that, because of her religious beliefs, she intended to stay a virgin until her wedding day. She told me, "I thought demonstrating my convictions about God and abstinence would be a *good* thing for someone who's marriage minded. Most Christian men appreciate that in a wife . . . And besides, it's something very important to me, so if he can't deal with it, better I know sooner than later." I nodded my head, looked her in the eye, and in my most sympathetic voice I told her, "Ix-nay on the old irgin-vay."[7] It's not that virginity until marriage is a bad choice—in fact, this is something I've seen on the rise recently—it's just not first-date information. I don't know the exact number, but maybe it's fifth-date information. Most men (even "good Christian men") who hear that one too soon think, "Check, please!"

Even if you can't relate to some of these particular examples, consider what else you may be telling your dates that might *seem* noble or positive to you but might be very troubling to someone who barely knows you. The most successful daters I meet have the ability to step outside themselves and see their situation objectively, as though they're watching themselves on TV.

---

[7]For those of you who don't speak pig Latin, this roughly translates to "Nix the virgin talk!"

Speaking of TV, I want to emphasize that admitting to watching too much can definitely cause concern. A friend of mine described a JDate e-mail exchange with a guy who asked her if she watches any TV. She responded, "Yes, definitely!" and listed her three favorite shows. Then he asked her, "Do you read many newspapers or magazines?" She wrote back, "No, not too many." And then he changed the subject to something else. In hindsight, she realizes he probably lost interest by assuming she was a serious couch potato without a brain. Unfortunately, he never asked her the sixty-four-thousand-dollar-question: "Do you read many books?" She happens to be a book editor (which he didn't know yet) and she reads about fifteen books a month. She certainly has a brain. As for TV, the reality is that she often misses her favorite shows and only logs about three hours of TV viewing each week. Once again, it's important to realize that behind the surface of what guys are asking about TV is an attempt to stereotype your intelligence and activity level. Be proactive and respond with the whole story: if you admit to watching a lot of TV, don't forget to mention how much time you spend on intellectual and fitness pursuits.

Some people admit to spending too much time online. Philip, a sixty-four-year-old advertising director from Chicago, IL, recalled a date conversation where he described an account he was pitching to an online retailer. The woman told him she knew all about online shopping because she was "addicted to eBay." At first he thought it was funny as they joked about how many hours she spent online and the wacky items she bought. But soon he began to worry that she was using the word "addict" seriously. She had tremendous passion in her voice describing the items she bought and sold, and went into elaborate detail about bidding strategies and seller ratings. She read books on improving her eBay sales. She said she'd earned $38,000 the previous year on eBay (which was not even her day job). This wasn't "funny" behavior, he concluded. He started to look at her more skeptically for the duration of the date and never called her back.

EBay Lady reminded me of being nicknamed Dr Pepper Girl by a guy I dated once in college who never called me back. Okay, now that we're farther along in this book and perhaps you have enough context not to judge me, I'm going to share some of my own quirky baggage. Hello, my name is Rachel, and I'm not a casual soda drinker. I only drink Diet Dr Pepper, and I kind of drink it obsessively. I've done this since fourth grade. I've been known to drink six to eight cans a day. I used to think this soda situation was a cute little personal factoid about myself that livened up conversation when I met someone new. Hey, it's not something you hear very often, right? But after I talked about my quirk one night on a first date with a guy I'll call Bozo (I'm deliberately giving him a less-than-flattering disguised name since he didn't call me back . . . who, me? Bitter?), I heard from my roommate's friend that Bozo had nicknamed me Dr Pepper Girl. Not only didn't he ask me out again (and I had *really* liked him), but he told all his friends that I was a bit of a freak. I realized that any obsession, no matter how cute or benign it might seem to *you*, may not go over well with strangers who don't know that the rest of your personality is (relatively) "normal."

Would you typically expect this type of information—about things like TV watching, eBay, or Diet Dr Pepper—to fall under the heading of "baggage"? I wouldn't. And yet from the stories men told, one person's quirk may be a stranger's red flag. So if your story involves anything slightly obsessive, save it for later.

SOUND FAMILIAR?

You may not have noted similarities to yourself among The Flasher anecdotes thus far, as it's not always easy to recognize yourself through other people's stories. So you can use the self-assessment questions below to verify whether men might be stereotyping you as The Flasher before they get to know the real you.

AT WORK . . .

❏ Is your job environment one that is close-knit and often gossipy?
❏ In past performance reviews, have you ever been told, "Try to keep your personal life separate from your work life . . ."?

❏ When you meet a new colleague at work, does he or she usually learn something very personal about you during your first conversation?

WITH YOUR FRIENDS AND FAMILY . . .

❏ Do you come from a family where everyone expressed their problems and emotions openly?
❏ Do friends frequently tell you, "Stop . . . TMI!" (too much information)?
❏ Has anyone ever told you, "You do realize, don't you, that outside New York that's not considered normal?"

ON A DATE OR WITH A PAST BOYFRIEND . . .

❏ When you're nervous or in an uncomfortable situation, do you sometimes drink a little too much alcohol?
❏ Do you use the phrase "My shrink says . . ."?
❏ If things are going really well with a new guy, does your conversation quickly get to a deeper level through divulging personal details about each other?

YOUR PERSONAL PHILOSOPHY:

❏ Do you believe, "If he can't handle it, it's better for me to find out now . . ."?
❏ Are you someone who likes to "lay your cards on the table"?
❏ Do you think it's sometimes okay to confide personal details to a stranger sitting next to you on an airplane or park bench?

If you answered yes to more than five questions above, you may be perceived (or misperceived) as The Flasher. There's no doubt you're honest, genuine, and not a game player; of course you shouldn't change who you are deep down. But you may consider tweaking some of the things you do and say on a first or second date. Men who don't know yet how fabulous you are may think you're The Flasher and miss the chance to get to know you better on the next few dates.

So, What Should You Do?

I always say that I love the people I love "despite" as much as "because." Despite the fact that my friend Gina is usually an hour late to meet me, I love her because she's the most loyal and funny person I know. But I only overlook the flaws of the late friend, the selfish friend, or the whiny friend because I know her well enough to see and value all of her pluses enough to deal with the minuses. In a first-date situation, if I knew their main flaw, the truth is that many of my closest friends would not have made it to the second date with me!

If you can relate to The Flasher, here are five suggestions that help a relationship get off the ground, ultimately allowing both of you enough time to evaluate and learn more about each other.

1) KEEP IT IN PERSPECTIVE

Some women tell me that whether they have a big or little skeleton in their closet (anything from infertility, to being adopted, to having a family history of breast cancer), they feel dishonest if they don't reveal their issue right away. But I believe these women don't have the right perspective about their issue. They are allowing a challenge in their lives—whether current or past—to take center stage in their minds and to define them. They're assuming (often without realizing it) that whatever their issue is, it looms larger than all their good qualities combined. For example, if you know you can't have kids, how do you frame this situation in your own mind? Are you an infertile woman looking to date someone who either doesn't want kids or already has kids of his own? Or are you a warm, smart, vibrant gal who will disclose the private facts about her reproductive organs if and when the relationship gets serious and the issue becomes relevant? I don't consider the latter attitude to be dishonest; I'd call it putting your best foot forward and having a right to privacy. A man who's in love will most likely see his options in a different light: if he wants to have children, maybe adoption or surrogacy is okay if it means he gets *you too*.

Of course there's always the risk that a man will leave when he eventually discovers your skeleton. Certainly after a few dates, it makes sense to discuss a big issue and find out if it's something he can handle—don't waste your valuable time with the wrong guy. But on a first date, rather than using your baggage to screen men who barely know you, it's a worthwhile investment to use your time getting to know each other's values, interests, and outlook. This focus increases the odds that your positives will outweigh your negatives in his mind later. The same advice goes for you; and of course you'll be evaluating *his* baggage later too.

When the time arrives to discuss any difficult issues, pay attention to not only what you're saying but also to how you say it. You send crucial signals with your verbal and nonverbal communication. Crossing your arms and getting a resigned look on your face as you say, "You're going to find out sooner or later, so you should know . . . ," is guaranteed to make any guy clench his teeth and grip the edge of the table.

2) USE A TOURNIQUET

Remember that smart daters are like chess players: they are always thinking several moves ahead. If you know there's something about you that might be controversial, make sure your first-date conversation doesn't stray down a path that will force you to reveal it or be tempted to lie about it. If anything potentially difficult comes up in the conversation, use a "tourniquet" to stop the bleeding before it gets worse. Let's say you're a hard-core atheist. This isn't exactly baggage, but it's something that can be quirky or controversial to a religious person. People with different beliefs fall in love all the time and make it work. But on the first date, religious differences can certainly be date-breakers. So when you ask him what he did last weekend, and he says, "I went to church on Sunday with my mom," head off any religious discussion that may follow by jumping in with the diversion question "Oh, your mom? That's great, I didn't know she lived in town. Tell me more about her . . ."

3) KEEP IT SHORT

It's imperative for The Flasher to keep first dates brief because TMI is her enemy. If you spend one hour with a guy on a first date instead of two hours, you're 50 percent less likely to spill out anything unflattering. Your first date should be more like *Reader's Digest* than *Encyclopaedia Britannica*. Keep your conversation light and interesting, and save the serious history for later when you know one another well enough to warrant that kind of sharing.

4) AVOID THE BONDING TRAP

A date is not a confessional with your priest, rabbi, or therapist. It's great if you want to dig beneath superficial first-date conversation—that's the right instinct—but realize that bonding over baggage may actually cut the ties, not bind them (as you saw in the examples with Glenn and Chuck). It's important to keep any personal issues to yourself when you sense your date might be trying (intentionally or unintentionally) to get you to reveal more than you should. When he replays your conversation in his mind at home later, he may have (irrational) second thoughts about what he needs and what he can handle. So if you're talking to him about family, don't share the emotional moment when you found out you were adopted. Instead, either talk about the loving family you have now or tell a funny story about a family holiday gone awry—provided it sounds more like a moment from the Brady Bunch than the Manson family.

What if your parents are divorced? Best to gloss over it early on. If he tells you his parents are divorced too, refrain from bonding over stepfamily traumas. It's a trap! It's okay to say, "Yeah, my parents are divorced too . . . it can be hard!" but avoid spewing out, "Oh, that sounds very civilized compared to *my* parents' divorce! My dad's on his third wife, I have two dysfunctional half sisters, and my mom just married a Jehovah's Witness she met in a Gamblers Anonymous group."

What if *he's* The Flasher? How do you handle his serious or shocking confession on a first date? First, do not assume it's okay for *you* to confess something next. Second, ask a few clarifying questions to make sure you've understood the scope of what he said. Maybe whatever it is, it's not as bad as it sounds. If he told you he's an alcoholic, you can ask him whether he's sober now and for how long. If he hasn't had a drink in ten years, maybe that's not so bad—only you can make the call about what's okay for *you*. But give him the benefit of the doubt if you like him by spending more time getting to know the "real him." And don't forget to be sympathetic—whether you plan to see him again or not. He's trusting you with something deeply personal and watching you closely to gauge your response. Even if this is a date-breaker for you, have the courtesy not to reveal any judgment. On the other hand, your mother would never forgive me if I didn't tell you this: if it's something truly horrible and unacceptable, run!

5) DEFINE YOUR "ISSUE"

Enough about heavy baggage—what if your issue is something a bit lighter? Maybe you're not very athletic, you have some credit card debt, or you once broke off an engagement. Maybe you snore. Maybe you always lose your keys. When should you mention something like this to a new guy? Well, everything is relative. First define exactly what your issue really is. Let's say you're a terrible cook. What does that mean? Are you less talented in the kitchen compared to your friend who spent a year at a French culinary school? Maybe you don't love to cook, but there are three things you make pretty well. Can you at least claim that no one ever died of food poisoning from a meal you served? You may be giving yourself a bad rap, because depending on how you see it (and describe it to your date), your "baggage" may not be an issue for him at all.

As described in the advice for The Bait & Switcher, it's good to set realistic expectations and mention a few of your "light" issues, but be sure to define them. This will avoid taking self-deprecation so far that something becomes bigger in his mind than the reality.

Extra-Credit Points

Want some extra-credit points here? Try the old fake-out move. Because men are always looking for the "but...," why not have some fun and give them a little scare? It might relieve some first-date tension. One of my clients once told her date in a confessional whisper, "Before we go any farther, I should tell you a little secret about myself..." Of course he immediately thought, "Oh, no, here it comes... what is it this time? Hepatitis C? A Bon Jovi groupie? An artificial limb?" But instead she pointed to a little dish in the center of the table, smiled, and said, "I *love* green olives." She proceeded to eat three of them. (For the record, she didn't eat *twenty* of them and morph into Crazy Green Olive Girl!)

If You're The Flasher ...

WHAT'S HOT:	WHAT'S NOT:
1. Conversation	1. Confession
2. Circumspection and patience	2. Verbal diarrhea
3. Fifth-date baggage reveal	3. First-date baggage reveal
4. "I'd love to know more about you."	4. "Here are some things you need to know about me."
5. Telling him you love to read heartbreaking memoirs	5. Telling him *your* heartbreaking memoir

#7 REASON HE DIDN'T CALL BACK
The Bitch-in-Boots

> Who wants to walk on eggshells for the rest of your life? —Randy, 34, Burlington, VT

> I'm not looking for a pushover, but a little compassion goes a long way. —Grant, 29, London, England

> It was like trying to hug a porcupine.
> —Walt, 41, Detroit, MI

The Bitch-in-Boots is a woman who does not seem kind. Sometimes she's impatient or easily irritated. She can act entitled or passive-aggressive. She's quick to snap at someone who annoys her, including both strangers and people she knows well. She might have traces of The Closer's pushy, aggressive, or cross-examining mannerisms, but men don't perceive her attitude as stemming from a ticking biological clock. They think it comes from deeper anger issues or just a bitchy temperament. She's the poster child for the famous line in the 1983 movie *Terms of Endearment* when John Lithgow says to the rude grocery clerk, "Oh, you must be from New York."

Men catch a glimpse of this prickly attitude on a date and get edgy and nervous, hoping not to be the next one in her receiving line. A few men actually quipped, "She kind of scared me!" Jim, a thirty-three-year-old book illustrator from Philadelphia, PA, remarked, "Who wants to wake up every morning and wonder if she's Dr. Jekyll or Mrs. Hyde?" Even the Bible says, "It's better to dwell alone in the wilderness than with a contentious and angry woman" (Proverbs 21:19).

I was surprised to hear some of these observations from the first-date trenches because I assumed no matter how bitchy a girl can be at her core, she would be smart enough to conceal those tendencies in the beginning. I pictured grumbling and snappish comments emerging later in a relationship when people let down their guard. So it surprised me how many slipups (or probably "misinterpretations") I heard about during my Exit Interviews.

I noted that when men were in a serious dating mode, they tended to look for someone who's a genuinely thoughtful person. Of course, who wouldn't pick good over evil for the long haul? Certainly there are men who thrive on trying to crack Cruella De Vil, but that's usually not a precursor for a healthy long-term relationship. Whatever we label these women—bitchy, prickly, moody—men are instinctively cautious about them. Yet I've never met a woman who isn't bitchy, prickly or moody, at least on occasion. Have you? I never met Mother Teresa, but I'd bet fifty rupees that even she had a bad day once in a while and didn't hide it. As I listened to some of the nitpicky anecdotes from men about The Bitch-in-Boots, I found myself wanting to snap at them, "Give her a break!" (Yeah, yeah, I know: I'm calling the kettle black . . .)

Are You The Bitch-in-Boots?

The Bitch-in-Boots encompassed three categories of behavior in my research.[8] Do any of these ring true for you?

RUDE TO YOUR DATE

Men didn't describe too many flat-out obnoxious remarks directed at them personally, but when they did, they remembered the lines word-for-word. I imagine these lines later became fodder for some bad-date competitions among single buddies. Jeff from Buffalo, NY, a twenty-six-year-old personal assistant, recalled his date's remark after he described his job: "You're a personal assistant? Are you joking? You mean you're, like, somebody's *secretary*?" They were married a year later. (Just kidding!) Peter from San Francisco, CA, a thirty-year-old architect, says he will never forget the night

---

[8]Divorced men were 104 percent more likely than men in other marital status groups to cite The Bitch-in-Boots as their primary no-callback reason.

his credit card was rejected at a bar when he tried to pay the tab, and his date (whom he'd known for thirty minutes) remarked, without a smile on her face, "I don't do poverty."

Those blatant examples were anomalies though. Chalk one up for women who self-edit. The more subtle anecdotes about The Bitch-in-Boots were what intrigued me—the ones when a guy was telling me his version of a "war story" but the woman probably had no idea how badly she came across. Landis, a twenty-seven-year-old banker from Denver, CO, recalled a second date with Shelly. He took her to a Broncos football game where they were going to meet a friend of his. When he and Shelly drove near the stadium, he was happy to spot a cheap parking lot. "Oh," he sighed to Shelly, "I wish I could have told [my friend] about this lot to save him a few bucks." Shelly responded, "Don't worry about it. It's not your money." Landis thought her remark was really inconsiderate, and along with a few other similar examples he recalled from their date, he found enough reason not to see her again.

An interesting comment came from Harlan, a thirty-three-year-old brand manager in Cincinnati, OH, who told me about being fixed up with the sister of his coworker. He called to ask her out for dinner, and as they were hanging up he said, "We should exchange photos—I'll e-mail you a picture of me; can you send me one of you too?" She hesitated and then replied, "Listen, I'm really not interested in men who care so much about my looks." Harlan was taken aback. He said she sounded bitchy, and he went on to tell me, "Like it or not, most people are used to dating online these days where you can see a photo. When you meet someone the old-fashioned way—through a friend or coworker—it's really not unreasonable to ask for a photo. Especially when we already had plans for dinner! It's not like I was using the photo to decide if I wanted to ask her out . . . sure, I was curious if she was attractive, but mostly I just wanted to recognize her when we met in a crowded restaurant." Harlan assured her that the photo wasn't necessary and they met "blind" a few days later. He said she was really pretty, but he couldn't shake what he perceived as a bitchy comment she'd made on the phone. He listened closely during dinner to gauge whether she was a kind person or not. He recounted that she seemed annoyed when he had trouble parking his car near the restaurant, and again when he forgot she'd already told him she had two sisters. He summed it up: "She wasn't sweet."

RUDE TO A THIRD PARTY

Men recounted many incidences when a woman's rude behavior was not directed toward them personally. Sometimes all it took was a few comments to a waiter and he extrapolated her entire personality. You probably judge guys for that too. Brett, a gay twenty-five-year-old MBA student at the Kellogg School of Management in Chicago, IL, said he saw one guy's true colors when he made this comment to the waiter: "I *need* ranch dressing." Brett told me, "There was no 'please' . . . or no 'when you get a chance.'" He described his date's tone as "haughty." Brett picked up on an entitled attitude a few other times throughout the evening and decided he wasn't interested.

Sometimes you can be your own worst enemy. Men listened to the stories women told—about something that happened at their office, or to one of their friends, or from their childhood—and they concluded from the story that she was The Bitch-in-Boots. Grant from London, England, a twenty-nine-year-old boutique-hotel manager, recalled a story from a girl named Julie. During her date with Grant, Julie complained about a colleague at work who was six months pregnant, tired all the time, and had some health issues. The colleague had been out of the office for several days. The burden of their joint projects fell on Julie's shoulders. Julie vented to Grant about her bad day at work and said, "I'm sick of people making excuses all the time for not doing their work. She chose to have a baby, so why should I suffer?" Grant couldn't believe how insensitive Julie was about someone who was going through a hard time.

He said, "I'm not looking for a pushover, but a little compassion goes a long way."

Not being *genuine* was also a big part of The Bitch-in-Boots aura. Some men mentioned concerns that women weren't revealing their true nature if they observed even brief moments of aggravated behavior. Phil, a forty-year-old stockbroker in New York, NY, told me that he saw something in the first two minutes with a woman named Andrea that framed his outlook for the whole evening. He arrived at her door while she was finishing a phone call with her mother. Andrea smiled and gestured for him to sit down. She stepped away into the kitchen (without closing the door). For the next two minutes he listened to one side of a very rude conversation between mother and daughter. She snapped at everything her mother said with lines such as "I *know* that! Don't you think I *know* that?" and "You *would* think that, wouldn't you?" Her tone was harsh and impatient. Soon Andrea hung up the phone with her mother, returned to the living room, and greeted Phil warmly. She acted like nothing had happened. He never glimpsed what he called "her evil twin" the rest of the night, but he admitted he was skeptical about her during their dinner and wondered several times whether certain things she said were genuine. Despite finding her cute and smart, he said her phone manner "had scared him early on . . . [and] he worried something else was underneath her façade." He didn't ask for a second date.

Isaac, a twenty-six-year-old human resources coordinator from Charlotte, NC, told me about witnessing a woman's catty nature during their first date when she saw a friend of hers walking by their dinner table. His date, Sarah, put on a big smile, stood up to kiss her friend's cheek, and had a brief, seemingly warm conversation with her. Ten seconds after the friend walked away, Sarah launched into her true feelings about the woman, saying she was arrogant and self-righteous. She even mentioned some rumors floating around about her "friend" having an affair with a married man. Isaac couldn't believe he had fallen for his date's act: he assumed by the greeting he witnessed that they were good friends.

He concluded that Sarah wasn't a genuine person and that she was also a gossip.

THE "GOOD-SPORT TEST"

Since I've already made my Diet Dr Pepper confession to you, I might as well tell you another personal story. This one's about my parents: Many years ago, my mother and father wanted to ensure that my older brother, Derek, brought a genuinely nice woman into our family. So they devised a "good-sport test" for a few of his dates. Derek would invite a new girlfriend to join our family for dessert at a now-defunct place in Denver called the Soda Straw. It was a garish, old-fashioned dessert parlor where kids went mainly to celebrate their birthdays. My mother would sneak away from our table and tell the hostess privately it was my brother's girlfriend's birthday that night. This meant that a few minutes later, the entire waitstaff at the Soda Straw would come jogging cheerfully over to us. They would clang a loud bell, hold up a slice of cake topped with a sizzling sparkler, and sing a goofy but enthusiastic rendition of "Happy Birthday." It was customary for all the patrons in the restaurant to join the singing, and the birthday girl was supposed to stand up *on top of the table* as she was serenaded.

Needless to say, my brother's unsuspecting girlfriends were aghast. Instead of going along with the "fun" of the evening, they would protest in shock, "No! It's not my birthday! You've made some mistake!" while my father would wink at the waitress, nod sympathetically, and say, "She's just embarrassed . . ." My mother would urge the crowd, "Keep singing!" Why my brother went along with this fiasco, I'll never know. But the theory in my family went like this: you've gotta have a sense of humor in marriage or you'll never make it. An easygoing, shrug-it-off-with-a-laugh girl is certainly the opposite of The Bitch-in-Boots. My family story may be outlandish, but look out, girls—you may just be the next "punk'd" victim as a man sizes you up on his bitch-o-meter!

SOUND FAMILIAR?

You may not have noted similarities to yourself among The Bitch-in-Boots anecdotes thus far, as it's not always easy to recognize yourself through other people's stories. So you can use these self-assessment questions to verify whether men might be stereotyping you as The Bitch-in-Boots before they get to know the real you.

AT WORK . . .

❏ Do you drink a lot of caffeine during the day, making you edgy or a bit aggressive?

❏ Do you have a high-pressure job and frequently come home stressed out?

❏ Do colleagues tend to come to you when they want to complain about something?

WITH YOUR FRIENDS AND FAMILY . . .

❏ Have you ever been told, "You'd catch more flies with honey . . ."?

❏ Do people sometimes say to you, "Are you mad at me for some reason?"

❏ Has anyone ever encouraged you to see a therapist about anger issues?

ON A DATE OR WITH A PAST BOYFRIEND . . .

❏ Do men compliment you on your sarcastic sense of humor?

❏ Do guys say to you, "I think you took that the wrong way . . . that's not what I meant"?

❏ When you really like a guy, do you sometimes "tease him" by saying something slightly mean to him?

YOUR PERSONAL PHILOSOPHY:

❏ Do you believe it's not *how* you say it, but *what* you say that matters?

❏ Are you frequently annoyed by a lot of things in your daily life?

❏ Are you the type to keep your guard up to avoid being hurt?

If you answered yes to more than five questions above, you may be perceived (or misperceived) as The Bitch-in-Boots. There's no doubt you're tough and no one takes advantage of you; of course you shouldn't change who you are deep down. But you may consider tweaking some of the things you do and say on a first or second date. Men who don't know yet how fabulous you are may think you're The Bitch-in-Boots and miss the chance to get to know you better on the next few dates.

So, What Should You Do?

One night on the phone, I asked Brian, a forty-seven-year-old oil company executive from Houston, TX, "What question do you ask yourself at the end of every date when deciding whether to call a woman back or not?" He thought about it for a few seconds, then replied, "I guess I ask myself, 'Is she someone who will make my life more enjoyable or more difficult?'"

If you want to get to know him better and decide whether he's someone whose life you *want* to make more enjoyable, here are five suggestions to help defrost your image so you can choose a second date or not.

1) BE AWARE

Awareness is nine tenths of the dating law. Know that every story you tell, every detail you give about yourself, every opinion you express, is fodder for him to extrapolate how you would look as his girlfriend or future wife. Without the benefit of really knowing you, he has no idea whether the comment you just made about your pregnant coworker is simply a one-off remark at the end of a bad day or symptomatic of a woman devoid of compassion.

Everything on a first date becomes a metaphor, as you see throughout this entire book. When you mention to your date, for example, that you no longer speak to your best friend from college because of an argument, he might think you're unforgiving and judgmental. When you joke that you'd rather spend Thanksgiving in solitary

> **Everything on a first date becomes a metaphor.**

confinement at Alcatraz than with your relatives in Des Moines, you might think you're being cute, but he might think you're either not family oriented or that you come from a dysfunctional clan (even if you do—because we all do—save that one for later). Remember to edit your "jokey" stories in order to paint your best portrait—not only on the first date, but during your pre-date e-mails and phone calls too. Big Brother is always watching you!

2) LOSE THE TONE

Often it's not the content of what you say but your tone of voice. I'm sure you know what I mean: the snide, caustic, or miffed tone that indicates you're annoyed. Ask your friends and family if you're not sure whether you're prone to it (reassure them you want their *honest* feedback), and ask them to help alert you when it creeps into your conversation. Once you become aware of it, lose it.

Want a role model for a consistently lovely voice tone? One man I interviewed told me his dream voice would sound like the character Juliet on *Lost*.

3) ADMIT YOUR MISTAKE

When you've put your foot in your mouth, admit it. Don't pretend it didn't happen. Men may be dense sometimes, but they're usually not blind. For example, what if your date accidentally spills red wine on your white blouse? Perhaps in the moment you're pissed off and you snap at him with a few harsh words. Even if you quickly compose yourself, he still saw your anger flash. Instead of trying to ignore what happened, you could acknowledge your mistake with, "Oh my gosh, what am I saying? I'm so sorry; I overreacted. Sometimes I get nervous on first dates. Of course it was an accident! [Laughing] Here, please spill more wine over here and it'll look like part of the pattern in the fabric!" Admitting you're wrong, blaming your reaction on first-date stress, and making a little joke at the end goes a long way toward defusing the incident. Then you can get back to the business of getting to know more about each other without a dark cloud over your head.

4) RESCHEDULE THE DATE

We all have bad days and bad moods. If you feel like you're really not up for projecting your best self one night, go ahead and reschedule the date. You're better off creating a stage with good lighting than performing in the dark. But you can't cancel more than once with the same guy, nor too close to your meeting time. Otherwise, your rudeness will likely be the only impression you leave, risking his not wanting that first date at all. I think eight hours' notice is the minimum for courtesy without a genuine emergency. And definitely don't text or e-mail the cancellation: call him and speak in person or leave a heartfelt voice mail, which is the only way to convey sincerity. (Also, see my cautionary advice about canceling dates in the upcoming Busy Bee category.) Understand that all the stars will never be aligned—when you're not bloated, your hair isn't frizzy, *Grey's Anatomy* isn't on TV—so I'm not talking about canceling a date under *any* adverse circumstance. But if you're anticipating an 8 out of 10, or above, on your personal bitchy scale, then consider making a polite call to reschedule.

5) BE YOUR OWN PR AGENT

If you're not sure you can rein in your bitchy side with the defensive tactics above, take the offense instead and be your own public relations agent. Craft a positive personal brand for yourself and keep reinforcing it throughout the evening. Spend time before your first dates to think about your best qualities, and remind yourself about specific stories from your past to demonstrate them. Tap in to those qualities and let them guide your date conversation. You could reframe what others might call your bitchy side by casually referring to yourself as sassy, saucy, or cheeky. Or you could focus on demonstrating qualities that are specifically the *opposite of* The Bitch-in-

Boots label, such as compassion, sensitivity, thoughtfulness, good humor, or easygoingness. I am not suggesting you make anything up; on the contrary, you have to be truthful. But I know that inside almost every Bitch-in-Boots lies a sassy woman with good intentions.

Jot down in advance some of the things you've done or said in your past—all the way back to childhood if you want—to trigger your memory. You can tell him on your first date about your experience volunteering one summer for the Special Olympics or a funny story from your recent tutoring session at the Boys and Girls Club. If he says, "Too bad the rain ruined your outdoor party," you could respond with, "Oh, no, that's fine; with the drought this summer, I'm happy this town got the water it needed!" Reinforce your compassionate and easygoing side.

George, a thirty-year-old veterinarian from Omaha, NE, told me about his fiancée. She had shared a sweet story with him on their first date when he had asked, "What did you do today?" She answered by selecting one thing she did that day: she had helped an elderly neighbor look for her lost dog. He remembered being touched by that story and said it shaped his opinion that she was a caring person from the start. Remember that you can guide some of your date's first impressions about you by revealing flattering stories of your own choosing.

If You're The Bitch-in-Boots . . .

WHAT'S HOT:	WHAT'S NOT:
1. Cute tone	1. Curt tone
2. Showing empathy	2. Showing entitlement
3. Acknowledging and apologizing	3. Acting like nothing happened
4. Laughing at his jokes	4. Laughing at someone else's expense
5. Taking an opportunity to show your compassionate side	5. Taking your moods out on him

#8 REASON HE DIDN'T CALL BACK
The Debbie Downer

> She was not exactly Little Miss Sunshine.
> —Baker, age 25, Austin, TX

> She complained about everything. I felt like I was visiting my ninety-year-old grandma in Florida: "It's too cold in here, the soup needs salt, could they make these chairs any less comfortable?"
> —Harry, age 40, Providence, RI

> I love it when a woman is *delighted* by something. People are so jaded these days.
> —Alberto, age 29, Los Angeles, CA

The Debbie Downer is a complainer: nothing is ever quite right. She can also be the bitter or cynical girl who sees the glass as half-empty. She doesn't act like a happy or energetic person.

Of course, if you're down on dating, you probably have a good reason. Bracing for yet another bad Internet date, still hurt over a recent breakup, or doubtful that Mr. Right even exists, you wonder, "When did dating stop being *fun*?" Maybe it's not just dating that's causing your blues: your boss is a jerk, your rent just went up, and there's always too much traffic. Regardless, men want (and expect) upbeat women in first encounters, so it becomes a chicken-and-egg thing. Are you down because dating sucks, or does dating suck because you're down?

In his book *Why Men Marry Some Women and Not Others*, John Molloy writes, "When we asked men who had just become engaged what attracted them to their fiancées when they first met, most said it was how positive, energetic, enthusiastic and upbeat [she] was." But sometimes it's hard to recognize when you're not being positive. Sometimes when I relay Exit Interview feedback to my Debbie Downer clients, they tell me, "He called me cynical? But I thought we had intelligent banter . . . ," or "Maybe I was *discerning* about the food, but I was definitely not *complaining* . . ."

Are you The Debbie Downer?

The Debbie Downer encompassed four categories of behavior in my research.[9] Do any of these ring true for you?

COMPLAINTS

Complaints accumulate throughout the evening. Gabe, a forty-year-old military officer from Atlanta, GA, described a woman he dated who had nothing positive to say. She complained that he ordered pork chops at a Greek restaurant (instead of a Greek specialty), that the bathroom was at the top of a long flight of stairs (instead of on the main level), that the people at the next table were too loud, and that he yawned when the wine made him sleepy. He told me it wasn't actually the wine that made him sleepy; it was the *whine*.

Complaints can set a negative tone early on. Jesse, a twenty-nine-year-old software designer from Seattle, WA, picked up Kerry one night for a date after meeting her at a "Hurry Date" speed-dating event. She was new in town and he was eager to show her some of his favorite spots. But when he asked, "How do you like Seattle so far?" she replied, "I don't really like it. It rains all the time, apartments are expensive, my job is stressful . . ." It was like letting the air out of a balloon, he said. Their date atmosphere lacked energy for the rest of the night.

Sometimes the complaints were sprinkled throughout a story that a woman told. Stefan, a sixty-one-year-old rancher in Driggs, ID, told me about chatting online with Linda, a woman he met on ChristianMingle.com who "had a bright future as a travel critic," he said sarcastically. They initially connected because they both had a passion for travel, but when she described trips she had taken, she

---

[9]Men from the East Coast were 56 percent more likely than men in other geographic groups to cite The Debbie Downer as their primary no-callback reason.

made comments such as, "Rome isn't what it used to be. You can't even cross the street without being run over by a motorcycle," or "It was nice to swim in the Mediterranean when I visited Crete, but the food was terrible—I don't like lamb, and moussaka is greasy. I'd say Crete is a definite 'must miss.'" Stefan had never been to Rome or Crete, but he hoped to go one day. Without Linda.

CYNICISM

The cynical comments I heard sometimes resembled complaints, but they usually centered around broad negative statements about men. Of course it's easy to understand how women become jaded about men in the first place. If a guy lost interest after getting you into bed, it's natural to think men only want one thing. If your serious relationship ended in disappointment, it's natural to be skeptical about mankind's ability to make a long-term commitment. But that cynicism is, naturally, a turnoff for the next guy, who may or may not deserve it.

Garrett, a twenty-nine-year-old video editor from Scottsdale, AZ, remembered a woman he met through a friend. She made remarks during their first date such as, "Guys are just looking for sex," and "All men want to do is sit on the couch and watch TV sports." He said in hindsight he should have known she was a cynical person because, before they met, his friend had shown him a photo of her on his MySpace page. In the photo (taken at a party hosted by his friend), she had posed with a beer bottle in one fist and a handmade sign in the other fist that proclaimed, "This should make me attractive to men."

I heard another anecdote about cynicism from a twenty-five-year-old retail store manager in Spartanburg, SC, named Shane. He said his date, Carol, was so unbelievably pretty that he was willing "to put up with a lot of stuff from her." But by the end of the date the luster had worn off. She was just too negative. Shane's gripe was that Carol prejudged him, saying, "You're probably the type of guy who wastes his paycheck on cocaine every week," and "You're probably the type of guy who's not into monogamy." He wondered why she accepted his date invitation in the first place if she thought so little of him. He never asked her, he just didn't call her back.

One afternoon near my home in Denver, CO, I had a lively interview with my daughter's soccer coach, a thirty-six-year-old divorced dad nicknamed Coach T. He said he has a lot of respect for women, especially because he was raised by a single mom and he's now raising a daughter himself. He knows that it's important to give women compliments and make them feel appreciated. Coach T recalled an example from a date with one woman who showed up looking fantastic. He smiled at her and said, "Wow, you look great." Her brisk reply was, "You probably say that to everyone." He remarked to me, "I get labeled insincere if I compliment a woman and insensitive if I don't." He asked his date later at the restaurant if she wanted another drink, and she said, "Oh, right, you're just trying to get in my pants!" Coach T concluded, "I couldn't win. Women are so jaded now they don't even recognize a good guy when he shows up."

> **"Women are so jaded now they don't even recognize a good guy when he shows up."**

PESSIMISM

I heard several anecdotes about women who saw the glass as half-empty. Tobias, a sixty-one-year-old cosmetics distributor in St. Louis, MO, excitedly told his date, Ellen, about his future plans to expand his business overseas. He explained that it was a bold move for him, how it would involve taking out a second mortgage on his house, but that he thought he could do it successfully. Ellen told him, "I don't know. You should be happy with what you've got: a nice house and a solid business. There are so many things that could go wrong: changes in the economy, currency fluctuations, international tax issues. I wouldn't risk it." He was turned off by her attitude. He said, "I want a partner who encourages me to seize the day!"

As an author, I meet a lot of women in the publishing world, especially great single editors. I recently played matchmaker to a cute, vivacious editor I know. I fixed her up with my art dealer friend in Manhattan. His name is Tate, and he's a voracious reader. Prior to the date, he told me he was excited to hear her stories from inside the book world. But when I found out later that Tate didn't want a second date with the editor, I asked him why (of course!). He told me, "After dating in New York for twenty years, I have one important criterion: someone who sees the glass as half-full. You can tell whether a woman does or doesn't by the way she answers the most basic questions." Tate said one example was that he asked my editor friend whether the infamous "slush pile"[10] he'd heard about really existed, and if so, what kinds of manuscripts she had seen in there over the years. She related some details about several boring manuscripts and bad proposals she had read, and lamented how there weren't any unique topics anymore. He told me, "She selected everything negative to tell me about her job. Instead of saying, 'My favorite manuscript was X,' she picked out all the bad ones to describe." I reminded him that he *had* inquired about *the slush pile*—a pile notorious for 999 bad manuscripts for every good one. His response was, "Then I'm looking for the girl who tells me about that *one* good manuscript."

NONVERBAL MESSAGES

Seth, a forty-five-year-old manager at a health club in Newport Beach, CA, described a first date with a woman who "had negative energy." He remembered a few comments she made about having a bad day at work and being upset with her mother. But he said, "Her slumped posture said it all." Because he works in a health club, Seth pays attention to what the body says and recommends Pilates classes for men and women to strengthen their core. He says this facilitates sitting up straight. Good posture signals a self-confident

---

[10]"Slush pile" is a demeaning term for the thousands of unsolicited manuscripts that are sent directly by authors to publishers without a literary agent and are usually discarded by the publishers.

and energetic person. During my conversation with him, I found myself shifting in my chair and forcing my spine to go rigid. It didn't feel natural, but I knew he was right.

Adam, a twenty-eight-year-old associate television producer in New York, NY, commented, "Women create a funeral-like tone for a date when they wear all black." Then he joked, "I'm not looking to date a Gypsy, but c'mon, gimme at least one non-grayscale color to gaze at all night!"

Eytan, a thirty-seven-year-old diamond exporter from Tel Aviv, Israel, recalled an afternoon with a group of friends at the beach. For two hours, he enjoyed a lively conversation with an attractive woman named Dahlia whom he'd never met before that day. But when someone suggested they all go swimming in the ocean, Dahlia was the only one in the group who declined. While everyone else was splashing in the waves, she sat alone on the shore. She told Eytan she didn't feel like swimming, which made him conclude she wasn't "fun." I suggested to him several valid reasons why she might have declined (She didn't want to be seen in a bathing suit? She was tired? She had her period? She's afraid of jellyfish?) and he said, "Sure, sure, maybe . . . but I like girls who are fun and carefree. She seemed like a party pooper sitting there by herself. Besides, I meet so many women—it's not a big deal if one doesn't work out."

Rajeev, a thirty-three-year-old technology consultant in Pittsburgh, PA, told me about a date with a woman he called "vibrant" and "fun-loving." They had gone out once, and he said he couldn't remember exactly why nothing had developed between them. But a year later he was at a party and saw her across the room—he recognized her and had a brief thought: "Oh yeah! I liked that girl . . ." He was about to go over and say hello, maybe restart something, when he noticed the look on her face: she was not happy or smiling. She looked "dour," he told me. She didn't know he was watching her, but "she looked stiff . . . giving off that vibe like something smelled bad." It was a disconnect with the positive memory he had of her, so he stayed in the shadows and didn't reconnect. I heard a few other comments from different men who looked at their date when she didn't know he was watching. If the guy saw an unhappy face, he started to wonder—on some level—whether she was the positive person he wanted in a long-term partner.

SOUND FAMILIAR?

You may not have noted similarities to yourself among The Debbie Downer anecdotes thus far, as it's not always easy to recognize yourself through other people's stories. So you can use the self-assessment questions below to verify whether men might be stereotyping you as The Debbie Downer before they get to know the real you.

AT WORK . . .

❑ Do colleagues often ask you, "Is everything okay?"

❑ Is your job the type where success depends on identifying or dealing with problems (such as medicine, law, venture capital, customer service, psychotherapy, etc.)?

❑ Are you unhappy in your job?

WITH YOUR FRIENDS AND FAMILY . . .

❑ Do people often say, "C'mon, cheer up! Things aren't that bad . . ."?

❑ Is your mother constantly nagging you to sit up straight?

❑ When traveling or dining out, are you typically the one in your group to voice any complaints to the manager if something is wrong?

ON A DATE OR WITH A PAST BOYFRIEND . . .

❑ As you're getting ready for a first date, do you assume it probably won't work out?

❑ Has a guy ever told you, "Let's try to have *fun* . . ."?

❑ When you're in an uncomfortable situation, do you tend to voice your concerns rather than "keep a stiff upper lip"?

YOUR PERSONAL PHILOSOPHY:

❑ Do you keep your expectations low to avoid being disappointed?

❑ Do you gravitate to depressing books and movies?
❑ Is more than 50 percent of your wardrobe black?

If you answered yes to more than five questions here, you may be perceived (or misperceived) as The Debbie Downer. There's no doubt you're realistic, discerning, and contemplative; of course you shouldn't change who you are. But you may consider tweaking some of the things you do and say on a first or second date. Men who don't know yet how fabulous you are may think you're The Debbie Downer and miss the chance to get to know you better on the next few dates.

So, What Should You Do?

I remember teaching a dating seminar in Manhattan a few years ago. When I discussed The Debbie Downer stereotype, I mentioned something about how men like upbeat women. A thirtysomething woman, dressed all in black, quickly raised her hand and said, "No offense, but you don't know what you're talking about!" (*Um, no offense taken?!*) She told me that *all* her friends in New York are jaded and cynical. And many of them are married! And it's *funny* to complain about bad service and crappy movies and stupid taxi drivers.

My reply to her was this: "I'm not suggesting women morph into perky Shirley Temple clones or change their personalities in any way. My focus is to illuminate how precarious first impressions can be with someone who doesn't know you very well." I'm not sure I convinced this woman, but I do believe that if you only have ninety minutes for a first date and a first impression, and you're bitching half the time, a guy can easily think you resemble Tony Soprano's grim mother. Let your inner critic emerge later as he gets to know you better. Or let him catch a glimpse of your devilish side on the first date, *as long as you balance it with more positive than negative energy.*

While many men appreciate—and specifically *seek*—intelligent sarcasm and critique, most men are drawn to the initial image of a happy person when they want to find a committed, healthy relationship. And I heard that more often from New York men than anyone else!

So if you're The Debbie Downer, here are six tips to help you cheer up, enabling *you* to select the men you want to smile or frown upon next time.

1) USE THE 3:1 RATIO

Men do like an "edge," so you certainly don't want to have a smile plastered on your face all night, proclaiming, "Everything's fantastic! I love the world!" But try to create a mental balance sheet that skews more positive than negative. For every sarcastic or negative comment you make, come up with three positive remarks. (This ratio is also recommended in my advice for The Bait & Switcher.) For example, tell him right away how impressed you are that he found this hidden gem of a restaurant, that you love the spicy shrimp, and that the wine is amazing. Then you can let loose about the irony of using chopsticks in Thai restaurants since people in Thailand don't even use them. Using the 3:1 ratio here, the glass is three quarters full!

2) DON'T SH*T WHERE YOU EAT

Okay, this is not an attractive title. Don't use this expression on a date, please! But the idea is that if you have anger or depression issues, use a therapist, friends, or family for venting purposes rather than your dates. This is not simply about avoiding negative personal topics (i.e., advice for The Flasher), but includes refraining from expressing your frustration with daily life or personal disappointments. Instead, try calling a friend one hour before every date begins. Deposit all your complaints for the day with her, thereby clearing your head for only good thoughts the rest of the night. You can send your poor friend an iTunes gift card the next day to thank her for listening.

Remember, I'm only talking about avoiding downbeat comments

during early-stage dates. Of course if he turns into a long-term partner he should be someone with whom you can be open and honest about all your feelings: the good, the bad, and the truly awful.

3) SCREEN YOUR TOPICS

Everyone has hot buttons that, when pushed, will unleash a cascade of negative energy. Please don't ever get me started about my college boyfriend who cheated on me, my horrible boss in 1994, or how waiters always ask you, "How's the food?" *only* when your mouth is full! You know what your own hot buttons are, so avoid conversational topics that are guaranteed to elicit bitchy remarks from you. You can and should steer the first-date conversation toward fun topics. Go to your happy place. Captivate him with colorful stories about your quirky childhood neighborhood, your nothing-short-of-religious experience snowshoeing in British Columbia, or the best-ever, mouthwatering caramel-cappuccino-chip cheesecake you ate in a little place near Ventura Beach.

4) SCREEN YOUR PHOTOS

Garrett's story, noted earlier, about the woman with the beer bottle and man-hater sign on his friend's MySpace page, was focused on specifically cynical perceptions. But it brings up important advice about online photos in general. You should review *all* your online photos (posted on dating sites, social networks, and photo sites such as Shutterfly or Snapfish, where you might show an album to a new guy). Think of various ways each photo could be perceived by someone who doesn't know you: is that photo cynical, promiscuous, crazy, weird? Or is it sporty, artistic, family oriented, sweet? Be sure your photos project the positive image you want.

5) FOCUS ON YOUR BODY

Shoulders back. The nonverbal message of good posture signals confidence, energy, and a positive attitude. If you are prone to the shoulder slump, think of a cue to remind yourself to sit up straight—

maybe adjust your posture every time you take a sip of your drink. Also, don't cross your arms—this body language can appear stern. And turn that frown upside down! (Don't you hate that expression?! Sorry, I'm not getting sappy on you . . . but please smile.) Even if you're on the sidelines at a party or social gathering, think of a funny joke or story that will (re)energize your facial expression. You never know who might be scanning the room.

6) BLAST IT

This might sound basic, but there's nothing like playing your favorite song *really* loud while you're getting ready for a date. If you've had a bad day or you acknowledge that you've got a bad attitude about men, I know there's one song out there that must put you in a great mood. Everyone's got that one song. Mine is "Sweet Home Alabama." Yeah, I know that dates me back to the mid-seventies when Lynyrd Skynyrd was popular in my junior high school. But ancient or not, when I hear the first few notes to that song I am instantly perkier. Whatever your own "good mood" tune is, blast it before your next date.

If You're The Debbie Downer . . .

WHAT'S HOT:	WHAT'S NOT:
1. A little color in your wardrobe	1. The all-black Italian widow uniform
2. "Seize the day!"	2. "Better safe than sorry!"
3. "Thank you, what a lovely compliment."	3. "I bet I'm not the first girl to hear that line."
4. "I haven't had this much fun in ages!"	4. "It's been ages since I had any fun."
5. "I appreciate a good man."	5. "There are no good men left."

#9 REASON HE DIDN'T CALL BACK
The Ex-Factor

> I was genuinely curious why she got divorced, so I wanted to hear about her ex-husband. The problem was how *bitter* she sounded . . . not exactly an aphrodisiac. —Pete, age 39, Boston, MA

> She told me her ex-boyfriend cheated on her . . . At first I was sympathetic, but then I started thinking, "If that guy risked losing a girl like this, there must be something wrong with her that I haven't seen yet . . ." —Jasper, age 30, Philadelphia, PA

> She was droning on and on about her last relationship . . . it took up too much of the conversation. I was bored, and frankly I just didn't care. —Saul, age 61, Palm Springs, CA

The Ex-Factor refers to women who talk about their ex-boyfriends or ex-husbands. It ranges from too much ex talk overall on a date to a few brief mentions. It also includes women who refer to men in general who have disappointed them or allude to a gold standard of behavior established by one special person in their past.

Not discussing your ex on a first date is advice that pops up in every dating article or book I've ever read. It's the big "duh!" factor. It's one of those commonsense guidelines that's obvious. Yet just because something is common sense, it doesn't mean it's common practice. The Ex-Factor merits discussion here because the data tells me so. I heard two hundred and one anecdotes from men about women who divulged something (consciously or unconsciously) about an ex-boyfriend or ex-husband that directly resulted in the man not wanting to see her again. On some level women know this is a mistake, but on another level, they just can't resist.

Like any bad behavior—from smoking to overeating to spending too much on shoes—it just feels so good in the moment.

But it's a no-win situation. For example, tell me this: is there *any* good way to say, "My ex-boyfriend cheated on me"? If you sound hurt, he'll assume you're still emotionally attached. If you sound angry, he'll be turned off by your bitterness. If you act detached about the whole episode, he might think you're cold or unemotional. If you express something positive about your ex, you risk making your date feel competitive, jealous, or worried that you're not over him. There's just no safe path. Besides, ex talk can be plain annoying and boring.

"Fine," you might be thinking. "That's not me. I don't talk about my ex." But below the surface of what's actually spoken on a date, women can fall prey to The Ex-Factor in subtle ways without once mentioning the "ex" word.

Are You Involved with The Ex-Factor?

The Ex-Factor encompassed four categories of behavior in my research. Do any of these ring true for you?

OBVIOUS MENTIONS

While discovering past heartbreaks about someone certainly holds great fascination, and while those heartbreaks have certainly helped shape who you are today, they absolutely do not belong on the first-date menu. This category has shades of The Flasher (revealing something undesirable) but is specifically focused on exes and deserves its own label. Men told me tales of women who vented about cheating exes, complained about lazy exes, laughed about loser exes, and lamented commitment-phobic exes. Frankly, men said they didn't know the woman well enough to care about any of this yet. Harsh, but true.

Dick, a sixty-four-year-old lawyer in Washington, DC, made this analogy: "Dating a bitter woman coming out of a divorce is like interviewing someone who won't stop bitching about her last job. No, thanks!" Kamaal, a thirty-one-year-old radio producer in Atlanta, GA, shared his shocked reaction to a woman who told him she'd been divorced for one year, but she had a six-month-old baby. She said matter-of-factly, "The baby is a result of makeup sex with my ex-husband." Alrighty, then.

Jason, a twenty-five-year-old computer programmer in Austin, TX, told me that he noticed a tattoo on his date's ankle. It looked like some kind of bird, and he asked, "What is that?" The woman replied, "Oh, I had that done for my ex-boyfriend in college—it's a lovebird to symbolize our commitment. In hindsight, not a great idea!" Jason was left feeling a mixture of two things. One, he knew every time he looked at her ankle, he'd start thinking about her with some other guy. Two, he went from thinking earlier that she was "cool" to thinking she was stupid for getting a permanent tattoo for some guy in college (and then admitting it).

Several men in my research talked about playing the "What's Your Number?" game (i.e., how many people you've slept with). None of them called these women back for another date. The game always seemed to evolve accidentally on the first or second date while joking around or during a late-night confessional. In case any woman thinks there is *ever* a good number to reveal, let me state for the record: there is not. Whether a number you provide is true or false, it will always be the wrong number in the early stages of dating (too few, too many, too complicated). And never feel obligated to provide an answer if he reveals his number first. The only correct response would be, "Let's talk more about that when we know each other better!"

SUBTLE MENTIONS

The Ex-Factor has no loopholes. Please don't try to find one! While outright mentions, comparisons, or anecdotes about exes might be easy to avoid, The Ex-Factor is sometimes cited as a date-breaker even when the actual word "ex" never enters the conversation.

Often the little words "we" or "our" can be the culprit. Bridger, a twenty-nine-year-old chef in San Antonio, TX, remembered a woman who kept using those taboo plural pronouns during their date. She had lived with a man for two years but never mentioned it to Bridger (he had heard it earlier from the mutual friend who introduced them). But her comments during lunch were sprinkled with indirect references to her ex. First she said, "We didn't like to leave our dog at a kennel when we traveled." A little while later, she said, "What a coincidence, we went to that beach in Mexico too!" At some point, she also mentioned "that park close to our apartment." He said he felt like a third wheel on his own date; it was a complete turnoff.

I talked to one woman who forgot about a particular photo album on her Facebook page. It was titled "The Best Days of My Life." She had posted the album a year earlier after a great vacation with her then-boyfriend. It had not even crossed her mind to delete it when they broke up, since they're still friends. But a potential new beau browsing her profile is likely to see that album and of course feel uncomfortable. Maybe he'd think she wasn't over her ex or that he'd have a hard time topping the "best days" of her life. Having photos of an ex lurking on your social network page is a subtle but dangerous land mine.

Broad statements about men also conjured up images of exes. Jonas, a thirty-seven-year-old teacher from Charleston, SC, told a woman on their first date that he had just started working out with a personal trainer. Her reaction was, "Oh, that will probably last about two weeks and then you'll quit. I just know how guys are." Not only did Jonas dislike her negative energy (reminiscent of The Bitch-in-Boots and The Debbie Downer), but he was more focused on the implicit reference to other men she'd dated. He said that when a woman "knows how guys are" she is basically saying, "I've dated a bunch of losers and you'll have to try really, really hard to prove that you're different!" It didn't exactly elicit feelings of lust and romance from him.

Other men cited examples of women who said, "I have trust

issues," or "Honesty is extremely important to me." The implication, without her ever naming names, was that some guy cheated on her in the past. Most guys didn't pry, a few couldn't resist, but the result of these types of comments was the same: a downturn in date energy.

Women's presumptions about men based on their past relationships aren't always relayed in a negative manner. Yet they can still have adverse effects. Randall, a thirty-four-year-old flight attendant in San Diego, CA, described a woman who opened her door to greet him and gushed, "Wow! You're right on time. I can't believe how great it is to have a date show up on time!" He told me that her remark was meant as a compliment, but the brief thought flashing through his mind was, "Oh, I guess she dates a lot of guys." He said it deflated him somehow and he couldn't articulate why.

Gabriel, a twenty-eight-year-old construction manager from Montreal, Canada, told me that he didn't ask Sharon for a second date because the two of them had such different personalities: she was outgoing and he was quiet. I remarked to him that usually couples with opposite natures complement each other. He agreed and explained that he had told Sharon the exact same sentiment— something about how he liked an outgoing woman to balance him. But she had replied, "I've been told in the past that I dominate conversations, so it's a relief to be with someone who *appreciates* my personality!" Gabriel told me he hadn't thought of her exactly as dominant until she mentioned the word herself. The thought began nagging him. He wondered why other guys in her past thought she dominated their conversations. Maybe she was *too* outgoing? And just like that, he moved "outgoing" from her plus column to her minus column in the subconscious tally in his mind.

What's the difference between Sharon mentioning her tendency to dominate conversations here and someone who is setting realistic expectations (as advised for The Bait & Switcher)? Two things: her tone and her lack of spin. The way Gabriel described Sharon's comment, it sounded tinged with bitterness rather than self-deprecating in a light and humorous manner. And by using the word "dominate," she wasn't taking the opportunity to spin or qualify something she perceived as one of her issues. Perhaps a better way for her to phrase it might have been, "Thank you for the compliment! Sometimes my style gets me into trouble—I'm working on doing more listening than speaking—but I do have a lot of fun talking with people."

MISLEADING MENTIONS

Philip, a fifty-one-year-old lawyer in Atlanta, GA, admits that he wants to know why a woman's ex is no longer in the picture. He asked one woman, Justine, why she was divorced. She explained, "My ex-husband and I never fought. He grew up in a WASP family where everything was brushed under the rug. I grew up in a family where we were taught to get it all out in the open—to confront problems head-on." Philip assumed shouting matches and histrionics were her preferred argument mode. But perhaps Justine only meant that she valued acknowledging a problem and discussing it honestly. If that was the case, then her ex talk left him with the wrong impression. She didn't know him well enough to get into the details—nor should she have—but her summary gave him just enough to make a negative assumption about her. Sometimes these types of miscommunications are inevitable, but hopefully Justine's comment serves as a reminder that no good can *ever* come of ex talk on a first date.

Romney, a twenty-nine-year-old pharmaceutical representative from Austin, TX, described being on a date with a woman who told him she had broken an engagement four weeks before her wedding. When he asked what happened, she shrugged and said that after dating and living with the guy for six years, she realized he wasn't right for her. Knowing a little but not enough, Romney started to wonder why she had wasted so much time in the wrong relationship and why she had agreed to an engagement. He thought maybe she didn't know what she wanted in a partner, or maybe she was flaky, or unstable. He didn't pry—but he jumped quickly to a lot of conclusions. This became a no-win situation for the woman because she mentioned a piece of information that warranted more explanation than was appropriate to discuss on a first date. That's the danger of mentioning *anything* about an ex . . . You're damned if you get into any details and damned if you don't.

PROXY MENTIONS

Ex talk can sometimes present itself as a proxy for something else: a woman "testing" her date or a woman trying to demonstrate how desirable she is.

Several men had stories about being tested for something related to an ex-boyfriend or ex-husband. Neil, a twenty-seven-year-old website designer in Oakland, CA, told me an interesting story about being on a date with Gail, who asked him out of the blue, "What makes you furious?" This sounded like a trick question of the type described in the section on The Blahs. Neil wasn't sure he understood her question at first, so he said, "You mean what makes me furious in general? Or at work? Or, like, on California freeways . . . ?" She replied, "You know, just anytime you're mad about something—what pushes your buttons? And how do you react when you're mad?" Eventually Neil came up with an anecdote for her about his boss, who had blamed him for something that wasn't his fault. Neil described firing off an angry e-mail to his boss sprinkled with some four-letter expletives. He'd also copied his boss's boss. Neil saw Gail smile after hearing the story. Apparently she liked his answer, but he didn't know why until the end of the evening. Gail later confessed that she had asked the question because her old boyfriend was passive. Nothing ever riled him up, and in the rare instances when he got mad at something, he just sulked, never confronting the problem. Gail said it was healthy to let anger out, so she liked Neil's story about his boss. She said it also showed her that Neil had "fire."

But Neil didn't like her explanation. Jumping to his own

conclusion, he thought she was probably like other girls he knew who thrived on tumultuous relationships. He wanted a steady, solid partnership he could count on. He decided "not to get on that roller coaster" and didn't call Gail back. Uh, have I mentioned yet how nothing good comes from ex talk?

A few years ago, I worked with a client named Ava, a thirty-four-year-old lawyer from Los Angeles, CA. She was heartbroken when Stuart, a man she'd had a crush on for months, had finally taken her on a date but never called her again. Despite her attractive appearance and success in her job, Ava was a bit insecure; she guessed he hadn't asked her out again because she wasn't as pretty as the women he normally dated. When I spoke with Stuart for an Exit Interview, he eventually revealed that while he had initially liked Ava a lot, she had made several mentions of other men being interested in her that tempered his enthusiasm. She had referenced some guy in her office who had invited her to a concert one weekend, an ex-boyfriend who sent her e-mails saying how much he wanted to get back together, and a few other comments along those lines. Stuart said she "sounded really insecure" and "if she was trying to make me jealous, it had the opposite effect." He also commented, "Even in high school, I never liked dating popular girls . . . it made *me* insecure thinking about all the other guys who were after them." Ava was blindsided. She said she had wanted Stuart to like her so much that she probably mentioned other guys to make herself seem more desirable. It backfired.

SOUND FAMILIAR?

You may not have noted similarities to yourself among The Ex-Factor anecdotes thus far, as it's not always easy to recognize yourself through other people's stories. So you can use the self-assessment questions here to verify whether men might be stereotyping you as The Ex-Factor before they get to know the real you.

AT WORK . . .

❏ Does your job success depend on studying and understanding the past (e.g., history teacher, psychiatrist, or researcher)?

❏ Do you sometimes mention your ex-husband or ex-boyfriend in conversations with colleagues?

❏ Have you ever dated a coworker whom you continue to see daily, making it hard for you to stop thinking about him?

WITH YOUR FRIENDS AND FAMILY . . .

❏ Are you often told fondly, "You should try to move on"?

❏ Do you keep any contact or communication with an ex secret from anyone?

❏ Do you ever use the phrase "He was the love of my life" or "We were soul mates . . ."?

ON A DATE OR WITH A PAST BOYFRIEND . . .

❏ Do you often find yourself mentally comparing a first date to your ex?

❏ Do you feel it's important to get certain answers from a man early so you won't repeat relationship mistakes from your past?

❏ Are you frustrated that men keep asking about *your* past relationships when you want to steer clear of the topic . . . but since they asked, it's hard to avoid answering?

YOUR PERSONAL PHILOSOPHY:

❏ Do you have a photo displayed in your home of someone you dated in the past (pictured with you alone or in a group shot) because *you* look really good in the photo?

❏ Are you proud that you've got men figured out? ("They're all alike in some way or another!")

❏ If you see a therapist, do you dwell on resolving issues with an ex?

If you answered yes to more than five questions above, you may be perceived (or misperceived) as The Ex-Factor. There's no doubt you're wise and you've learned what works for you and what doesn't; of course you shouldn't change who you are deep down.

But you may consider tweaking some of the things you do and say on a first or second date. Men who don't know yet how fabulous you are may dub you The Ex-Factor and miss the chance to get to know you better on the next few dates.

So, What Should You Do?

Everyone has a past, and of course it has shaped who you are today. Old relationships are a *logical* topic for early get-to-know-you conversation, but they are never a *smart* topic. Admittedly, there are some men who may genuinely not be scared away by ex talk, but the problem is that you don't know early on if your date is one of them or not. If you have wrestled with The Ex-Factor, here are five tips to ex-proof your first dates so that *you* (not your date) will decide who plays a role in your future.

1) DON'T MENTION YOUR EX

No explanation needed!

2) BEWARE OF TRICK QUESTIONS

Similar to my advice for The Blahs, be on the lookout here for trick questions. Ex talk can slip into conversations in the most innocent of ways. One minute you're talking about how much he liked your online dating profile, especially those profound comments you wrote about what you've learned from past relationships. You say, "Yeah, I've had some trust issues to deal with, but who hasn't?" *Good, you kept it positive and didn't let him bait you into talking about your ex.* But now he's curious. He asks, ever so sweetly, "Was your old boyfriend unfaithful?" A pained look crosses your face, and he says gently, like the wolf talking to Little Red Riding Hood, "Come closer, my dear, it's okay, you can tell me all about it . . ."

And he's *such* a good listener! And, well, *he's* the one who asked! Wanting to take the date to a deeper emotional level, you decide to get more personal. One thing leads to another, and suddenly you're trapped. During the next thirty minutes you tell him all the gory details of your heartbreak. You can't help it. And he's encouraging you! Yet whether your monologue is melancholy, angry, or really funny, he is left pondering: "Is she over that guy? Why did he cheat on her in the first place? I can't stop picturing her in bed with another guy . . ."

No good can ever come of ex talk! So if you hear that wolf's voice in Grandma's clothing beckoning, "Please tell me what happened . . . ," gently switch the subject. Or tell him you'll save that story for when you know each other better. Or dart for the ladies' room. Or see the next tip below.

3) USE THE ONE-FOR-ONE RULE

Let's be realistic. Even if you don't bring up your ex or his right away, you are bound to be in a first-date situation sometime when a guy directly asks you about your exes and won't accept your vague-but-appropriate reply. Or, perhaps worse, he starts talking about *his* ex and won't shut up. This is where my One-for-One Rule comes in: allow one sentence about an ex on date number one, two sentences on date number two, and so on.

Here are some examples of vague but appropriate one-sentence answers for date number one. If a man directly asks you about your last relationship or why you split up, you can say:

➜ "He's a nice guy, but we grew apart."
➜ "It turned out he wasn't a nice person, but I learned a lot from that relationship."
➜ "We were young and didn't have our priorities straight."
➜ "The big picture is that we didn't communicate very well, which was a great learning experience for me."
➜ "We didn't work as husband and wife, but we have a good working relationship now surrounding our kids."

Immediately follow any of the above sentences with "But let's save the ex talk for another time! I'd love to hear more about your trip to Vietnam . . ." By closing the door on this taboo first-date topic and changing the subject, you will keep the date energy positive. If he presses for more details, feel free to quote my One-for-One Rule out loud. This should squelch the topic, and if you say it with a smile and a jokey tone of voice he shouldn't feel rebuffed.

If a man does ask you about your ex early on, never reciprocate with a question about *his* last relationship. You should model the behavior that ex talk simply does not belong on a first date.

4) ANSWER ONLY WHAT YOU'RE ASKED

As discussed in the section on The Flasher, remember to answer only the question you're being asked. TMI is your enemy. For example, when Jason, the guy earlier in this section who dated a girl with an ankle tattoo, asked, "What is that?" she had to come up with some kind of response. While she couldn't change what she'd done in the past, a better response to Jason's question might have been, "It's a bird." Note that he didn't ask "*Why* did you get a tattoo?" And he certainly didn't ask "Did you get that tattoo for an old boyfriend?" When it comes to ex talk, if you reveal only information that is being asked (just like on the witness stand in a courtroom), limiting any details that are none of his business on a first date anyway, you should be in good shape.

5) DESTROY THE EVIDENCE

Don't get backed into a corner. Avoid circumstances that raise the topic of your ex, forcing you to either talk about him or lie about him. For example, remove any photos of old flames that still linger in your apartment, in your wallet, or on your Facebook page, including any group photos in which he appears. This avoids the question "Who is that guy?" And don't wear any jewelry given to you by another guy, thereby avoiding potential pitfalls from questions such as "Nice earrings . . . where'd you get them?"

If you are being fixed up by a mutual friend, remember to ask her not to mention your past relationships when describing you.

Often your well-meaning friends just don't *think*. They start to babble about your past to someone without realizing the damage they're causing. I can just hear it now: "Oh, Jim, my friend Marla's great! You'll really like her! And it will be *sooo* good to get her out of the house since she broke up with her boyfriend who slept with her sister when she went on vacation . . . you're the kind of guy who can *really* help her trust again!"

Look, ex-boyfriends and ex-husbands are a big part of your psychological makeup. And you'll get to talk about them as much as you want eventually. But zip it for the first date or two. Don't let your past mess up your future.

If You Recognize The Ex-Factor:

WHAT'S HOT:	WHAT'S NOT:
1. The present and future	1. The past
2. Enthusiasm	2. Bitterness
3. "I think that communication is really important in a relationship."	3. "It's so refreshing that you appreciate feedback; my ex-boyfriend used to say that I criticized him about every little thing!"
4. Telling a funny story about the vacation you took last month with your sister	4. Telling a not-so-funny story about your ex-boyfriend who slept with your sister when you went on vacation
5. "I'm excited to see what my future holds."	5. I'm going to hold my past against you."

#10 REASON HE DIDN'T CALL BACK
The One-Way Street

> There's a reason God gave us two ears and one
> mouth: you should listen twice as much as you speak.
> —Edmund, age 68, Palo Alto, CA

> It wasn't a date; it was an interview. She was Barbara
> friggin' Walters. —Finn, age 33, Concord, NH

> 'Tis better to be silent and thought a fool, than to
> open your mouth and remove all doubt.
> —Abraham Lincoln, Springfield, IL

The One-Way Street is in her own world. She dominates the date by either talking too much or directing the conversation too much. It's as if she is on a date for one, and this can play out in different formats. Her endless chatter may be the result of first-date nerves. Her self-absorption may be either an accurate reflection of her personality or simple lack of awareness. Her interrogation may be her attempt at efficiency (not wasting time with low-potential men). But the give-and-take in the conversation ratio is heavily weighted toward *her* and *her agenda*. Regardless of the underlying causes, men said this type of behavior was a date-breaker.

You've probably heard a million times throughout your life some form of "Don't talk too much; listen to what other people have to say." You might think this information is obvious. But I hope that you will read this section carefully, the same way you might read a new diet book that basically tells you to eat right and exercise more. Why read what you already know? Because it's sometimes the familiar things that people do wrong, again and again and again. So even though your brain might be saying, "I already know that . . . ," it doesn't mean you don't need a reminder not to trespass on familiar territory.

Are You The One-Way Street?

The One-Way Street encompassed four categories of behavior in my research. Do any of these ring true for you?

THE INTERVIEWER

You saw from anecdotes about The Closer that men don't like being interviewed as potential sperm donors or about their interest in settling down. You saw from The Park Avenue Princess that men don't like being interviewed about financial assets. These sentiments overlap with The One-Way Street, but here the woman isn't just investigating his gene pool, his readiness for commitment, or his bank balance; she's looking to complete the whole census form. The sheer quantity of her questions creates an edgy and formal atmosphere on dates. Carter, a twenty-seven-year-old engineer from Baltimore, MD, said, "Her questions came out bam-bam-bam . . . one right after the other." She wanted to know where he grew up, how many siblings he has, where he went to college, what magazines he reads, and whether he is a Democrat. It felt like being in the hot seat at a job interview. He got the sense there were right and wrong answers, but he wasn't sure if he had responded correctly. "It was not exactly a relaxing atmosphere," he remarked, "so I figured she wasn't my type." I wondered if Carter's date could have been nervous, or if she'd had too much caffeine. I wondered if her rapid questions reflected *who she really is.*

Damien, a twenty-two-year-old law school student in Philadelphia, PA, said, "I didn't mind all the questions . . . If anyone is going to be comfortable with a cross-examination, it's me— I'm studying to be a trial lawyer . . . [it] was excellent practice. I mean, I didn't want to get *romantically involved with her*, but I enjoy being kept on my toes." Case dismissed.

During my evenings doing research at speed-dating events, I heard a lot of One-Way Street complaints. Given the format of the eight-minute meet-and-greet process, it's understandably challenging to control excessive questioning. Merrill, a thirty-one-year-old army officer from Ft. Rucker, AL, said, "The problem is that you meet a lot of women throughout the night . . . all those basic questions get so *boring* to answer." Trent, a twenty-nine-year-old brand manager from Cincinnati, OH, said, "By the end of the eight minutes with [one girl], I had answered all her questions, but I didn't learn anything about *her* . . . So how could I know if I wanted to see her again? . . . By default, I ended up making my decision based on her looks."

Payton, a forty-five-year-old pilot from Los Angeles, CA, told me in a telephone interview about Rebecca, a woman he met on JDate. Payton has a diverse job profile. He's a pilot, but he only flies occasionally for a private jet company. He's also a flight instructor, Hollywood stunt man, volunteer fireman, and photographer. Apparently Rebecca couldn't quite pin down how he earned his living (understandably), so she started to grill him on their date. Payton said, "It looked like a scene from a movie where a guy is locked in a room with a police interrogator. She kept asking, 'So what's your primary job? And what's the name of that company? Is that a job or a hobby? How many days a week are you there?'" He went on to explain, "I felt drained . . . defensive. She was more interested in my data points than hearing about why I enjoy what I do." It sounded to me like Rebecca was suspicious about his background. I probably would have been too. But there might have been a gentler way to extract the information, just in case she wanted to see him again.

Often the real motivation for a first-date interrogation stems from a desire to label your date, to put him in a neat little box and tie him up with a bow. Is he the Workaholic, the Playboy, the Geek? Is he Freaky Obsessive-Compulsive Guy, Devoted Single-Dad Guy, or Boring Accountant Guy? The problem, of course, is that stereotyping him too quickly is often misleading—and hypocritical. Extrapolating random data points from a series of interview questions and then jumping to conclusions too quickly is exactly what men are doing to women (as you see throughout this book). While turnabout is always fair play, your first impressions are probably just as faulty as his. And what if your interview techniques actually do peg him accurately (in a positive light) on the first date and you decide that you could really like him after all? If your questioning results in his not calling you back, what's the point of the questioning?

THE BORE

Jeb, a thirty-one-year-old electronics sales manager from Indianapolis, IN, told me about a woman who had "a fast, staccato-like way of speaking." He said, "She seemed very high strung . . . nervous. I guess I like women who are more relaxed . . . thoughtful." Men have called overly talkative women everything from "The Big Yawn" to "Chatty Cathy" to "really annoying." Stanley, a thirty-year-old nonprofit fund-raiser from Nashville, TN, related an anecdote about a woman he dubbed "The Forehead Bruiser" because she practically put him to sleep facedown on the table. He had asked her, "Are you reading any good books right now?" And she launched into a twenty-minute story about how she was reading a book called *Does This Clutter Make My Butt Look Fat?*, which she'd read about in the *New York Times Book Review*, so she ordered it on Amazon, but she was leaving on a trip four days later, and she wasn't sure if it would arrive before she left, so she tried calling customer service, but she couldn't get an exact arrival date, and she never got the book until after she returned from her trip, and . . . I'll spare you the rest. You get the picture.

THE IN-ONE-EAR-AND-OUT-THE-OTHER

One of the characteristics of The One-Way Street is being a bad listener. When women were focused on themselves and pursuing their own agenda on a date, they appeared to stop listening to the details. Danny, a thirty-six-year-old entrepreneur from Princeton, NJ, told me about being on a date with Jessica. One example he remembered was that he had talked excitedly to her about his upcoming plans to vacation in Mexico. They spoke about the trip for over fifteen minutes during dinner. He told Jessica he was "leaving this Friday and would be gone for a week." The following day Jessica e-mailed him saying, "Let's hang out this weekend—are you busy?" She didn't even remember that he was leaving on Friday for Mexico. Danny scoffed, "Wasn't she listening? That was typical of the whole date."

LITTLE MISS SELF-ABSORBED

Men sometimes concluded that women were self-absorbed if they didn't show a genuine interest in something the man was proud of. I did an Exit Interview once for a client who became labeled The One-Way Street: a never-married forty-six-year-old woman from Toronto, Canada, named Suzanne. One of her former dates, Tony, was a single dad, and he told me he didn't call her back for a simple reason: she had expressed zero interest in his six-year-old son. His son was the most important thing in his life, and she had not asked any questions about him. Tony said that on a few occasions during the date, he'd made references such as "My son and I went to the zoo last weekend," but Suzanne didn't ask any follow-up questions. Instead she had switched the subject to talk about what *she'd* done last weekend. Tony said to me, "She doesn't have kids, so I guess she wasn't interested in hearing about mine . . . she talked a lot about herself."

Maybe Suzanne wanted to be cautious about not dwelling on his son to avoid being labeled "baby crazy." This is the right instinct if you're The Closer (although a few polite questions would have been okay). But encouraging Tony to tell her more about his son would have been appropriate for The One-Way Street.

Lance, a thirty-four-year-old software salesman in Stamford, CT, provided a different angle about a woman whose attitude was "What's in it for me?" His story had some Park Avenue Princess undertones about being self-centered, but here it wasn't about money or lifestyle. He described Carissa, a woman he'd recently dated who had helped him out in a bind. This initially sounded nice to me, so I was curious where his failed-date story was headed. Apparently, after their date in Manhattan ended at 2:00 AM, he rushed to Grand Central Station but just missed the last train back to the suburbs. He needed a place to sleep and was hesitant to call Carissa, who lived five blocks away. He was understandably worried that if he asked to spend the night she'd think he was calling with an excuse to have sex. But he decided to call her and she didn't sound bothered. She graciously offered her couch to him for the night. As Lance walked back to her apartment, he thought, "Wow, I really like her . . . I like the way she handled a potentially awkward situation."

But when he arrived at her door, she greeted him with this comment: "Well, now you really owe me one! Since I'm letting you crash on my couch, I hope you won't mind helping me hang my new curtains tomorrow. I need an extra pair of hands, and it's only fair . . ." It sounded to me like she was just trying to be cute, but Lance didn't interpret it that way. He said he wouldn't have minded helping her hang the curtains if she had asked the next day, but framing it as a "trade" erased his warm feelings about her initial generosity. As I spoke further to Lance, he articulated that he wants a woman who genuinely enjoys helping other people, someone who isn't only looking at things from her perspective. He wants someone who's not evaluating what's in it for her. As he lay on her couch that night alone, his mind wandered back over the evening. He decided her comment about the curtains wasn't an isolated example of being self-absorbed. He described a few other all-about-me comments she'd made (such as "I'm trying to cut down on carbs, so let's avoid Italian food" and "Let's get the check instead of having coffee, because caffeine keeps me awake"), which culminated the next morning with some curtain hanging, a polite good-bye, and no callback.

SOUND FAMILIAR?

You may not have noted similarities to yourself among The One-Way Street anecdotes thus far, as it's not always easy to recognize yourself through other people's stories. So you can use the self-assessment questions here to verify whether men might be stereotyping you as The One-Way Street before they get to know the real you.

AT WORK . . .

❏ Do you interview people as part of your job—and you're good at it?

❏ Is your job one that rewards you for being curious and asking a lot of questions (e.g., researcher, scientist, or journalist)?

❏ Do you tend to dominate conversations during staff meetings?

WITH YOUR FRIENDS AND FAMILY . . .

❏ Do you complain about how men love to talk about themselves?

❏ Has anyone ever told you, "You'd make a great reporter!"?

❏ On an airplane, have you ever thought the person seated next to you was rude when they put on their headphones—right in the middle of your story?

ON A DATE OR WITH A PAST BOYFRIEND . . .

❏ When you're nervous or uncomfortable, do you tend to talk a lot?

❏ At a restaurant, does a guy usually finish his meal first (perhaps because you've been doing most of the talking . . .)?

❏ In the middle of a first date, has a guy ever said, "I feel like we've talked a lot about me, but I don't know much about *you* . . ."?

YOUR PERSONAL PHILOSOPHY:

❏ Are you really interested in what makes people tick?

❏ Are you proud that guys you meet online don't stand a chance trying to lie to you—you always get to the bottom of it?

❏ Are you uncomfortable with silence?

If you answered yes to more than five questions here, you may be perceived (or misperceived) as The One-Way Street. There's no doubt you're outgoing, curious, and have an interesting life; of course you shouldn't change who you are. But you may consider tweaking some of the things you do and say on a first or second date. Men who don't know yet how fabulous you are may think you're The One-Way Street and miss the chance to get to know you better on the next few dates.

So, What Should You Do?

If you can relate to The One-Way Street, here are six suggestions to correct the imbalance.

1) ASK WITHOUT INTERVIEWING

Of course first dates are about getting to know each other, and that'd be pretty tough without asking some questions. The difference between asking and interviewing is a function of three simple things: **Making him feel relaxed** (create small talk about your day, compliment him about something genuine, order a drink), **monitoring the quantity of your questions** (perhaps no more than one question every five to ten minutes—allow the dialogue to be about depth, not breadth), and **using open-ended questions** (instead of asking, "Do you have a good relationship with your mother?" ask, "Tell me about your family."; instead of asking, "Do you ski?" ask, "What do you like to do on weekends?").

2) ASK WITHOUT HIM KNOWING

If you're looking to validate what a stranger tells you, that's a great instinct. But I do believe that someone devious enough to lie in the first place is probably clever enough to keep up the charade during your first date. If your gut is telling you that something doesn't quite add up about this guy, you might be better off sniffing around on Google or using one of those online background-check services (e.g., www.datedetectives.com or www.datingdetective.net).

Of course, you should always meet him in a public place. But waiting patiently for him to explain, elaborate, or contradict himself during the natural course of conversation might be a better strategy than launching an interrogation. Interrogations usually result in getting your answers but not your man.

3) LIMIT ALCOHOL

Loose lips and rambling monologues can often result from a few too many cocktails. This goes without saying, but know your limit and stay far under it on a first date—even if you're nervous. (Limiting alcohol is smart for every first date, regardless of which stereotype you resemble.) If you're anxious about an upcoming date, find something to relax you at home before he picks you up: yoga, knitting, a bath, or even a half glass of wine; hopefully this will deter you from turning into a nervous chatterbox. Then, when you arrive at the restaurant, sip slowly!

4) AVOID BORING STORIES

If you find yourself giving an answer that sounds like this: "Well . . . and then . . . and next . . . Oh, and then . . . But . . . ," you're probably getting boring. Of course you need to provide more than "yes" or "no" answers, and you need to keep your answers engaging and colorful. Self-edit the comments about people he doesn't know and avoid detailed logistics that no one cares about. Cut the story short and segue into something else. And as mentioned in The Blahs section, always do your homework before a date by compiling a mental list of fun and interesting conversation starters.

5) LISTEN TO AN EXPERT

There's a very smart book called *How to Talk So Kids Will Listen and Listen So Kids Will Talk* by Adele Faber and Elaine Mazlish. Even if you don't have kids, and even though your audience here is men (okay, it's debatable whether some of them are actually grown-ups!), this book is extremely useful for The One-Way Street. In a logical format, it outlines excellent communication skills, starting with simple awareness about your word choices. It demonstrates how specific listening techniques can make someone feel like a million bucks and how rephrasing certain comments will elicit vastly different responses from the other person. It's a must-read for any age!

6) PAY ATTENTION TO WHAT MATTERS—TO *HIM*

One of the best things you can do on a date is determine the single most important thing this man cares about. It may be obvious or it may be subtle, but if you listen carefully to his tone and body language, you'll usually see how his energy level changes when he's passionate about something. For example, when Tony (the single dad mentioned earlier) referenced taking his son to the zoo, Suzanne could have asked what the boy's favorite animals were and what other father-son adventures they liked to go on. To me, Tony wasn't labeling Suzanne self-absorbed because she talked about herself, but rather because she didn't pay enough attention to the one thing he cared most about: his son.

Sure, men want to learn more about you—which is why they asked you on the date—but it makes sense that they'll want you to shine a spotlight on whatever it is they're most proud of. Whether it's his six-year-old son, his beloved dog, or his motorcycle, try to quickly identify it, ask about it, and refer back to it later. Not only will he relax and start enjoying himself because he's speaking about what he loves, but you'll get a better glimpse of what makes him tick than you would with demographic data questions.

Also, when you're on a first date, you probably know several basic *facts* about the guy (perhaps a friend set you up and described his background, or maybe you met online and read his list of favorite hobbies and preferred cuisine), but you don't know the *whys*. Why did he choose his first job or why is that his favorite movie? Asking the whys behind the data points is the perfect way to show genuine interest in him and to send him home feeling gratified. Hopefully he will want to know the whys behind your data points as well—when he asks you for a second date.

Most dates that are one-way, whether they flow all toward you or all toward him, will not precede a second date. If you catch yourself in a one-way situation by the time your entrée comes, make sure to adjust during the second half of the date to make it a two-way street.

If You're The One-Way Street . . .

WHAT'S HOT:	WHAT'S NOT:
1. Open-ended questions	1. Monologues
2. Me, him, me, him	2. Me, me, me, me
3. Conversations	3. Filibustering
4. Gazing into his eyes	4. Gazing into the mirror
5. "Once I trekked through the Amazon . . ."	5. "This one time, at band camp . . ."

Beyond the Top Ten: More Date-Breakers

There are a few more interesting date-breakers that men revealed. Here you'll find a short summary from my research of the eleventh through sixteenth most common reasons men said they didn't call a woman back. While these reasons were not mentioned as frequently in the Exit Interviews, it bears repeating that the most important reason of all is only the one that resonates with *you*.

#11 REASON HE DIDN'T CALL YOU BACK
The Seinfeld

The Seinfeld describes a woman with neurotic, irritating, or odd behavior that men discovered during a first date. Who didn't love that *Seinfeld* episode where Jerry dumps his girlfriend because she ate her peas one at a time? This is an amusing category—you can peek inside someone else's neuroses here, hoping hers aren't as bad as yours. The men I spoke with described a woman who wouldn't sit back in a movie theater chair for fear of getting head lice, another woman who had more than two hundred angel dolls in her apartment, another woman who wrote "tee hee hee" in her e-mails (instead of "LOL" or "ha, ha"), and another woman who lined up her yogurt flavors alphabetically in the refrigerator. (I often wonder whether she filed French vanilla under "F" or "V.")

There were several over-the-top pet stories: "Only filet mignon is good enough for my pooch!" and "Aren't these teeny paw-mittens adorable?" Then I heard three times about a woman who chose restaurants based on "warm lighting" (those anecdotes came from three men who all lived in Los Angeles, CA, so I'm curious whether this is an LA thing or if they had dated the same woman). One woman had an irritating verbal tic, saying "Wait for it . . ."—e.g., "I have . . . wait for it . . . thirteen umbrellas!" And . . . wait for it . . . zero second dates!

I recorded a lot of germ phobia that some guys found weird enough to factor into not calling a woman back. This included everything from not touching door handles or hand railings to wiping the rim of a soda can with a napkin before drinking. One guy wanted a woman to listen to his favorite song on his iPod and tried sharing his earphones (one piece in his ear, one in her ear)—but she refused, citing "ear germs."

Of course there were all the eating idiosyncrasies: a woman who gnawed her bread like a chipmunk, one who only ate white-colored foods, one whose metal fork clinked noisily against her teeth every time she took a bite of something, and one who used her fork to "smush down flat" all the food on her plate before eating it. There was no shortage of Meg Ryan types (from the movie *When Harry Met Sally*) whose super-picky orders included a longer list of "on the sides" and "leave outs" than there was space on the waiter's notepad.

We all have our "thing." I am certainly not exempt: I have this weird thing about eating cheese and crackers. I prepare a snack for myself by cutting little chunks of cheese. Then I count crackers onto my plate in the exact same ratio: six crackers for six cheese chunks. *I have to have an equal number or it drives me crazy.* If my husband takes a piece of cheese off my plate, I rush to cut another one—it would actually kill me to have an extra cracker left over. My husband seems to think this is sort of cute and loves to tease me about it, but I'm quite sure he would have labeled it crazy and possibly a date-breaker on our first date.

The point is not that you should stop your neurotic behavior (that's usually too hard)—just try to tone it down or conceal it on the first date, because someone who doesn't know you very well is going to go home and tell his friends that you're weird. And one quick tip for all the picky eaters out there: call the restaurant ahead of time and get the menu faxed to you—take the time to select something you can eat with only one change. If you can't find anything at all, politely suggest a different restaurant because you read a great review about it (or some other excuse). It's fine to order dressing on the side or no onions, but save your ultra-finicky food orders for future dates when your guy will laugh *with* you instead of *at* you.

#12 REASON HE DIDN'T CALL YOU BACK
The Never Ever

The Never Ever mistake occurs when a woman makes a categorical, absolute, or emphatic statement on a first date that disturbs the man. One example you saw in chapter 1 was Sophie, who said, "I'll never leave New York." Other examples in my research included "I would never raise my children in [another] religion," "I would never give up my last name," "I would never live in a winter climate," "I would never go to a Bible study class," "I would never date a smoker," "I would never marry someone with kids," and "I would never marry a man without a college degree." Some Never Ever statements were made in an online profile or to a matchmaking friend who inadvertently relayed it to the guy when describing the woman—starting things off on the wrong foot.

Cousins of The Never Ever are absolute or emphatic "I will" or "I hate" statements. Examples in my research included "I will live in Japan one day," "I will only have one child," "My children will go to boarding school like I did," "I will keep working full-time after I have kids," "I hate cats," "I hate camping," and "I hate the beach."

A guy may eventually accept your "never ever," but why put him to the test on your first date before he gets to know you? And as to how "never" will your "never" be? Don't shoot the messenger here, but let me just say that *everything* is negotiable when you're truly in love. Regardless of what you think or want or detest right now, you will be willing to look at things a little differently when Mr. Right comes along. I am **not** saying that you will (or should) change your values or core beliefs for a man, but for many practical and unforeseen reasons, your opinions and attitudes will be affected and expanded when you become "we."

I have witnessed the most startling things from my vantage point in the love business. Here are three true examples.

→ I know one woman who adored her cat more than life itself but met a great guy who was severely allergic to cats. She swore she'd *never* give up her cat and almost refused a second date with this guy. Yada, yada, yada: they got married and worked out a compromise. Her neighbor keeps her cat, which she visits on her way home from work.

→ I know another woman who belongs to every Jewish organization ever created. She lived in Israel for a year, all her friends are Jewish, Judaism is her *life*. Of course, she swore she'd never marry a non-Jewish guy. Fast-forward: she married a non-Jewish guy. He's fabulous, and he recently converted (which he was not initially open to). They are blissfully happy and now have a beautiful five-year-old son.

→ My husband's sister, a longtime New Yorker, fell in love with a man who lived in Cleveland, OH. She said she would rather *die* than live in Cleveland. I mean, really: a devoted New Yorker living in Cleveland? Can you even picture it? You know how this ends: they got married, she moved to Cleveland, and she ended up loving it there—much to her astonishment. Then two years later her husband's job changed and now they live in Los Angeles. Life is unpredictable.

I could go on and on, but you get the picture. So watch out for those emphatic, categorical statements on first dates . . . because you just *never* know. Life may take you on a different journey.

#13 REASON HE DIDN'T CALL YOU BACK
The Birds of a Feather

Birds of a feather flock together. And through the eyes of a stranger, your flock says a lot about *you*. The comments, behavior, and beliefs of your friends and family become synonymous with yours before he really knows you.

Men made a point of telling me that a woman's friends speak volumes about her because friends are the only people we actually choose in life. I heard about one woman's friend who made a racist remark, another friend who admitted cheating on her boyfriend, another friend who had a drug problem. Another woman's friends seemed like "man-haters," so her date told me, "I could just see how things would go the first time I made a mistake with *that* jury watching over me." Another man concluded someone wasn't mature enough for him when one woman's friend "made references to TV shows that were very young" and another woman's goofy friend "emptied the salt shaker on the table and filled it with sugar as a practical joke." I'm not claiming that these men made associations that were *rational*, but in the absence of enough data about you early on, they drew hasty conclusions.

One man described a woman he initially liked because she seemed "fun." But when he asked where she liked to go out with her friends, she mentioned the name of a local bar where he knew Hells Angels biker dudes hung out. Then he noticed a small tattoo on her shoulder, and he concluded that biker bar + tattoo = wild. He decided they wouldn't be compatible because he was more conservative. Sure, maybe they weren't a match, but she could have been more conservative than he assumed (maybe "biker night" at that bar is on Wednesdays, but she goes on Fridays when the yuppies congregate . . . who knows?). Realize that the places you claim to frequent usually have some kind of reputation (wild, dull, snobby, etc.) that will cause men to stereotype you simply by association.

A few men told me about women who wanted their friends' thumbs-up during a date—a "look him over" situation that made the women seem insecure for needing someone else's approval. Getting your friends' collective thumbs-up on a swimsuit or new hairstyle is one thing; getting it on your date—in front of your date and on a first date—is another. I spoke to one divorced dad who shared a story about a woman who took him on their second date to watch her son's soccer game: the other dads at the park, who were loyal to her ex-husband, snubbed him. He was obviously very uncomfortable being around that crowd.

A few single moms struggled when they introduced a man too soon to their children. Kids who acted rude or spoiled reflected badly upon the mother as a parent and made her date wonder what he might be getting into. And adult parents made an impact too: if a woman mentioned that her parents wouldn't approve of him for some reason, a man started associating her parents' attitudes with hers.

There were also a few cases involving online social networks. One man described how a woman invited him into her Facebook network after their first date, where he saw two guys he knew. He thought the guys were complete jerks, so he started thinking about the woman more skeptically because she was associated with them. Another man had the same reaction when a woman he met forwarded him an Internet joke and he recognized a couple names he didn't like on the distribution list. It's not that these observations were exactly date-breakers, but they were triggers that served to make the guy feel skeptical. And things went downhill from there.

The key to avoiding The Birds of a Feather problem is simply to wait to introduce him to your friends and family until he knows more about you, including not inviting him into your online social network right away (and not accepting his "friend request" right away). There's just too much room for misinterpretation (see more about social networking in the "R U 4 Real?" section in chapter 4). Give him enough data points on your graph so that any outlier behavior from (or associated with) a friend doesn't tarnish your image. Later, try to introduce him first to your "safe" people—the ones who always make good impressions. When he meets some of your quirky friends, be sure to explain clearly in advance *why* someone is your friend: maybe you're loyal to a childhood pal even though you've grown apart, or someone was there for you during a crisis and for that you'll always be grateful to her. Maybe you like variety and find one friend's outlandish personality endearing; of course that's fine! You're not exactly making excuses about your friends. You're simply clarifying your bond so he doesn't jump to the wrong conclusions when everything they say can and will be held against you.

#14 REASON HE DIDN'T CALL YOU BACK
The Psychobabbler

It's a sign of our time: everyone's in therapy these days, and it's impacting first dates. This stereotype differs slightly from the therapy anecdotes in The Debbie Downer section because here the focus is on irritating *language*. Men complained they heard too much "therapy-speak." They were sick of statements that began with "I sense that you feel . . . ," "You should define your boundaries . . . ," or "I've worked on myself . . ." While some of these same men were in therapy themselves, they wanted to leave the "I statements" and the "how does that make you feels" in their therapist's office (or at least for later-stage dates).

Men rolled their eyes about women's "Freudian interpretations" of their fathers and about their friends or exes who were "narcissistic," "emotionally unavailable," or "suffering from abandonment issues." A lot of this therapy-speak emerged around the topic of divorce—his or her own divorce, or his or her parents' divorce. But this differed from The Ex Factor or The Flasher because here again the men were focused on the new-age terminology rather than content.

The tone of what I heard wasn't that men are looking for someone without issues, or even someone without a therapist; they just sounded annoyed with the lingo! Some said they heard enough of it in their own therapy sessions, some said it reminded them of past couples-counseling sessions they'd rather forget, and others just mocked the psychobabble. But most of all, they simply wanted the first date to be fun.

#15 REASON HE DIDN'T CALL YOU BACK
The Wino

The Wino represents women who simply drank too much alcohol (or a few who used drugs) on a first date. Men described them with these words: "loud," "sloppy," "embarrassing," "gross," "abrasive," and "belligerent." Often those women became a one-night stand. Men said The Wino was not the mother of their future children.

Most drunken anecdotes (69 percent) were reported for women in their twenties and thirties. But let me just say there's one little sixty-two-year-old party girl out there in Philadelphia, PA, who can't hold her liquor—and if you're reading this, one of your former dates said to tell you he still can't get the vomit smell out of his Acura!

Men quoted women on first dates slurring, "Give me your hand. I'm not wearing panties . . . ," and declaring loudly, "If that woman next to us doesn't shut up, I'm going to throw my drink at her."

A glass of wine or a fun cocktail is great: it sets a festive mood for your date and calms your nerves (or your attitude). But it should be obvious that overdrinking is almost always a date-breaker. At best, it's a one-night stand. You have a lot to think about when you're under the spotlight—saying the right things, avoiding the wrong ones, and figuring out if *you* like *him*. You need to keep your wits about you to make a good impression and a good decision. So keep the bottle corked (and your legs crossed) on the first date.

#16 REASON HE DIDN'T CALL YOU BACK
The Why Bother

Some men confessed they didn't call women back because they expected or were afraid of rejection. I spoke to sweet guys who adore you and can't imagine that someone as beautiful, successful, or popular as you would be interested in them. I also spoke to guys who (accurately or inaccurately) assumed you wouldn't be interested because they knew they weren't attractive enough, successful enough, or educated enough for you. Here it wasn't that these issues bothered *them*, but rather that they perceived that these issues bothered *you*. Some guys said they picked up your disinterested vibe but had no idea what caused it.

I think what's notable about this category is how few men actually cited it (3 percent) compared with how many women guessed they were victims of The Why Bother (13 percent) in chapter 2. But if your gut is telling you you're on a first date with a shy, unsure guy, absolutely tip your cards a little more. Tell him clearly you had a *great* time, touch his arm lightly, and look into his eyes when you emphasize, "I'd love to do this again."

Hey, What About . . . ?

Are there some issues you're wondering about that didn't pop up on the "Top Ten" or "Beyond the Top Ten" lists? What about men who aren't attracted to a woman's appearance? Where was that? And what about women who lacked a sense of humor, weren't the right religion, or didn't have hobbies in common? Some of these topics came up as natural subsets of the sixteen reasons previously listed. For example, appearance came up in the section on The Bait & Switcher, and I also explained in chapter 2 how men had already factored looks into their decision for a *first* date. But none of these other topics were mentioned often enough to warrant their own sections.

Why? While occasionally men mentioned other reasons, such as "religion" or "sense of humor," these were rarely among the one (or two) *primary* reasons cited for a no-callback. Here are two of my theories to explain this: 1) Because dates are prescreened better today for certain attributes, especially through online dating, perhaps some of these classic things-in-common reasons were minimized in my research (i.e., first dates were happening between men and women because they already had multiple key traits in common), or 2) Perhaps the "in-common criteria" are lower on a man's checklist than we assume, or less frequent than women are led to believe by men who use this as a convenient excuse for why things didn't work out.

As previously mentioned, if a man provided an initial answer that was vague, he was asked for deeper, more specific reasons. This explains why you did *not* see the following types of responses on the list: "There was no chemistry/spark," and "I met someone else."[11]

---

[11] If a man "met someone else," he was asked for details about why he chose one woman versus the other.

 **CHAPTER 4**

The Morning After

Top Five Date-Breakers *After* a First Date

Sometimes the first date goes very well; you and Mr. Potential want to get to know each other better. He intends to ask you out again, but then something happens to douse the momentum in the crucial follow-up stage after "good night" (within hours, the next few days, or after a second or third date).

This time period immediately following the first date is as much of a minefield as the first date itself: you still have to watch your step. Men clearly told me that many great first dates ultimately did not lead to second dates because something quickly changed. Here are the five reasons most frequently cited by men who said this dynamic occurred.

#1 REASON HE DIDN'T CALL BACK AFTER A GREAT FIRST DATE
The Sadie Hawkins[1]

I completely understand what it's like to finally meet someone you're excited about. When I receive those good-news phone calls or e-mails from my clients the morning after, I am so happy I can't begin to tell you. Especially if they've had a recent string of bad dates and had almost given up hope. Their first question to me after a great first date is usually, "What can I do now? I don't want to let this one slip through my hands." My answer is: "I want you to go out and immediately . . . *do nothing*! This is the *one time* in your modern, empowered, I-can-make-anything-happen life when you have to sit back and be patient."

Men like the chase. That's something you've always heard, and my Exit Interviews underscored it. Sure, men like it when you're interested in them and don't play games, but there's a fine line between encouraging and pursuing.

Are You The Sadie Hawkins?

The Sadie Hawkins encompassed two categories in my research. Do either of these ring true for you?

THE OBVIOUS TACTICS

Blake, a twenty-four-year-old human resources consultant from Boston, MA, told me about a second date with a woman he took to dinner and then to a local amusement park. They were having fun playing skee-ball at the arcade when she stood behind him, wrapped her arms around his waist, and whispered in his ear, "I really, really like you." He said he experienced this sudden drop in his energy level: "I can't explain why," he said. "I mean, I was interested in her,

[1] "Sadie Hawkins" is a common term meaning "girls pursue boys." It is most frequently used for a ladies'-choice school dance where the girl invites the boy.

but she sort of sounded desperate and it made me wonder about her." Other men described women who confessed similar sentiments to them by phone or e-mail quickly after the first date: "It's been so long since I've felt this way," or "It's so hard to meet someone as smart as you are." I heard several variations on the latter sentence: "It's so hard to meet someone as funny, real, handsome," etc. Here's what that message conveyed to guys: *Let me clarify that I want you; now the only question left is, do you want me?*

The stories of women who wanted to seize the day went on and on. Ian, a thirty-five-year-old editorial director from London, England, said, "I called her the next night after our first date. I was planning to ask her out again for the weekend, but before I had the chance to ask, she alluded to our 'future' two or three times . . . it was little things, something about 'I'll give you that book we talked about when I see you,' or 'I'll teach you to snowboard this winter, it's easy!'" He felt deflated, like she had stolen his thunder.

Kenneth, a twenty-two-year-old insurance sales assistant from Rapid City, SD, talked about a girl he'd dated once who "was the prettiest girl he ever dated." She surprised him by showing up at his house two days later with pizza for him and his roommates. He thought it was nice, he was glad to see her, but he said, "She took the excitement away." The pizza sounded like a sweet gesture to me, so I was curious why he didn't respond favorably—especially since he thought she was so pretty. (And who doesn't love pizza?) Kenneth didn't have an articulate explanation—he just said, "I wished she had played it more cool." Nobody said men were always logical (or articulate).

Morgan, a thirty-year-old sales manager from New Orleans, LA, recalled a woman mentioning on their second date, "I had a dream about you last night." At first he thought nothing of it because she said she didn't remember the details, but then when she referenced a movie she wanted to see with him, and later she emphasized what a great time she was having, he started to feel like she was coming on too strong. He admitted he likes women who are more of a challenge. Remember Groucho Marx's famous line: "I don't care to belong to any club that will have me as a member."

Several men talked about those awkward moments at the end of the evening. When the date had gone well and he wanted to ask her out again, he definitely preferred to be in charge and do the asking (then or later). If she said anything like "I hope to hear from you soon" or "E-mail me!" then he knew she was interested and the challenge evaporated. Alejandro, a twenty-seven-year-old fireman from Seattle, WA, said, "I think women sound a little desperate when they remind me to contact them."

THE (NOT-SO) SUBTLE TACTICS

Guys are not as dumb as we think. They're on to us.

Parker, a thirty-six-year-old retail entrepreneur from West Orange, NJ, regularly receives not-so-subtle hints when a woman wants him to ask her out again. But these girls don't come right out and say so. He said, "Girls ask me, 'What are your plans this week?' or they text me at ten PM and say, 'Hey, r u still out? Where r u?'" Then he says he usually loses interest.

I heard numerous references to the morning-after "thank-you e-mail." Most guys admitted mixed feelings about it: they appreciated it on one level, but it definitely signaled that the woman was (too) interested. This often tempered their eagerness to pursue her. I was most surprised to hear what Kyle, a thirty-nine-year-old physical trainer in Miami, FL—who is apparently very popular—said on this subject. He dubbed the thank-you e-mail "the bet he always wins." He said he has this routine with a buddy of his: Kyle texts his buddy after a date and wagers five bucks on how long it will take him to receive The E-mail. He admitted that he's lost a few bets, but usually he wins with the "eight-to-twelve-hour window." I was appalled but fascinated.

Kyle explained that the women he dates seem to know better than to blatantly ask him out again, so they do it by proxy: "They send an e-mail thanking me *again* for a great evening . . . then I'm supposed to reply, 'Let's do it again; how about Friday?'" He said it happens like clockwork.

Arrgh! The arrogance. Kyle was not one of my favorite guys,

that's for sure. But his "little wager" serves as a reminder that the thank-you e-mail is not necessary and not subtle.

SOUND FAMILIAR?

You may not have noted similarities to yourself among The Sadie Hawkins anecdotes thus far, as it's not always easy to recognize yourself through other people's stories. So you can use the self-assessment questions below to verify whether men might be stereotyping you as The Sadie Hawkins before they get to know the real you.

AT WORK . . .

❏ Is your job environment one in which you're rewarded for taking initiative?

❏ Do you go after what you want: promotions, company resources, new clients?

❏ Are you known among colleagues as a "straight talker"?

WITH YOUR FRIENDS AND FAMILY . . .

❏ Have you ever been told fondly, "I always know where I stand with you . . ."?

❏ Are you the one who usually initiates gathering a group together for an outing?

❏ Do you often use the phrase "Go for it!"?

AFTER A DATE OR WITH A PAST BOYFRIEND . . .

❏ Do you usually send a thank-you e-mail after a date?

❏ If a guy makes a vague reference to something—about his plans next weekend or seeing a friend—are you likely to ask for clarification (e.g., "Who are you going with?" or "Which friend?")?

❏ If you're nervous at the end of a date, do you rush to fill an awkward silence by saying something like "So, call me soon!"

YOUR PERSONAL PHILOSOPHY:

❏ Are you someone who "takes the bull by the horns"?

❏ Are you a planner—you like to make plans well in advance?

❏ Are you proud that you're not someone who "plays games"?

If you answered yes to more than five questions here, you may be perceived (or misperceived) as The Sadie Hawkins. There's no doubt you're forthright, confident, and a go-getter; of course you shouldn't change who you are deep down. But you may consider tweaking some of the things you do and say after a first or second date. Men who don't know yet how fabulous you are may think you're The Sadie Hawkins and miss the chance to get to know you better on the next few dates.

So, What Should You Do?

Here are five tips to help Sadie get her man to ask her to the dance, so *she* can get to know *him* better.

1) BE DIFFERENT

Most other women are out there using obvious or not-so-subtle moves to reverse the natural order of boy-likes-girl, boy-chases-girl. You have to do something *different.* You have to stand out from the crowd to intrigue the guy you want. That means *not* referring to future plans either during or after a great date (that's his role). Understand the difference between showing interest and taking the lead. When the date is over, you simply say with sincerity, looking into his eyes, "Thank you! This was a *great* evening. Good night." (This is all the thank-you he needs; no follow-up e-mail required the next morning—save that for your job interviews.) If he doesn't call you, he's not interested. He's a big boy and knows how to contact you. Review chapter 3 to understand what might have gone wrong to improve future dating results, and then say, "Next!"

Men who are older than thirty-five are especially used to being pursued by women because there are fewer single men than single women in this age group.[2] It's more important than ever to stand out from this crowd and let him take the initiative. But, you might

---

[2]According to the U.S. Census, there are 28 million single women over age thirty-five, but only 18 million single men over age thirty-five.

ask, *what if he's not calling*? No matter how great you think he is and how rare it is to meet someone like him, please don't let that cloud your judgment and start convincing yourself there are valid external reasons why he hasn't called . . . and therefore actions you can take to spur his interest. You don't want to hear it, but the truth is that it's a waste of your valuable time.

2) DON'T BE A NANCY DREW

If you check his online profile after your date to see if he has logged on during the past twenty-four hours, you are The Sadie Hawkins. When the software allows him to see who has viewed his profile, you're busted. Before you're in a relationship together, leave his on-line activity alone. You'll only decrease the chance of hearing from him again.

3) TEXTING COUNTS

Yes, it counts as "chasing him" even if you send a really, really, re-ally short text message to contact him before he contacts you first, for any bogus excuse *at all*. Guys aren't falling for the old "What was the name of that movie you said I should rent?" or "Here's the name of that paint store I recommended."

4) KEEP DATING OTHER GUYS

After one or two great dates, you might be tempted to decline other invitations, to stay home instead of attending another crowded party, or to take down your online profile. But you have to keep your options open in the early stages of a budding romance. The excited vibe you feel after a great first date can change at any mo-ment, and you need to have other irons in the fire. It's like you're managing a stock portfolio—you need to have several stocks in the game so that if all of a sudden one goes down, there are other stocks that may go up. Forcing yourself to look for and go out with other guys is vital during the first few weeks of a potential new relationship. If nothing else, it will help distract you from the temptation to contact him first.

5) ASSESS EACH SITUATION

One caveat to The Sadie Hawkins is that each man must be assessed individually because some guys are genuinely unsure of themselves. It's tricky to spot who's shy and who's playing it cool, but as discussed in The Why Bother section in chapter 3, some men need a little encouragement from you to know you're interested.

#2 REASON HE DIDN'T CALL BACK AFTER A GREAT FIRST DATE

The Flame-Out

There's nothing more intoxicating than a first date that went extremely well. You're thrilled when he can't get enough of you because the feeling is mutual. And *he's* chasing *you*. He e-mails or texts you fast and frequently in the next couple days, he's saying all the right things, he's using future-tense verbs, and his actions speak louder than words. He canceled boys' night to be with you, he told his family he met someone special, and he left a super-size Nestlé Crunch bar on your doormat because he remembered it's your favorite. Everything underscores his sincerity and serious intent. But situations like these have "WARNING! CAUTION!" stamped all over them. Relationships that ignite too quickly can—and often do—flame out just as fast. You've probably already experienced this yourself at some point. If there's one thing I've learned in the dating business, it's that slow and steady wins the romance race.

Have You Experienced The Flame-Out?

The Flame-Out encompassed three categories of behavior in my research. Do any of these ring true for you?

PREMATURE EMOTIONAL INTIMACY

Quickly exchanging too many personal feelings and details about each other creates the *illusion* of intense emotional intimacy. Even though you may have met only once or twice in person, you've spent an eternity together on the phone, over e-mail, or in your hopes and dreams. You assume you are, or soon will be, a real couple . . . but you don't have the safety net of time invested and trust earned to navigate any bumps in the road.

Connor, a thirty-three-year-old chef in Nantucket, MA, shared with me his regret about Madeline, a woman he met last summer. "There was immediate chemistry, and I knew she was someone with long-term potential," he told me. He described their first three dates, which all occurred within five days, during which they confided everything to each other: a troubled childhood, being fired from a job, breakup details about past lovers, and even sexual fantasies. Connor said, "This was no slow boil; this was flash frying!" "So, what happened?" I asked in a jaded tone of voice, because I knew what was coming next. He certainly wasn't the first guy who'd described this syndrome to me.

"Well," he explained, "on our fourth date we sat at a table next to a stressed-out mom dealing with her kids, and Madeline whispered to me that she didn't know how women survived without a nanny . . . I felt like someone had punched me in the stomach: [Madeline] wasn't who I thought she was . . . I started piecing it together: I remembered she had told me she went to boarding school and always had a nanny growing up . . . We just weren't on the same page. I realized she wasn't the right person for me." He went on to tell me why he reacted so strongly: he was raised by nannies, he felt neglected by his parents, and he didn't want to raise his own kids with nannies and boarding schools. I asked him if he had discussed this with Madeline, because I'm sure she would have understood his perspective, and I hoped they could have found a solution one day—even though all this sounded very premature.

But asking Connor that question illuminated my mistake: the

idea that someone should discuss and resolve big emotional topics is something you'd suggest to a person who is part of a real couple. And that's the rub: they weren't a real couple yet. They hadn't taken the baby steps to fine-tune their communication skills, nor had they built up enough relationship equity to value compromise. They were only on the fourth date! Connor went on to summarize his experience with Madeline: "We were too different; I backed off before anyone could get really hurt." Their bond was so fragile that it snapped easily. He never told Madeline what really happened (and I'm sure she's still wondering).

I heard from other men what else burst their fantasies: a few wrong answers, an e-mail from an old girlfriend, a bad dream, a few cautionary words from their therapist, and seeing one movie about divorce (note: never rent the movie *The Squid and the Whale* on a date!). The problem is that when things move too fast, men don't fall in love with you—only the fantasy of you. Whenever a bit of reality or discomfort creeps in, the glue is still wet and it can't hold you together.

PREMATURE PHYSICAL INTIMACY

Wow—I heard a lot of comments in this category during my interviews! Frankly, the anecdotes were trite: the guys mentally divided the nonserious prospects—the sex buddies, friends with benefits, and women who had sex too fast—from the ones they were serious about. Sure, everyone knows that you shouldn't have sex on the first date, but the line gets blurry after date number one. Men can't respect a woman who sleeps with them immediately. But . . . um, can we please define the word "immediately"? If your first date lasted seven hours and then you spent ten hours on the phone and you poured your heart out over e-mail and you feel like you've known each other a lifetime, even though *technically* you've only met three times—is that "immediately"? YES, PEOPLE, IT IS!

There are so many problems with having sex too soon that I don't know where to start. Toby, a twenty-nine-year-old sound design engineer from Livonia, MI, labeled sex with women he barely knows as "doing halfsies." He explained that even if he has some intense dates with someone, he obviously can't be in love with her yet, so "it's like doing halfsies—the body without the heart." He says the cuddling, if there is any, is fake. Ditto for the meaningful sighs. Toby quickly assured me, "Hey, I wouldn't turn it down, but it's not what makes me fall in love with a woman."

Rubin, a fifty-one-year-old chemist from Hartford, CT, said, "I don't know someone well enough in the beginning of a relationship to figure out real sexual compatibility. If she wows me with some great moves, it might be exciting, but it also says she's done [that] a lot before, which is a turnoff if I really like her. And if she's too demure, it's kind of boring. How do I know whether she's demure because we barely know each other or if she's just a dead fish in bed?"

And there isn't a guy alive, I was told, who believes that line "I've never done this before with someone I just met." Also, some men are simply *bored* with easy sex. That might sound surprising, but they say they've been having casual sex for so long, often since their early teens, that they actually want something different now. They want anticipation to *grow over time* as they really get to know someone. You'll rarely see a guy turn down temptation—biologically, men just aren't that complicated—but you'll also rarely see him wanting a committed relationship with that same woman. Marshall, a thirty-four-year-old sales representative from Delaware City, DE, said, "I think she confused my being turned on sexually with my being turned on romantically."

Anton, a thirty-six-year-old hair salon owner in Boston, MA, described how easy it is for him to get oral sex or intercourse on a first or second date. He framed the problem like this: "All these flings only intensify my craving for real intimacy." Myles, a forty-year-old travel adviser from La Jolla, CA, said shyly that he's looking for a woman who considers getting naked a special moment: "Call me old-fashioned, but [girls] who undress and have 'almost sex' seem like the same ones who go all the way—I can tell they're just holding back to play games, not because they think it's wrong to do that without commitment."

PREMATURE DECISIONS

Men and women often experienced The Flame-Out in another context: when a big decision presented itself to them too soon and created panic. Owen, a forty-three-year-old home builder in Los Angeles, CA, described having a few dates with Brooke, a single mom with two kids. He was initially very excited about her and thought she had serious potential. At the end of their third date, which had lasted twelve hours, Brooke told him that her kids would be with her ex-husband for a week the following month. She wanted to take advantage of her free week, maybe travel somewhere exotic. Although she acknowledged they hadn't known each other long, her time off from work was a rare opportunity. Would he be up for an impulsive trip together? He was into her, he had a flexible job, so he thought, "Why not?" They quickly agreed on a trip to Thailand.

But in the next few days some awkward questions arose, such as: who pays for what? If Brooke was his wife, Owen said, he would expect to pay for the whole trip—he wasn't rich, but he could afford a nice vacation. And yet, should he spend thousands of dollars on someone he had known for less than two weeks? She had e-mailed Owen some links to a few four-star hotels she found online and he wondered, "Which room category should we pick? What can she afford?" He didn't know her financial situation and didn't want to ask. Finally he said to her, "Um, what is our budget for this trip?" She replied, "*Our* budget? Gosh, this is embarrassing. I've never paid for a trip with a guy since I was in college . . ." The conversation deteriorated from there. He said the vacation issue then prompted other hypothetical questions in his mind: If they got married, would he be responsible for supporting her two kids? Could he afford two college tuitions? All these decisions were very premature, but they weighed on his mind. Owen and Brooke never went to Thailand together and they broke up a week later.

Men described other uncomfortable situations arising too soon: buying nonrefundable tickets for a concert two months away, meeting a single mom's children, being a woman's date at a charity auction with her parents, or being her date at a wedding. These types of events triggered a chain reaction of precocious decision-making or speculation and ultimately caused The Flame-Out of a budding relationship.

SOUND FAMILIAR?

You may not have noted similarities to yourself among The Flame-Out anecdotes thus far, as it's not always easy to recognize yourself through other people's stories. So you can use the self-assessment questions below to verify whether men might be stereotyping you as The Flame-Out before they get to know the real you.

AT WORK . . .

❑ Do you love your job because it's a high-intensity environment?

❑ Do you typically jump to conclusions before knowing all the information?

❑ In past performance reviews, have you ever been told, "Pace yourself; we don't want you to burn out!"

WITH YOUR FRIENDS AND FAMILY . . .

❑ Do you have a reputation as a passionate and emotional person?

❑ Are you frequently warned, "Be careful . . . don't get your heart broken!"

❑ Would you be described as vulnerable?

AFTER A DATE OR WITH A PAST BOYFRIEND . . .

❑ Do you have a romantic history of intense but short-term relationships?

❑ Do you ever take an overnight trip with a guy you barely know?

❑ Are you likely to sleep with a guy quickly if you feel an intense emotional connection?

YOUR PERSONALITY:

❑ Are you impulsive?

❑ Do you form attachments easily?

❑ Do you have an addictive personality?

If you answered yes to more than five questions here, you may be perceived (or misperceived) as The Flame-Out. There's no doubt you're passionate, loving, and intense; of course you shouldn't change who you are deep down. But you may consider tweaking some of the things you do and say after the first few dates. Men who don't know yet how fabulous you are may think you're The Flame-Out and miss the chance to get to know you better.

So, What Should You Do?

I was standing on the edge of a sidewalk recently, looking at the red pedestrian light signaling me to stop. But I was in a hurry. I looked both ways, and since there were no cars coming, I thought, "I can just dart across the street—it's perfectly safe." I stepped off the curb and suddenly a car turned the corner and screeched to a halt in front of me. When my heart stopped hammering at the close call, it occurred to me that The Flame-Out women are standing on that same curb. The red pedestrian light is there for a reason, not to look pretty. (It is red for your safety,) not as a general guideline that you can sometimes ignore when you don't see any cars coming. Jaywalking is illegal in some states because people can get *seriously injured*.

Here are four tips to help you wait patiently for the green light.

1) WATCH YOUR LANGUAGE

When you hear yourself muttering phrases during the first few dates such as "I've never told anyone this before . . . ," or "I usually don't let my guard down so quickly . . . ," that's a red flag saying things are moving too fast. It's good to go beneath the surface with a guy you're really interested in, but not so deep that he knows more about you than some of your friends or family who've known you for years. It's just too much, too soon. Think of your relationship as a hike up a mountain with a steady incline rather than a steep vertical path. Remember the One-for-One Rule from The Ex-Factor advice: tell him one personal tidbit on date number one, two on date number two, and so forth. Words and actions that are slow and steady build a stronger foundation that can't be shaken easily.

2) KEEP YOUR DATES ACTIVE

If your first few dates are long marathon gab sessions over meals in which you lock eyes and never move from your chairs, you will be more tempted to delve into emotional intimacy faster than you should. Similar to the advice for The Closer, you should plan some activities for the next few dates: tennis, walking your dogs, or going to a baseball game. Learn about each other bit by bit while you have *fun*, focusing on something else besides your intense feelings for each other.

3) DON'T GO THERE

If you want to avoid a guy panicking over a big decision too soon, don't let the tricky issue arise in the first place. If you must, take that vacation or buy the concert ticket with a girlfriend, or go alone. And if you want to avoid the temptation to have sex too fast, stay out of bedrooms until more time has passed (I suggest avoiding bedrooms for *at least* eight dates that are paced evenly throughout one or two months). It's wise to keep your date locations in the public domain.

I heard Dr. Phil once say something simple and powerful about being on a diet that relates to delaying sex. His concept was that if you really want to lose weight, keep your kitchen cupboards empty. If cookies are not present in the house, you are highly unlikely to get in your car at 11:00 PM when you have the munchies and drive to the twenty-four-hour market. So, if you want to avoid The Flame-Out, keep your bedroom empty to avoid temptation.

But what about dining and living rooms in the privacy of your home or his—should you avoid them too? The home-cooked meal is usually a key component of early date settings, but this presents a tough geography decision here. It usually turns into the make-out date. You should only put the home-cooked meal on your agenda if you have willpower of steel and know that you can (and will) terminate the evening before it progresses too far, too soon (sexually and emotionally).

4) CONTROL THE PACE

Just because *he* wants things to move quickly, it doesn't mean you have to go along for the ride. If he texts you, wait an hour to text back. If he asks you out six times in one week, tell him you are only free three times (but assure him you *wish* you were free all the other nights). You're controlling the pace that is right for a solid relationship. You are building a house brick by brick.

#3 REASON HE DIDN'T CALL BACK AFTER A GREAT FIRST DATE
The Busy Bee

"How are you?" you ask your friends and family. "Busy," says your mother. "Busy," says your best friend. "Busy" is the new "fine." *Everyone* is busy, including you and your potential mate. Sometimes two people miss out on a fabulous relationship because one or both of them simply couldn't juggle a schedule after a promising first date. Of course there are folks who experience love at first sight, after which nothing can deter them from the tenacious pursuit of their intended, but that's usually in Hollywood. In the real world, busy professional men usually don't have the time or energy to leap over the seventeen hurdles on your calendar, including your job, workout, out-of-town guests, a crisis with your friend, vacation, business trips, book club, and girls' night out. Not to mention phone tag. At some point, his initial interest wanes and some other girl enters stage left.

Women, whether single or married, are like Swiss Army knives when it comes to multitasking. We're organizers, socializers, planners, sympathizers, hard workers, and volunteers all wrapped in one. But when you're single, this full life becomes a big fat liability if you can't detach and stay flexible. I'm not talking about agreeing to a date at a moment's notice: if he calls you Saturday night at 7:00 PM to ask if you're free for dinner at 8:00 PM, that's just rude. I'm also not talking about changing your plans for a man who disrespects your time by being late or forgetting to call, or who wants to dictate get-togethers only according to what's convenient for him. But after a good date with an intriguing man who wants to see you again, it's a shame to let your preplanned commitments prevent you from that second date any longer than one week.

Are You The Busy Bee?

The Busy Bee encompassed two categories in my research. Do either of these ring true for you?

TOO MANY EXCUSES

Artie, a thirty-seven-year-old electrical engineer from Dallas, TX, told me about a woman he really fell for during their first date. He was so excited about her that he asked in the middle of dinner if he could see her again. She enthusiastically said, "Yes!" and they agreed on dinner three nights later (a Sunday night). But she called him the next day to explain that her boss had just scheduled an early meeting Monday morning in Atlanta, which meant she'd have to fly out Sunday night. Artie was busy with his parents visiting all weekend, so they changed their dinner plans to the following Friday night, when she was scheduled to return to Dallas. But Friday morning she texted him, "I'm so sorry, but I've come down with a terrible cold—can I call you tomorrow to make a new plan? I really want to see you soon." Artie was disappointed but understood.

Over the next ten days, everything seemed to conspire against them. When she recovered from her cold, he had a client meeting out of town. He called her when he returned, but they played phone tag all day. By the time they spoke in person, she was packing for a two-week vacation to Africa with her college roommate. It was one thing after another. Artie told me she seemed genuinely interested in seeing him again, always expressing sincere regret and trying to find another time. But when she called him after she returned from Africa, he had just started dating someone else.

Many men in my research had grown wary of "too busy" women and were looking for someone more available. Max, a forty-year-old accountant from New York, NY, complained, "More than half the women I ask out will call me within a few hours of our date with some last-minute 'crisis' and ask to reschedule for another night." He remembered one woman who told him, "Sorry, my *month* has been really busy, but now I'm available . . ." He couldn't believe it—she was claiming a whole month went by without a free hour or two? He said he used to be very understanding but now he thinks it's just rude—and worse, a sign that any future relationship will not be a priority. He emphasized that their excuses usually sound very legitimate (being sick, working, traveling, etc.), and he believes the women are genuine when they apologize profusely and ask to see him the next night or next week instead, but he sighed, "I'm over that. I want to be with someone who thinks a date with me is important."

Harvey, a sixty-four-year-old widower and aviation engineer from Bend, OR, told me, "I met a woman recently; it was the best date since my wife died three years ago . . . But when we spoke on the phone to arrange our next date, she mentioned how frequently she travels for work. Scheduling our second date was a challenge, and it made me realize she'd be too busy for me if [we ever became serious]. It's hard enough getting to know someone when you see them regularly, but if one person is gone so much, it's too hard." Harvey never explained his concern to her, nor did he give her the opportunity to suggest a solution. They eventually had a perfunctory second date, but no third date.

Sometimes too many other commitments translated not as "too busy" but rather "too rigid." George, a forty-five-year-old hotel supply distributor from Charlotte, NC, stayed out until 2:00 AM on a fantastic first date with Anna. But at the beginning of their second date, Anna told George she'd have to be home by 10:00 PM—not only that night, but every night. She explained that she needs eight hours of sleep: she exercises at 6:00 AM every day, replies to e-mails from 7:00 AM to 8:00 AM, and arrives at the office by 8:30 AM. He understands how hard it is to fit everything into a day, but Anna seemed too rigid. He also knew that when *he* really liked a woman, he was willing to be tired the next day if it meant staying out later with her. She didn't seem to feel the same way after their first date, and so George and Anna's potential romance turned into a pumpkin.

TOO POPULAR

Other men cited Busy Bee examples about women who received numerous calls or text messages on their cell phones during the date. Even when their devices were switched to vibrate mode and they didn't reply, their date could usually still hear the buzzing. Stan, a thirty-five-year-old construction company owner from Cleveland, OH, said, "We had a great first date, but her phone was constantly vibrating. She got about five calls in an hour!" He said he gets a lot of calls too, but he turns off his BlackBerry during a date. During their second meeting, when it happened again, he figured she was too popular (and a little rude not to switch it off). Contributing to his "too popular" impression was that she had made references to some parties she'd been to recently, and two different friends had stopped by their table to say hello. Despite being attracted to her, he said he doesn't like "social butterflies" because he thinks he won't get enough one-on-one time with them.

William, a fifty-one-year-old communications consultant from San Francisco, CA, recalled dating a woman named Gabrielle who was clearly juggling a lot of other men. She was honest with William up front by saying that while she'd had a great time the first night, she had already committed to some other Internet dates in the coming weeks and couldn't back out. She explained that she had just ended a serious relationship and William was only the second date that she'd had. William appreciated her honesty and understood that Gabrielle wanted to see what else was out there, but he was tired of dating around. He wanted something serious, so he didn't call her back. He said Gabrielle called him about six months later, asking if they could get together; by then he was seeing someone else and declined.

A few men mentioned women who cut evenings short because they had other priorities or plans. One woman announced at the beginning of a second date that she had to leave by 9:30 PM. She provided no excuse, so he assumed she had double-booked the evening with another guy. He never called her again.

SOUND FAMILIAR?

You may not have noted similarities to yourself among The Busy Bee anecdotes thus far, as it's not always easy to recognize yourself through other people's stories. So you can use the self-assessment questions below to verify whether men might be stereotyping you as The Busy Bee before they get to know the real you.

AT WORK . . .

❑ Do you work really long hours?

❑ Do you travel a lot?

❑ In past performance reviews, have you ever been told, "Try to delegate more . . ."?

WITH YOUR FRIENDS AND FAMILY . . .

❑ Do you receive this advice about life in general: "Try to say no more often"?

❑ Does returning messages to the people you most care about usually fall to the bottom of your to-do list?

❑ Do you have more than five hundred friends on Facebook?

ON A DATE OR WITH A PAST BOYFRIEND . . .

❑ Are you usually running late?

❑ Is it difficult to schedule a date with you?

❑ Has a guy ever confessed to you, "When you canceled last time, I wasn't sure if you were trying to blow me off . . ."?

YOUR PERSONAL PHILOSOPHY:

❏ Do you think being overscheduled is simply "living a full life"?
❏ Do you constantly think, "There's never enough time . . ."?
❏ Do you usually feel exhausted?

If you answered yes to more than five questions here, you may be perceived (or misperceived) as The Busy Bee. There's no doubt you're successful, capable, and popular; of course you shouldn't change who you are deep down. But you may consider tweaking some of the things you do and say after a first or second date. Men who don't know yet how fabulous you are may think you're The Busy Bee and miss the chance to get to know you better on the next few dates.

So, What Should You Do?

If you want to avoid the sting of The Busy Bee, here are three tips to keep your schedule flexible so you can decide if he's *worth* adjusting your hectic life for. While each of these tips has a subtle distinction, they all contain a variation of the core message: "Cancel other stuff so you're not too busy to see him again *soon*."

1) PRIORITIZE HIM

I am always perplexed when a single woman tells me that meeting the right guy is her top priority, because her actions are rarely consistent with her words. When she finally meets a great guy, she won't cancel any previous commitments to fit him into her busy schedule. Sure, it's admirable to keep promises to girlfriends with whom you have already made plans; and okay, that work project is pretty important. Yes, I know your nonrefundable vacation next week can't be moved *just because* you had one great date with some guy. In fact, if he can't wait for you, it wasn't meant to be . . . right?

I have to say: wrong. We are such feminists today (myself included) with our attitudes of "I will never change for a man." And this includes "I will never change *my plans* for a man." But sometimes that means cutting off your nose to spite your face. It is so rare to meet a wonderful man that *sometimes* you should take a leap of faith: your girlfriends won't stop loving you if you cancel one night with them—they should be happy for you. So what if you spend three hours instead of six on that big work project? The track record you've built for yourself through the years counts for something. Sometimes Mr. Right doesn't knock twice; sometimes Mr. *Righ*t is only available *right* now. There will always be a way to apologize to a friend or a boss later.

And here's a radical thought: consider in the big picture whether paying a $100 change fee on your airline ticket might be worth staying in town one extra night for that second or third date—you don't have to tell him what you did to become available (just do it behind the scenes). Paying an airline change fee for a date would be crazy, right? Not always. Sometimes The Busy Bee needs to do something a bit radical to force herself to prioritize her dating life. E-mails and phone calls while you're traveling to keep in touch with him are certainly no substitute for building face-to-face chemistry. Don't let your schedule derail a budding romance if you can help it (and afford to change it).

And what happens if you make some cancellations and the next date is a dead end? I still think you made the right choice to prioritize him—not *every* him, certainly, but a few special hims—because love is always a gamble (and you only need to win once).

2) FORGET THE (USUAL) RULES

Waiting three days to return a call or e-mail from a man you're interested in is ridiculous. (However, I'd vote for a *little* time lapse to reply—say, twenty-four hours—because I do agree that playing it cool can create intrigue, especially for men who like a challenge.) But if you wait too long because you are, or are pretending to be, too busy, then your potential relationship can simply lose momentum.

Some men worry that a busy woman doesn't have the kind of lifestyle that allows room for them. I heard this from several men who especially hesitated to pursue busy professional women and single moms because they *assumed* they'd be too unavailable. Thus, there is a big difference between playing it cool and making him think you don't have free time.

3) MAKE HAY WHILE THE SUN SHINES

If you recently started a new job, or you're training for a marathon, or you're applying to graduate schools in another city, or any number of other examples suggesting that getting serious right now with a guy you like is a bad idea *because your life is too busy or too tumultuous*, I encourage you to think again. I have seen so many women who look back with regret over not pursuing a great guy because in theory they had too much else going on in their lives. Let me clarify here: it's not that I see a lot of women *consciously* deciding to prioritize something else, but it sneaks up on them one day at a time. They turn down one date or one party because they have other plans that Friday night or a work trip next Thursday. But this adds up over the years until one plus one equals fifty. Trust me, if you find someone special at exactly your busiest time, take advantage of it.

#4 REASON HE DIDN'T CALL BACK
AFTER A GREAT FIRST DATE
The R U 4 Real?

It's hard enough to align the Mars and Venus planets with verbal communication, but with the dominance of electronic communication today, it's "virtually" impossible. It's not unusual anymore for a person to have three phones (home, office, cell), a wireless handheld device, a pager, a fax, Skype, three e-mail addresses (personal, work, alumni), a personal website or blog, a few online dating profiles, a few social networking profiles, and maybe even a virtual assistant in India! With all these devices and contact points, I quickly learned that electronic dating disconnects were significant.

At no other time are men and women looking more closely for nuanced signals of interest, or lack thereof, than immediately after a first date. But because there is not a unanimous, clear set of rules for electronic communication, those signals can be as reliable as reading tarot cards. Of course misunderstandings also occur in person and by telephone, but with the elimination of eye contact and voice tone, cyberspace is more susceptible to misfires.

Have You Experienced The R U 4 Real?

The R U 4 Real? encompassed three scenarios in my research. Do any of these ring true for you?

CONFUSING CONTENT

Men expressed confusion over many types of electronic content. For example, they wondered whether basic spelling mistakes were accidental typos or signs of stupidity. (I hear this concern a lot from women too.) Frankly, if you wouldn't tolerate a spelling error on your résumé, you shouldn't allow it to happen during early-stage dating communication either—even if you're using a BlackBerry or iPhone. Just take the extra ten seconds to proofread or spell-check, because first impressions are so important. Burke, a thirty-one-year-old venture capitalist from Menlo Park, CA, said the most common spelling error he sees is the confusion of "you're" with "your." He also remembered women who spelled "definitely" as "definately" or "deep-seated" as "deep-seeded." He said over the course of ten e-mail exchanges, one or two spelling errors is no big deal but three or four start to make him wonder. Burke commented, "It's not that I really care whether her spelling is perfect, but having a smart partner is very important to me. How can I predict after one or two dates whether she's going to be intellectually stimulating enough for the next sixty years? Obviously I can't, so I end up noticing little things, like spelling errors—they just make me pay closer attention to the intelligence issue." (Burke is one sharpe guy.)

Several men remarked that certain comments they received over e-mail or text messaging were downright odd. They didn't know how to interpret them and later acknowledged to me they may have jumped to wrong conclusions. Raj, a twenty-eight-year-old website designer from Ft. Worth, TX, remembered a great first date. But when he texted his date the next day, she wrote back, "You weren't what I thought you'd be like." He wasn't sure if that was supposed to be good or bad. Women in the past had told him that he was shorter than they expected, so his first assumption was that her comment was negative and referred to his height. He took offense irrationally and fired back a cutting reply: "At least I was honest about my weight." She replied, "F*ck U," and their "great date" was abruptly negated. Good riddance to Raj with his insecurity and knee-jerk temper, but this exchange echoed similar electronic misunderstandings that I heard several other times.

Another man reported a woman who texted him, "The flowers you sent me were provocative." He thought to himself, "Huh? What does *that* mean?" After showing the text to some friends, he concluded she didn't know what the word "provocative" meant and she wasn't very bright. Another man remembered asking a woman for a second date by e-mailing, "Can we get together this Saturday night?" She replied, "Sorry, I'm busy Saturday night." He didn't know whether she would be interested in going out with him on a different night or whether she was blowing him off. He said, "I hate being rejected, so I just let that one go."

Social networks were a big source of confusing electronic content. Several men commented about messages they read on women's Facebook walls, or MySpace groups they joined, or the type or quantity of their cyber friends. They used this information to gather little clues about who women are. Why? Because as you saw in The Birds of a Feather section in chapter 3, your online group friends and memberships, how many cyber friends you have, and the cryptic messages and photos posted online by those friends inevitably stereotype you (accurately or inaccurately) to someone who doesn't know you well. As singles are increasingly using social networks (for friendships, networking, and dating), this is a growing arena for dating confusion. Unlike online dating profiles, you have less control over the image you project on a social network because it's almost impossible to control which photos you're tagged in and what messages your friends post (even if they're well-intended or an inside joke).

And then there's the plethora of details you reveal about yourself on sites like Facebook without proper space for explanation. For example, if your Facebook page reveals that you're a "fan of Arnold Schwarzenegger," some people will think you're a Republican, some will think you're a fan of the movie *The Terminator*, some will think you like men with foreign accents, and some will think you're attracted to bodybuilders. These individual interpretations, like a Rorschach test, could contribute to a buildup of inaccurate clues about you, eliminating potential romances with die-hard Democrats, film snobs, accentless men, or cute guys with love handles. If you're a Republican who doesn't want to date Democrats, that's one thing. But if you simply happen to like Austrian accents, you may be inadvertently turning away some intriguing suitors.

Other social networks have similar confusion risks. For example, MySpace allows you to select a favorite song that plays every time someone visits your page. It also allows you to select your own profile layout with a variety of background designs, colors, and fonts. While these features allow creativity to express yourself, they dramatically increase the chance you'll be instantly misunderstood by strangers. If you choose a Beethoven symphony, could you be perceived as pretentious? If you choose a pink font with flowers, could you be written off as childish? As a tool to communicate with your friends, it's great; but as for creating first impressions, it's dicey. I'm not saying don't use social networks; just think carefully about how your profile reflects who you are and wait until you know a guy better before inviting him to your page.

CONFUSING TONE

Electronic tone was easily misinterpreted as well, and everyone had their own pet peeves. For example, is using too many exclamation points overly enthusiastic? Is using no exclamation points too disinterested? Are smiley faces fun and good-humored or irritating and cutesy? Is signing off your e-mail with "Ciao" considered cool and sophisticated or affected and trite? Men talked about everything from women who used ALL CAPS (were they "shouting" or had they forgotten to unlock the caps button?) to women who used text spelling such as "C U L8R"[3] (were they still in high school or trying to avoid carpal tunnel syndrome?) to women who replied with only one line (was that direct and sexy, or curt and disinterested?). The smallest things become electronic petri dishes when people don't know you well.

Skylar, a twenty-two-year-old talent agency assistant in Los Angeles, CA, told me that she uses ALL CAPS when she wants to express excitement, exaggeration, or awe ("I'm a HUGE fan of the iPhone!"). But thinking back on it, she wonders if one guy who didn't call her back may have used ALL CAPS with a different intent. She described a guy who once texted her, "I'm looking forward to our date even though I have SO much work to do." She assumed he really liked her because, despite all his work, he was still making time to see her. But when he canceled their date an hour before their dinner reservation and she never heard from him again, she wondered if he had been implying that while he was looking forward to their date, he wanted her to suggest a rain check because he had SO MUCH WORK. Maybe she ignored the pressure of his job and was written off as inconsiderate? I doubt it, but the point is to realize the possibilities for misinterpretation and avoid relying so heavily on electronic messaging when you're first getting to know someone.

A few years ago, a journalist named Marcie interviewed me for a magazine article about dating. She was a single thirtysomething woman and our conversation quickly turned to her personal dating stories. She complained about a guy who had never asked her out again after a promising first date. This guy had told her over dinner that his favorite book was *Lonesome Dove*. When she told him she'd never read it, he exclaimed, "Seriously? You have to read it—it's the best book I've ever read! It's about cowboys, but it's romantic, heroic,

---

[3]"See you later."

intelligent . . ." Intrigued, Marcie stopped by a bookstore the next day and bought it. She e-mailed to tell him and he sounded pleased. Then she left the next day on a business trip. A few days later he e-mailed, "So, have you read *Lonesome Dove* yet?" She replied, "Not yet, I've been busy." He wrote back, "It's not a class assignment." She didn't understand what he meant and thought he sounded miffed. She wrote back, "What's that mean?" He replied, "Nothing." And, just like that, she never heard from him again.

Marcie has always wondered what went wrong. Usually these misunderstandings originate during the date itself—a buildup of off-kilter comments. If he already perceived her as a bit self-centered or rude, for example, then the "wrong answer" via e-mail or text becomes the nail in the coffin (rather than a random reaction). I wished she had picked up the phone to ask him what happened instead of stewing in confusion. So, Lonesome Dove Guy, if you're out there reading this sentence by some bizarre coincidence, e-mail me through my website! I still remember your story after all these years and would love to hear your perspective.

CONFUSING SILENCE

Perhaps the worst technology misfire is dead silence. Men reported exchanging rapid-fire e-mails or texts after a great date (often within minutes after "Good night"), which fueled their optimism and sexual interest. But if the exchanges suddenly slowed or stopped in the coming days or weeks, the men became confused. Sometimes the confusion was good (it left them waiting eagerly for her response), but sometimes the confusion had a negative outcome. Nathaniel, a twenty-six-year-old management consultant in Columbus, OH, had a double whammy with a woman named Carmen: a combination of The Flame-Out and The R U 4 Real?. He explained, "We had this initial e-mail intensity. The date went well, and the next day we exchanged about twenty e-mails. But suddenly around 9:00 PM Carmen didn't respond. The next time I heard from her was the following morning. Her e-mail was time-stamped 3:00 AM." He explained that since they'd only had one date, he didn't want to ask where she had been, but he had a bad feeling she was with another guy if she was getting home at 3:00 AM. He waited until later that night to reply, then Carmen waited until the following morning to send *her* reply. The silence in between their e-mails expanded until Nathaniel concluded, "Our energy level just petered out."

A few men reported feeling confused about electronic silence after they sent what I'll term "an impersonal communication." After successful first dates, one man sent a woman an invitation to join his LinkedIn network, another man included a woman on a group-distribution e-mail with some Internet jokes, and another man sent an e-card. When they didn't hear back from the woman, they assumed she wasn't interested. They each gave me the same explanation for their (lame) impersonal communication: they were testing the waters, not knowing whether she was interested or not. They assumed no reply meant no interest. (I know, it's hard to believe any woman would have guessed that being part of a fifty-person e-mail distribution list with a bad knock-knock joke was her date's attempt to test the waters!)

One complaint in this category came across loud and clear, and this one I really agree with. Men hated those spam-control settings! Some men opted for silence after attempting to e-mail a date and receiving a spam-control message—you know, the kind that says the recipient needs to authorize your initial e-mail to verify you're not a spammer? Of course everyone in the entire world hates spam, but at least when you're single, get rid of that annoying setting on your computer. Men said it leaves an irritating first impression and sometimes makes women seem uptight or guarded. (If you've experienced some confusing silence, it might be worth checking your trash folder to see if he tried to contact you but was filtered out.)

In the ideal world, if someone really wants to see you badly enough, of course he'll try again or he'll jump through hoops. But in this era when everyone is too busy and has too many other dates just a click away, it's worth trying to be a little easier to reach until you decide whether he could be a keeper or not.

SOUND FAMILIAR?

You may not have noted similarities to yourself among The R U 4 Real? anecdotes thus far, as it's not always easy to recognize yourself through other people's stories. So you can use the self-assessment questions below to verify whether men might be stereotyping you as The R U 4 Real? before they get to know the real you.

AT WORK . . .

❏ Do you send or receive more than a hundred texts or e-mails per day?

❏ Is your job environment one that emphasizes electronic communication over face-to-face meetings?

❏ Do you often find yourself explaining what you meant in an e-mail because a colleague took it the wrong way?

WITH YOUR FRIENDS AND FAMILY . . .

❏ Do you frequently share a text or e-mail from a guy to help you dissect what it really means?

❏ Have you ever received this text: "WTF . . ."?

❏ Does anyone tell you, "It's hard to understand your electronic sense of humor?"

AFTER A DATE OR WITH A PAST BOYFRIEND . . .

❏ Do you spend more time communicating electronically than in person?

❏ Do guys often tell you, "I wasn't sure what that e-mail [or text] meant"?

❏ Do you usually write electronic messages without rereading what you wrote?

YOUR PERSONAL PHILOSOPHY:

❏ Do you appreciate and/or prefer short communication?

❏ If you aren't checking e-mail after an hour, do you feel antsy?

❏ Are you reachable 24/7?

If you answered yes to more than five questions here, you may have experienced The R U 4 Real?. There's a good chance electronic miscommunication can be blamed for your date-breaker. You should consider tweaking your e-mail, text, and IM exchanges in the early stages of dating according to the advice below. Otherwise, men who don't know yet how fabulous you are may miss the chance to get to know you better in person.

So, What Should You Do?

Here are four tips to avoid your promising second or third dates being derailed by electronic confusion . . . so you can determine if he is 4 real.

1) ESTABLISH AN EARLY PATTERN

While frequent and rapid e-mails, texts, or IMs can certainly have an intoxicating effect, be sure to establish some limits and norms with him from the very beginning. This is important because not only can technology misunderstandings and sudden silence create confusion, but they can lead to The Flame-Out. Going to extremes after only one or two dates (e.g., twenty e-mails in one day or ten texts in ten minutes) is bound to somehow end in disappointment—as it did for Nathaniel and Carmen.

To date smart, first establish a reasonable pace for your text and e-mail messages early on. If you both get in the habit of replying within sixty seconds or sixty minutes, any deviation in that pattern could be viewed as a red flag. One of you might presume the other one's interest is waning. Deliberately vary your response time from rapid to slow over the first few weeks, telling him directly, "Sorry, I don't check my messages very often." If irregular correspondence is normal from the beginning, it actually creates less worry and negative thoughts when the inevitable delayed response occurs later. It also builds anticipation (the Holy Grail of dating).

Secondly, when you're exchanging messages back and forth at whatever pace you've established, tell him directly if you're logging off—don't suddenly disappear for twelve hours. By saying "good night" or "'bye for now" before signing off, you are establishing another norm in your cyber relationship. If electronic silence suddenly occurs one time in the future, then you both will understand that something deviated from your norm and will feel comfortable enough to pick up the phone and clarify it before things spiral downward.

2) EMOTICONS AREN'T ALL BAD

Emoticons—those electronic smiley faces and other keyboard punctuation images—and popular abbreviations seen in teen texting ("LOL" = laughing out loud) get a bad reputation. A lot of people scoff at them: "They're so *cutesy!*" But emoticons and abbreviations can dull the edge of certain electronic remarks that could appear snide or irritated. Like 'em or not, emoticons and abbreviations accomplish one very important thing: a lighter tone. While I'm not suggesting you go crazy with hundreds of them, throw in a few winks, smiles, and "JK"s ("just kidding") now and then to ensure he doesn't misinterpret your dry wit as rude or obnoxious.

3) PICK UP THE DAMN PHONE!

When in doubt, always pick up the phone immediately and call him to clarify tone or intent before things get beyond repair. Electronic communication should be used to enhance flirting and getting to know each other in the early dating stage, not as a replacement for human interaction. It was such a shame listening to cyber misunderstandings during my Exit Interviews. I'm sure most of these could have been easily clarified with someone picking up the phone right away. It's hard enough finding the right partner; technology is the most inane culprit of all when a promising couple implodes.

And expect the same from him: consider directly telling him after a few dates, "I want you to know that I'm a very straightforward person. We're bound to misunderstand each other sometimes in texts or e-mails. So if you're ever confused about my tone, or something I write, or not hearing a response from me, will you please pick up the phone and ask me about it?"

4) ALLOW ONE FOLLOW-UP

Most of us assume that if we never get an anticipated e-mail, text, or voice message, it's because the other person never sent it. And 99 percent of the time that's probably an accurate assumption. But every once in a while there's a genuine technology glitch. I've had my share of inexplicably lost e-mails over the years; haven't you? (The fact that Brad Pitt hasn't returned my e-mails is, I'm certain, the consequence of some crazy cyberspace mix-up.) There are probably several glitches I've never even discovered because I assumed someone chose not to respond. The times I've found out about the mistakes were usually in a business context when I was waiting for an important reply that didn't come. Once my literary agent didn't reply within twenty-four hours to one of my e-mails and I actually thought she might be dead. She is very devoted to her clients and practically has her BlackBerry surgically attached. When I'm in Europe and she's in Los Angeles, she'll write me back within minutes despite a nine-hour time difference (even when it's 3:00 AM her time). The thing is, I know her response pattern. When it deviated *once*, I assumed the worst.

But that's business. It's more complicated in your personal life to know if someone's avoiding you or didn't receive your message. So here's my guideline for handling silence from men: If you expected him to e-mail you after your date, or at some point you sent him an e-mail that went unanswered, first check your spam folder. If it's not there, wait one week and then send him one test-the-waters e-mail. Simply type a nonhostile message, such as, "I was just thinking about you today: how are you?" If he still doesn't write back, forget it. While there are a few possible technology glitches that might account for his silence, the odds are overwhelming that he's not interested.

I should note that this test-the-waters e-mail is not the same as the Sadie Hawkins thank-you e-mail. In my mind, the test-the-waters e-mail does not classify as pursuing him because, frankly, after a week of silence there's no pursuit going on at all. You don't have anything to lose now that he is probably not interested in you anyway. This is a low-risk e-mail because there's nothing to risk. Most likely you'll receive either silence or a polite, anemic reply. But on the rare chance that he did try to reach you (which is the only justification for sending this e-mail), he will hopefully react to your message with a relieved, "Great to hear from you, where have you been? Did you get my message?"

#5 REASON HE DIDN'T CALL BACK
AFTER A GREAT FIRST DATE

The Tailspin

The Tailspin results when a woman expects to hear from a man after a great first date, but he doesn't contact her right away. She works herself into a frenzy, gathering speed like a tornado. By the time he actually does reach out, she's pissed off. She acts aloof or angry. Maybe she starts playing games, such as not returning his call quickly, leaving him a message at home when she knows he's at work, or trying to make him jealous. Men said that's obviously not alluring.

I'm a fan of the book *He's Just Not That Into You*, but remember the focus there is not the first-or-second-date scenario. When a man isn't treating you well in a *relationship*, you should realize he's not interested and move on. But when a guy you barely know doesn't call right away, that's a different story. Is he not that into *you* or not that into *his stereotype of you*? This is a subtle but interesting distinction. After one or two dates, we've established by now that he doesn't know the real you. So it's not a personal insult yet if he doesn't rush to clear his calendar, pursue you arduously, have your name tattooed on his chest, and immediately make you his number-one priority. It may take him a while to follow up for any number of valid reasons. We all know that someone who's really smitten with you will call immediately; but if he's not smitten right away, you don't need to get your feathers ruffled so early in the dating game.

Dynamic single men (just like women) usually have overscheduled, hectic lives as they juggle their jobs, friends, family obligations, workout schedules, volunteer commitments, and hobbies. And realistically, they probably have a few other women in the picture when you first meet them. As you know from your own life, it's hard to squeeze everything and everyone in. So if he doesn't call fast? Sure, maybe he's not head over heels for you *yet*. But men told me that slow starts to a relationship can pick up speed later. It may take some time (and patience) until you become his top priority. Just like Busy Bee women risk losing a guy when they don't have time, these busy guys who don't call *you* right away are taking the same risk. You might be dating someone else by the time he calls, but if you're not, all I'm saying is you don't have to act cold, because there's still a chance for a happy ending.

Have You Experienced The Tailspin?

The Tailspin encompassed three scenarios in my research. Do any of these ring true for you?

THE CANDY STORE

A great guy is like a kid in a candy store: he has a lot of temptations. You may be in the same position yourself. It's like that reality television show *The Bachelor* (or *The Bachelorette*). When one man finds himself standing in a circle of twelve potentially interested women (just like if you find yourself surrounded by a dozen hot-for-you guys), it's really not personal when it takes a while to choose.

Aaron, a forty-four-year-old cardiologist in Tulsa, OK, admitted that he "has options galore." Despite the arrogant phrase he used, he sounded like a sweet guy on the phone with me—not the type who'd normally brag. I was introduced to him for an Exit

Interview by a mutual friend who described him as "such a great guy . . . everyone wants to fix him up." Aaron recalled a fantastic first date with a woman named Jessica he'd met one year earlier. At the end of their date, he told her he'd call her soon. He had a crazy week at the hospital with six surgeries and two on-call nights. And he admitted he had two other blind dates that week, previously scheduled before he met Jessica. He said Jessica was on his mind and he hoped to see her again. He described his feelings for her as "very positive . . . maybe not head-over-heels, but interested in spending more time with her." A week had passed when he finally had some downtime to call her. He was surprised at the reception he got. Jessica was "cold on the phone . . . she was obviously pissed off . . . I assume it was because I hadn't called her right away. She wouldn't say what was wrong . . . I got a negative vibe." They never went on a second date.

I spoke with another King of First Dates named Leonard, a thirty-nine-year-old consultant in New York, NY. He was introduced to me by a friend who described him as "a real catch who half of Manhattan is trying to land." When we spoke, Leonard described two separate great first dates that dead-ended because he didn't act fast enough. He said after he waited "about a week or two" to call back, one woman answered his call sarcastically, "Leonard *who*?" Another time, he tried to explain to a woman how busy he had been, and she replied, "I don't give a shit." I suggested to Leonard that he start calling back faster when he likes someone. He laughed good-naturedly and said, "Ya think?" Basically, he waits so long to follow up with women, even when he really likes them, *because he can*. He has so many opportunities it doesn't really matter if one woman gives him a cold reception. Okay, that's annoying, and he may not sound very desirable as I explain his situation, but at some point (next week or next decade?), I do believe that a switch will flip in his mind. Suddenly he'll decide it's time to settle down. Most of these popular guys eventually do marry. If he's such a great guy (as I heard from our mutual friend who has known him for over twenty years), could it hurt you to answer the phone sweetly and leave your options open for a second date? I bet the one girl Leonard calls after a lapsed time period who *doesn't* give him grief will end up being the keeper.

THE GRAY ZONE

Brandon, a thirty-six-year-old money manager from Weston, MA, described having a good blind date with Lisa. He said, "It was fun conversation . . . she was cute . . . I gave her a light kiss on the lips at the end. I was somewhat inclined to ask her out again, but I wasn't sure if there was chemistry or not . . . Also she was a smoker, but she said she was trying to quit . . . Everyone always says to give it another try if you're not sure, so I was thinking about it." By the time Brandon made up his mind to ask Lisa out again, his e-mail inquiry was not well received. She wrote back that after not hearing from him for two weeks, she assumed he wasn't interested. She had moved on but "wished him the best of luck!" He later heard from their mutual matchmaker friend that Lisa wasn't dating anyone else, she was just miffed at him. The friend said to Brandon, "I'm on Lisa's side . . . you should have treated her better." Brandon sighed, "I guess that meant I was a jerk. But I wasn't sure after one date—is that so terrible? I've had some bad breakups . . . it's hard to get excited right away."

Do *you* think Brandon was a jerk? Definitely I'd call him *slow to react*. Maybe if I'm feeling generous, I'd call him *cautious*. But a jerk? Hard to say.

Sam, a twenty-nine-year-old real estate developer in Denver, CO, told me about a woman with whom he'd had two great dates. Beth was fantastic and he felt momentum building with her. He told her, "Let's try to get together on Sunday night." But he ended up working all weekend and was extremely tired by Sunday night. Since they hadn't made any firm plans, he figured he'd go to sleep early and call her in the morning. At 9:00 PM, he received a text message from her: "Is there any reason I haven't heard from you today? I thought we had plans. I'm really disappointed." He wasn't sure what her tone was (reminiscent of The R U 4 Real? confusion in electronic media), but he figured if she was really upset she would have called instead of texted. He also admitted that receiving her text made him think, "She's overreacting . . . Maybe she was getting serious too fast." He decided not to respond right away. He told me his logic was this: in case she was really mad, it'd be better to wait until the next day to explain himself when he wasn't overly tired. When he arrived at work Monday morning, he had an e-mail waiting from her: "I'm very surprised at your behavior. I didn't think you were that kind of guy. If you don't want to go out again, have the guts to tell me."

Sam picked up the phone and called Beth to apologize. He said he realized that his logic about waiting until the next day was wrong and definitely rude. He reminded her they didn't have firm plans, but he understood he should have called to let her know he was too tired to go out. He said she calmed down, but he didn't ask to see her again. I said to him, "Don't you think if you'd really liked her you would have behaved differently Sunday night?" He replied, "I did really like her! But it's not like we were in love—we'd been on two dates!"

INSECURITY

When you really like a new guy, of course it's normal to feel insecure. You hope he likes you too, and you look for positive signals. The problem, of course, is that signals can be confusing and it's easy to be overly sensitive. The Tailspin does not only mean working yourself into a frenzy and reacting with anger or aloofness to a confusing signal, but it can include exhibiting increasingly *insecure* behavior. Marcus, a twenty-eight-year-old manager of a charity in Cheboygan, MI, told me about a common dilemma he discusses with his friends: how to handle the JDate.com feature indicating how recently members have logged in. (Match.com and other sites have similar notifications: "Online now" or "Active within twenty-four hours.") As an example, he described a woman named Carly he met on JDate. He'd had a really good first date with her, but she became upset when she saw that he had logged in to JDate within one hour after leaving her at her doorstep. He said, "What am I supposed to do? I don't know if a good first date will ever turn into something serious. I had been corresponding with two or three other girls. That's the online dating game, isn't it? It's a numbers game. If I want to find a great girl and start a family in the next few years, I have to manage my time by keeping several irons in the fire."

When Carly asked him about logging in so fast, he immediately asked her how she knew. She confessed she'd had such a nice time with him that she'd given in to her curiosity and checked his profile status, hoping he wasn't looking for other women. Marcus said he laughed it off and told her, "Thanks for being honest." They had a second date, but not a third. He summed it up by telling me, "I like girls who are a little more confident."

SOUND FAMILIAR?

You may not have noted similarities to yourself among The Tailspin anecdotes thus far, as it's not always easy to recognize yourself through other people's stories. So you can use the self-assessment questions below to verify whether men might be stereotyping you as The Tailspin before they get to know the real you.

AT WORK . . .

❏ Are you used to getting immediate feedback in some form (e.g., sales results, management coaching, client reactions)?

❏ Do colleagues sometimes ask you to stop bothering them for reports or information after you've asked them repeatedly?

❏ Does your boss advise you, "Try to let it play out and see what happens . . ."?

WITH YOUR FRIENDS AND FAMILY . . .

❏ Do you often say things you don't mean and immediately regret them?

❏ Has someone ever warned you, "Don't cut off your nose to spite your face . . ."?

❏ Did you struggle with emotions about not feeling loved when you were growing up?

ON A DATE OR WITH A PAST BOYFRIEND . . .

❏ Do guys sometimes tell you, "You're overreacting . . ."?

❏ Do you date guys who are aloof?

❏ On a first date, are you immediately trying to look for signs of whether he'll call you again?

YOUR PERSONALITY:

❏ Do you tend to believe things are black and white?

❏ Are you hot tempered?

❏ Are you the "one strike and you're out" type?

If you answered yes to more than five questions above, you may be perceived (or misperceived) as The Tailspin. There's no doubt you're passionate and sensitive; of course you shouldn't change who you are deep down. But you may consider tweaking some of the things you do and say after the first or second date. Men who don't know yet how fabulous you are may think you're The Tailspin and miss the chance to get to know you better on the next few dates.

So, What Should You Do?

With The Tailspin, there's actually *nothing you should do*. The point is specifically to *do nothing* except understand these three observations.

1) SLOW STARTS ARE OKAY

Not every great couple ignites quickly with a bolt of certainty and passion. Try asking a dozen happily married people you know to describe the early weeks when they first met their mate. Yes, half of them will probably tell you they "just knew" and they fell hard immediately. But the other half will tell you a different tale: they started off as friends, or, on the contrary, they were *sure* they didn't even like him/her; or maybe they were dating/living with someone else at the time. A slow start may not fit the romantic image you've always had of meeting the One, but it's more common than you think. Importantly, from what I've seen, slow starts can lead to long-term happiness.

2) PRIORITIES CHANGE

I'll admit that when a guy is too tired to call you because he was traveling, working, or had another date, it's not great news. You are not his top priority at that time. But he doesn't know you well enough yet to bump you up to number one. Try not to take it personally. Realistically, the man you may be looking for is busy with a hectic, overscheduled life . . . just like you. Frankly, he should heed my advice for The Busy Bee, but we know men don't read the self-help books they need. If he goes slowly in the beginning, even if the reason is something annoying, it doesn't mean he's a bad guy. When he does call, no need to mention how many weeks, days, or hours have passed since your date. He's calling (finally) because he liked the same girl he met last time—so don't go a-changing into someone bitchy or insecure. What matters anyway is where you end up, not where you start.

I have a female friend in Manhattan who's getting remarried next month. Following a very painful divorce, she had been going out on dates for four years. When she finally met her current fiancé, he was dating and sleeping with two other women. In the spirit of "full disclosure," as he put it, he confessed that information to her on their second date. She thought he was a phenomenal guy in every way, except for the part about the other women! At first she turned down his follow-up invitations, but eventually she continued dating him—along with his two other women. She confided to me, "I'm forty-one years old and there just aren't that many great guys out there like him. I feel horrible not being the only woman in his life, but I think I'll feel worse if I don't take the chance he'll eventually want to be with me exclusively." I was appalled by her logic. I thought he would waste her time, break her heart, and take her self-respect. I said, "Forget about this guy. I'm not just your friend, I'm a professional dating coach—please listen to me!"

Well, it took three months for her guy to end things with his two other women. And now that I know him better, I actually think he's a great guy. He was just slow to fall in love, but eventually he did. Lucky for my friend, she didn't listen to *me*! (Note: She waited three months, not three *years*, for his priorities to change.)

3) DO THE MATH

When deciding whether to react with grace or gritted teeth to an overdue phone call from a guy you really like, it's important to calculate what you might gain versus what you might lose. This point is summarized perfectly in a book by my friend and fellow dating coach Evan Marc Katz:

> Suppose a situation comes up ... [he] cancel[s] a date, for instance. Now, certainly, that could be a bad sign. He might have gotten a better offer. He might not be into you! You could try refusing to take his call for a while ... he might be fascinated by the challenge. You could arrange to go out with someone else and make sure he sees you. You could say something to one of his friends and wait for it to get back to him. At least he'd never be able to say he got the better of you.
>
> But suppose it's none of those things. Suppose he badly wanted to see you but work legitimately interfered—just like he told you it did—and he's looking forward to rescheduling. If you respond to him with any of [this] nonsense ... he's probably going to leave. And can you blame him?
>
> There comes a point at which ridiculous behavior apparently inspired by machinations you learned at the prom literally has *no chance* of benefiting you. It can attract *only* men who are bad news, and alienate *all* men who are good news. Its

only conceivable advantage is that it does leave you slightly less exposed because trying to [retaliate] will give you a certain illusion of control. Trust me, it's not worth it.[4]

Bottom line? Next time simply reply to his tardy call or e-mail with a casual "Hey, great to hear from you, how've you been?" And see where things go.

---

[4] *Why You're Still Single* by Evan Marc Katz and Linda Holmes, Plume Books, 2006, p. 57.

CHAPTER 5

You Lost Him at Hello

The Outtakes: The Funny, Rude, and Weird Things Men Said

Ultimately, dating requires a sense of humor. Here's a list of memorable outtakes from my Exit Interviews that didn't quite qualify as dating insights. These little romantic gems are the scenes that would have ended up on the cutting room floor, except they were too good to be missed.

> "She pushed corn onto her fork with her fingers."

> "She wore a sweater tied around her waist, which I assume was her attempt to disguise a fat ass."

> "I could probably sleep with four or five different women every week if I wanted to. But now I'm dedicated to the process of discovery rather than diversification."

"She had a small white hair sprouting off her jaw."

"I know girls like to be all delicate and everything when they eat on a date . . . I mean, I've seen a few girls who cut up a pizza slice and eat it with a fork. But this one girl and I were sharing chips and guacamole, and she broke a chip in half and tried to spear it with her fork for dipping . . . I am *not* making this up."

"When she leaned over, I saw a tag sticking out from her underwear. It showed size large. I don't want to sound superficial or anything, but that kind of turned me off. It made me think of 'granny panties.'"

"By the third date I always ask myself, 'Is this really going anywhere or is it my dick talking?'" [*What a hopeless romantic . . .*]

"She asked me if I wanted some gum, and then she tongued her used piece into my mouth. I think she thought it was sexy. It wasn't."

"The waiter came over to tell us the daily specials, and after each item he described, [she] enthusiastically proclaimed, 'YUM! YUM! YUM!' . . . It sort of grated on me."

"She was so hot that I was willing to put up with some crap to be with her. But at some point the crap is bigger than her hotness." [*Ladies, I present to you America's next poet laureate . . .*]

"She texted me at seven AM, 'I'm sending a big smile right over to you'—who is she, Mary friggin' Sunshine?"

"I heard her pee while she was talking to me on the phone."

"To be perfectly honest, I went out with her in the first place to test whether I really wanted to move in with my longtime girlfriend."

"My lip snagged on her tongue piercing . . . in my opinion, blood just doesn't belong on a first date, even a little bit."

"I didn't like the way her pubic hair grew outside her panties."

"She had just walked out of the ladies' room when we said hello for our blind date. I shook her hand and it was still a little wet, I guess from washing her hands . . . I know those air dryers aren't very effective, but a wet, clammy hand was kind of gross."

"Her cat threw up a hairball while I was sitting on the couch."

"She ordered red wine and told the waiter she wanted the 'peanut noir.'"

"Usually a glass of wine, or twenty years of marriage, is the only thing separating an annoying flaw from an endearing quirk."

"I think women should never eat whole fruit in front of a man. Apples, pears, or whatnot. It just can't be done delicately."

"She kept using slang like 'That sucks' or 'He's a brownnoser' or "I need to pee.' I can't imagine ever introducing her to my boss."

"She told me that I reminded her of her mother. That kind of threw me."

"After we finished eating, she called out to the waiter, picked up both of our plates, and handed them to him."

"She had something in her nose and kept messing with it."

"I eat very healthy and exercise a lot. She told me she's a junk-food junkie who never works out. I guess there's a chance I could reform her, but who wants to build-a-date?"

"I just don't like any fingers but my own in my butt."
[*Now that's a memorable first date!*]

Yes, it's a strange and wacky dating world out there . . . but I suppose you already knew that.

CHAPTER 6

Why He *Did* Call You Back

What Men Really Like

The danger with all this Exit Interview information is that you risk focusing too much on why he *might not* call you back at the expense of showing him why he *should* call you back. If you know how to avoid the traps and you decide a guy has potential, then the bulk of your date must be dedicated to showing him why you're fabulous in so many ways. For that, you don't need any tips from me; that's all about you.

It's easy to assume if you don't hear from a guy again that it's because something went wrong. But of course many things went right, and I heard plenty of those comments too. Below you'll find quotes extracted from my interviews that refer to all the little things men noticed and appreciated, sometimes illuminating the moment when they realized their date was special. Some quotes refer to the element of surprise: something a woman did unexpectedly that was cool, sassy, or covertly sensual. But I noticed something deeper too: a theme focused on small gestures women made that were thoughtful and considerate. This made me wonder: Do men actually want to marry "bitches" and women who "play it cool," as I've read in some popular advice books? Or do they really, deep down, just want someone *kind*?

Here's my theory about all the "kind" stories men revealed in this chapter: it's basically "like attracts like." The guy looking for a kind woman *understands* the importance of kindness and is most likely a kind person himself. Of course, there will be individual exceptions, but from what I've seen, the guys who stand the test of time—the ones who make the best husbands and continue treating you with respect after "I do"—are impressed during the dating phase with kindness and thoughtfulness. I can also tell you this: the vast majority of the divorced men who have hired me as their matchmaker in the past ten years have said the *number-one* thing they are looking for the next time around is **a kind person**.

The comments below touch on the memories that stood out favorably for men when I asked them, "What did you like about her?" or "How did you know she was special?" A few of these quotes describe the same woman they didn't call back, some refer to other women they dated for a while, and a few come from happily married men.

> The coolest girl I ever went out with suggested watching *The Texas Chain Saw Massacre* on Valentine's Day—very unique . . . [It] really surprised me.
> —Dale, age 26, Providence, RI

> When the restaurant hostess said something rude to us, I was upset. But [my date] calmed me down by saying, "Oh, it's not her fault. She's probably having a really bad night with this crowd." . . . I was very taken with her empathy. —Ron, age 32, New York, NY

We were kissing passionately on her sofa at the end of the date, when she slowed down, stood up confidently, and said we should say good night for now. She never once apologized or made excuses about why she put on the brakes. The women I'd dated before her usually said they were sorry for stopping or felt like they owed me an explanation if we didn't have sex. This one impressed me for her utter self-confidence. It's not like she was playing hard to get; she just made a decision and that was that. I had no doubt I wanted to see her again, and I'm sure she knew it. —Jordan, age 32, Burlington, VT

I'm forty-seven and have never been married. I liked her because she was the first woman in more than five years who didn't ask me, directly or indirectly, why I'm still single. —Charlie, age 47, Houston, TX

We met for coffee at Starbucks, and we were at that side bar—you know, where you put milk or sugar in your drink?—and she accidentally spilled a little sugar from the packet onto the countertop. No big deal, right? Except she actually took a napkin and wiped up after herself! I asked her why [she did that], and she told me it just seemed polite so the next person wouldn't have to look at someone else's mess. If it was me, I'd just leave whatever I spilled and figure the staff would clean it up . . . It was just a small thing, but it impressed me how thoughtful she was.
—Brian, age 34, Denver, CO

She spoke passionately for ten minutes about how the media distorts the truth . . . how she hates TV news. And finally I had to confess to her what I do for a living: I'm a producer at CNN. Without missing a beat, she replied, "So, I should send you my

résumé if any jobs open up at CNN?" I loved that
she could laugh at the awkward situation . . . and
didn't try to backpedal on her opinions.
—Jack, age 37, Atlanta, GA

As a doctor, I used to be on call several nights a
week. I was always exhausted, but I was really looking
forward to our first date. When I went to pick her
up, she invited me in for a quick glass of wine before
we drove to the restaurant. I sat down in this really
comfortable leather chair, and while she was in the
kitchen opening the wine, I actually fell asleep . . . But
she didn't get mad! Most gals would have taken
offense if their date fell asleep on them. Not only that,
she sat quietly for about twenty minutes and read a
book . . . When I woke up, she said she could see I
was exhausted and thought I could use a quick nap . . .
I'd never met someone so kind. We've been married
forty-six years.
—Murray, age 85, Denver, CO (a.k.a. my dad!)

I remember this little five-second gesture. I watched
as she put her hair up in a clip on top of her head. She
didn't fuss about how it looked—just swept up her
long hair and twirled it into a knot . . . She didn't need
a mirror. I thought, "She's very natural . . . very
comfortable in her own skin."
—Artie, age 26, San Diego, CA

I was blown away by her respect for other people! I'm
someone who's not always conscious of how I affect
others, but she so actively considers other people,
especially strangers. She mentioned something to me
shortly after we met that really impressed me:
whenever she stays at a hotel, she tidies up her room
before leaving so the maid won't be grossed out. I

know that probably sounds weird, but I loved it. She feels sorry for hotel maids because they have a hard and often disgusting job. If there's hair in the sink, she wipes it out. If there's a used Kleenex on the desk, she'll throw it away. She puts herself in the maid's shoes and tries to do her small part by not leaving one room dirty. I'd never heard anything so considerate! —Nigel, age 46, Minneapolis, MN

I just liked her ass. —Joel, age 37, Brunswick, ME

I had mentioned my favorite dessert was from this one shop that had the best chocolate walnut brownie. The next night she dropped off this brownie with my doorman, but the key was that she did a drive-by. Most girls would have used it as an excuse to hang out, or worse, to check up on me. I liked the gesture because it was actually focused on doing something nice for *me*. —Thor, age 45, Dallas, TX

I joke that she's a Boy Scout: always prepared. [On our first date,] she had this big purse she carried; throughout the night she pulled everything you can imagine out of that thing. I sneezed? She had a tissue. I ate garlic? She had a breath mint. I wanted to write something down? She had an extra pen. Later I couldn't find my car keys in a dark lot, and she pulled out a mini-flashlight! . . . Most girls expect to be taken care of . . . I thought, "She's a girl I could be stranded on a desert island with." —Carson, age 52, Portland, OR

She liked being totally surprised. For example, she never let anyone tell her a plot summary of a book or movie they recommended—not even one or two sentences. This was the opposite of other women I'd met who have jaded attitudes like, "Nothing surprises me anymore." —Charlie, age 30, St. Louis, MO

She borrowed my pen to write down an author we were discussing and later made a point of remembering to give me back my pen. I hate it when people forget to return my pen; I was a waiter one summer and everyone always took my pen! I never had a pen! . . . She seemed like a considerate person. —Perry, age 46, Philadelphia, PA

I told her I'd always dreamed about quitting my job and becoming a children's book author, even though it was unlikely that a writing career would ever pay the bills. The next day she dropped off a book in my mailbox called *How to Publish Your Children's Book.* Inside she inscribed, "Go for it!" . . . I knew she didn't care about money and would always be a cheerleader for my dreams. —Franklin, age 52, San Francisco, CA

She lightly put her hand on my arm when I said something funny . . . it made me feel like a million bucks. —Kevin, age 35, Miami, FL

We went to her neighborhood gelato shop after dinner, and I asked her what her favorite flavor was. She told me, "Cappuccino." But then she ordered banana fudge. I asked her why she didn't order her favorite, and she said, "I make myself try a new flavor every time." . . . I liked that; someone who tries new things. —Tyson, age 49, New York, NY

After dinner I wanted to do something fun . . . something different; but I didn't have any good ideas. I asked her if she had any suggestions, and she said, "Let's find some bubble wrap and dance on it!" It was such a unique idea—I'd never heard anything like it . . . She had a *fun* attitude about life. —Collin, age 27, Seattle, WA

On the phone before we met, I happened to mention that I never drink diet soda because I'm worried about the unknown effects of saccharine. When I went to pick her up for our first date, she offered me a drink. She opened her refrigerator, and while I saw plenty of Diet Coke in there, she said, "Would you like regular Coke or water?" I realized she remembered that I don't drink diet soda. . . . I was impressed she had really *listened* to me on the phone.
—Calvin, age 61, Princeton, NJ

We went to a Picasso exhibit at the art museum and they handed us a paper brochure to guide us through the exhibit. At the end, everyone else tossed the brochure in the trash, but she walked it over to the desk and handed it back to be reused. I asked her if she was recycling the paper, and she said, "Not really—it's just a waste of money to throw out all those expensive brochures." I like a girl who knows how to be frugal! —Aidan, age 29, Philadelphia

She moved to my side of the booth when dessert arrived. I loved that because I wasn't sure she liked me. When she did that, I knew she felt the same chemistry I did. —Jeffrey, age 36, New York, NY

I liked that she kept me in my place—in a playful way. . . . She had some attitude.
—Stephen, age 42, Dallas, TX

Her hair smelled like my summer camp.
—Neil, age 36, Albany, NY

Actually, I have no idea why I called her again. She tripped down some stairs, and I thought she was clumsy. She stepped in dog poop, which stunk up my

new car. And she ordered *three* plates of this
Parmesan cheese appetizer she couldn't get enough
of. I just really liked her in spite of all that. We've
been married now for fifteen years.
—Dean, age 39, Raleigh, NC

She had me at her sixth Diet Dr Pepper.
—Brad Greenwald, age 45, Denver, CO
(a.k.a. my husband)

Of course, every man is touched by something different! Feel free to recycle any of the memorable moments here if the mood seems right on your next date. But often you'll never know what little words or gestures will make an impact on him; you can't always plan the ways you're amazing.

 **CHAPTER 7**

Why *You* Didn't
Call *Him* Back

Top Five Date-Breakers (for Women) During a First Date

Even though most men don't buy self-help books and are unlikely to read this chapter, I couldn't resist asking why *you* declined second dates with men. I asked for your date-breakers, and the stories poured in!

I collected this data by e-mailing requests to female clients, friends, and acquaintances asking for reasons they declined second dates. I asked them to forward my e-mail to their own network of female friends, and the survey bounced across the globe. I tallied responses from the first 100 women who replied, which yielded 145 "primary" reasons for declining a second date (an average of 1.45 reasons per declined second date). The women in my survey come from twenty-three states and six countries, with ages ranging from twenty-one to sixty-eight. The top five themes reported were strong and consistent (see Exhibit B

at the end of the notes section for data details). I think these stereotypes echo the general female sentiment about men.

#1 REASON SHE DIDN'T CALL HIM BACK
The Puppy Dog

Women complained in droves about men who were too eager to
please them. Men who were "too nice" often appeared desperate or
weak. They didn't have "an edge." And their "gushing" early e-mails
with excessive flattery were a turnoff.

Emily, a thirty-nine-year-old writer from Boston, MA, said
about one man, "Eagerness can be flattering, but this felt a little
desperate . . . it became annoying. Also, because it was a first date,
[I think] it had more to do with a fantasy about me than me."
Hillary, a thirty-five-year-old magazine editor from New York,
NY, remarked, "I went out with him in the first place because he
was so complimentary to me. I thought I should give him a chance.
Normally I like a man who doesn't play games, but the flattery really became overkill." Karen, a twenty-eight-year-old health care
consultant in Madison, WI, sighed, "He looked like a sad puppy
when I said good night."

Liz, a forty-one-year-old language translator from Sherman
Oaks, CA, told me about a guy who sent such effusive e-mails after
they met that she "was disappointed to receive them." She said, "I
wanted the polite, even enthusiastic thank-you along with a compliment or two, but not the over-gush. I guess I wanted him to maintain a little mystery." Jenna, a thirty-three-year-old graphic designer
in Miami, commented, "He was too nice, too transparent . . . he
didn't *intrigue* me."

Emma, a twenty-five-year-old advertising associate in London,
England, described a guy she could have "walked all over." And
Shannon, a thirty-eight-year-old accountant from Cincinnati, OH,
remembered declining a third date with a too-nice guy who came to
her office after she got promoted. He spent hours organizing her

files and brought her a congratulations plant. She said, "He was so good on paper, but he acted kind of subservient."

Isn't it interesting how The Puppy Dog cited by women is basically the reverse of the top reason cited by men (The Boss Lady)?

#2 REASON SHE DIDN'T CALL HIM BACK
The Yuck Factor

I enjoyed (and by "enjoyed" I mean "cringed") hearing the anecdotes from women about men who were grooming-challenged and bad kissers.

Although many of these problems could be fixed, there was no lust reported for the guy "whose skanky toenails protruded from his open-toed sandals" (always a bad first-date shoe choice, in any case) or several men with horrific halitosis. Carla, a forty-year-old single mom from Tucson, AZ, described a "super fun, intelligent, and wildly successful, jet-owning entrepreneur" with whom she had a fantastic first date. "But," she said, "he had this crazy, blond Albert Einstein hair and was seriously overweight. I just wasn't attracted to him." I asked her, "Is he hopeless? Is there *anything* he could do in the future to attract someone like you . . . especially given all his other qualities?" She replied, "I suppose he could employ a personal stylist . . . or just look in the mirror."

Apparently certain men could use a nose-hair clipper to avoid repulsing women "who can't stomach the idea of kissing them." And Marla, a thirty-seven-year-old marketing planner from Long Island, NY, couldn't figure out what the odor was when she kissed her new beau, Ethan. Later she saw his dog jump up to greet him by licking his face and realized Ethan's mouth smelled like dog saliva.

It's surprising how many bad kissers are roaming around. One successful Yale grad was described as "kissing like a blowfish who attached himself to my face." A prominent forty-year-old Dallas, TX, attorney received this review: "It felt like he was swabbing the inside of my mouth!" (Maybe he was trying to secure a DNA sample?) Another woman wondered, "Seriously, how does a man get to be thirtysomething years old and still kiss like a guppy? How did other attractive women he dated, a few whom I know personally, get past his disgusting lip-sucking to appreciate an otherwise smart and interesting man?"

#3 REASON SHE DIDN'T CALL HIM BACK
The Garbage Man

Men can't possibly think it's appealing when garbage spills from their mouths—when they make lewd, crude, sexual comments to women they barely know—can they? This category also included the lines they tossed out in their feeble attempts to get women into bed.

Jennifer, a thirty-four-year-old marketing consultant from Boston, MA, told me about a guy she met through Match.com for a 4:00 PM date at Starbucks. She said, "[He started] undressing me with his eyes . . . saying how beautiful I looked, how sexy my outfit was, exactly one minute into the date. It freaks me out when guys jump into sexual thoughts too fast, especially over an innocent hot chocolate in the middle of the afternoon!" She said men should wait until the tail end of a date: "If he feels it's gone well, he can make comments that are sweet and nonthreatening, like, 'You're really cute" or "I was glad you're as attractive in real life as you are in your online photos." As opposed to the guy who Beth—a twenty-eight-year-old makeup consultant in Los Angeles, CA—went out with. She remembered having a great date with someone who called her the next day and purred, "I got a boner after that good-night kiss last night." (Where did this guy go to finishing school?)

Laurie, a thirty-three-year-old freelance book editor in New York, NY, talked about her big disappointment after a great date with "a seriously cute, funny, interesting chef." His e-mails became "quickly and increasingly suggestive . . . gross instead of sexy/romantic. I mean, I'm no prude; a little bedroom talk is swell, but there is a line in the sand . . . he [sounded like] a pervert." Eileen, a thirty-seven-year-old doctor from Providence, RI, talked about one guy who called her right after a nice evening. When she mentioned she was in her pajamas and just about to go to sleep, he said, "I'd *love* to get into your pajamas." She said, "I actually gagged."

Mary, a twenty-one-year-old student from Hanover, NH, said, "I am extremely turned off by compliments about my body, especially early in the date . . . perhaps guys think it's flattering, but [more likely] they assume it's the ticket to sleeping with me."

Maureen, a fifty-one-year-old travel agent living in Sydney, Australia, echoed the common female sentiment about men who curse on a date: "They seem unpolished, and lacking in class and intelligence."

#4 REASON SHE DIDN'T CALL HIM BACK
The Not-So-Macho Man

It's a timeless expectation, no matter how modern women are: they want a guy to generally act like a "traditional" guy. Women want, and expect, chivalry, career success, and a take-charge attitude.

The expectations of the women who complained about chivalry ranged from low to high. Women gave their suitors demerits for everything from ordering his drink first, to charging ahead first on a narrow sidewalk, to expecting to "go Dutch" at Starbucks (classy!). Christine, a forty-two-year-old attorney from Houston, TX, talked about the awkward dinner-check issue. She said she refused a second date with a man who allowed her to split the bill. She said, "Perhaps this is old-fashioned, and I am a successful lawyer with a good income, but I still think a gentleman should be a gentleman. I always offer, but I don't actually expect him to accept." Heather, a thirty-four-year-old woman who works for a sports apparel company in Greenwich, CT, said, "Although it would be nice to be financially supported by a man, I don't expect it. At the same time, I don't want to support *him*. I would at least like us to be equals."

Other women said turnoffs included men who were "stuck in a career rut" or who "lacked passion for their job." A thirty-one-year-old woman from New York, NY, mentioned dating "a small-potato actor with a day job in construction." She said, "I don't care what someone does for a living, as long as they do it well." She clarified that her guy in particular had no acting success beyond a bachelor's degree in theater, and he wasn't even trying to work his way up in the construction business. He was not ambitious in any arena. Marianne, a forty-three-year-old consultant in Indianapolis, IN, said that being a very successful woman has serious drawbacks. Lately she's been attracting men who "are taking pages out of Pamela Harriman's biography . . . trying to marry for fun and profit. These men view marriage as a career, just like women have done through the ages."

Then I heard about the "wimps." When men defied the traditional male characteristics of strength and confidence, they were rejected right and left. Allison, a thirty-three-year-old brand manager in Boulder, CO, remembered a guy who wouldn't make a plan. "He didn't ask, 'Would you like to go to dinner on Thursday night?' Instead he pulled that wishy-washy crap like he was afraid I'd say no: 'How about sometime . . . maybe let me know when you're free . . . call me later if you want to go out.'" Other complaints were voiced about guys on dating websites who send "winks" or brief one-liners such as "You're cute." Women felt strongly that those gestures were wimpy (not to mention lazy): they wanted full sentences and someone who had the confidence to put himself out there.

#5 REASON SHE DIDN'T CALL HIM BACK
The Mr. Big

Last, but certainly not least, I heard about the just-so-full-of-themselves guys. They were often the male equivalent of The One-Way Street.

Sometimes the behavior was insensitive. Linda, a fiftysomething investment analyst from Aspen, CO, said, "He was completely inward focused. He never asked me a single thing about myself . . . what a turnoff." Other women labeled these men "self-absorbed" or possessing no real interest in who they are. I loved the demure comment I received from Pauline, a thirty-five-year-old history teacher in Portland, OR, who was generous enough to give her date the benefit of the doubt: "He was so excited for me to get to know him better, he forgot to ask me anything about my own interests."

Often the behavior verged on arrogant. Serena, a forty-six-year-old architect in Cleveland, OH, remembered two bad dates. Once she was fixed up on a blind date with a man she later coined "Dr. Congratulations." He was a dynamic Italian doctor who ran an AIDS clinic in a tough neighborhood. She was impressed with his background and excited to meet him. But at the end of their dinner, he looked at her and said, "Congratulations, I'd like to see you again." Another time she met a man she labeled "Mr. Lucky-You." She met him through JDate and he later told her, "I usually don't date women over thirty-five because I want kids, but I'd be willing to take you out again."

And then I heard about the Big Men On Campus. They were the guys who were terminally stuck in the glory days of high school or college. Nicole, a twenty-seven-year-old international business student from Seattle, WA, laughed about the guy who spent the entire evening telling her about all the times he and his buddies got drunk in high school and pulled various stunts. "So immature; what a loser!" she said. Charlotte, a thirty-nine-year-old nonprofit fundraiser in Philadelphia, PA, was turned off by the guy who went on and on about playing football at Texas A&M . . . *twenty-one years ago.* And I could just picture poor Lara—a twenty-five-year-old art gallery assistant in San Francisco, CA—who suffered through a blind date with the guy she nicknamed "Too-Cool Tahoe." He had the car he'd been driving since his fraternity days in college: a souped-up, flashy Tahoe with sparkling new rims and ridiculous shiny chrome accents. He had the windows down, his mirrored shades on, and his baseball hat turned backward. She said, "His 50 Cent CD was blaring as we bumped our way to Jamba Juice for a 'date.' It was so embarrassing . . . the most I can say about him is that he paid for my juice!"

Two Observations

One trend I observed within the women's stories was that they were more likely than men to take a chance on a **first date** even if they didn't think there was an initial physical attraction. Women, especially after age thirty, often described their pre-first-date attitudes in this way: "He didn't look like someone I'd typically be interested in [*because he's too short, bald, old, skinny, potbellied, etc.*], but I gave it a try." One woman phrased it this way: "I'm trying to notice the *second* guy in the room, rather than the first, because the first guy who catches my eye never seems to work out." On the other hand, men usually described their pre-first-date attitudes like this: "Her photo was attractive" or "My friend said she was hot so I asked her out." These different attitudes led to one surprising distinction among the reasons why men and women declined **second dates**: *women* cited physical reasons more often than *men*. Of course the importance of physical attraction can't be dismissed for men or women, but when it came to **first dates**, women were allowing for the possibility that personality traits might overcome physical liabilities. As you'd expect, sometimes that open-minded attitude paid off; sometimes it didn't.

I also noticed that the word "annoyed" kept appearing frequently throughout women's anecdotes (e.g., "I became completely annoyed with him"). So I decided for fun to scan and count the number of times the words "annoy," "annoyed," or "annoying" appeared across the 145 anecdotes shared by the 100 women. The tally? The word surfaced fifty-eight times! I have no idea what that really means; I can only conclude that men are really annoying.

The Outtakes

Men say and do the darndest things! Below are a few of my favorite lines from the stories women shared with me.

"He told me, 'Salad gives me gas, so I think I'll order something else.'"

"He was so boring that I actually started wondering, 'Would it really be *that* rude if I just pulled out my book and started reading right now?'"

"He was just plain stupid. My online profile name is 'CuteDoc' and I had mentioned several times in our e-mails that I was a doctor. When he picked me up, he asked me what I did for a living. I thought, 'Well, maybe he forgot.' So I said, 'I'm a radiologist.' And he replied, 'Is that a doctor?'" [*No, it's somebody who works at Radio Shack . . .*]

"There's a fine line between dating a guy who's sensitive and dating a guy who's a *girl*."

"I had mentioned in my online profile that I had blue-green eyes. When I arrived for our lunch date, he insisted we walk outside into the sunlight so he could actually verify my eye color. I had to stand up and walk outside the restaurant with him for an inspection."

"He called me and said, 'Hi! That was really fun last night . . . Guess where I'm calling you from now?' So I said playfully, 'Where?' And then he flushed the toilet." [*Hard to believe this guy was still single . . .*]

"We went to a movie and he pulled his shirt up over his nose. He sat there like that during the whole movie, with no explanation. Very strange! I know this may surprise you, but this was a deal-breaker for me."

"In all seriousness, on our third date, he said before he could feel comfortable falling for me, he wanted to know if he could call my ex-husband to ask him a few questions about the reasons for our divorce."

"Hey, I'm okay with wearing a nurse's uniform if it's part of a sexual fantasy, but I'm sure not going to play nursemaid to these old guys with health problems . . . I hope I don't sound mean."

"He showed up wearing a bright purple fanny pack."

"When the waiter delivered his plate, he promptly took his knife and fork and cut every last bit of his food into bite-sized pieces, not talking to me the whole time."

"I'm not saying eating big pizza slices is ever easy in front of other people, but watching him hold up his slice above his face as it oozed cheese, with his tongue jutting out underneath as he slowly wiggled and curled his tongue around the triangle tip, wasn't exactly sexy."

"I didn't go out with him again because of what I call his 'foreploy'—he misrepresented himself for the purposes of getting laid."

"We were watching a movie and I saw him wipe his runny nose with the back of his hand, then reach into the popcorn bag we were sharing. This was not cool with me."

"After a romantic first date, he asked me a rather surprising question: whether or not I had a problem with him being *married*."

"Why didn't I call him back? Well, I left a voice message on an answering machine, but with those stupid automated message systems that drone impersonally, 'Leave-a-message-at-the-beep'—without any personalized greeting—I actually have no idea whether I called *him* back or someone else!"

"He stood up from the table and said, 'I have to go to the little boys' room . . . number *two*."

As these quotes from single women underscore, you certainly don't **want** a second date with every guy. What you want are options to cherry-pick the good ones.

CHAPTER 8

Exit Interviews Get Personal

So, are you ready to hear why he didn't call *you* back?

It's great to read what men are saying about other women, and hopefully it has triggered some introspection. But this reminds me of a line by my favorite comedian, Steven Wright: "I've been doing a lot of abstract painting lately. Extremely abstract. No brush, no paint, no canvas. I just think about it." While this book is structured to help you think about your own missteps by reading what happened on other people's dates, I strongly encourage you to personalize this process. Because when the right guy comes along for you, there's no room for error.

Okay, I know what you're going to say—it's what every woman says initially: "I'd rather die than have someone interview my ex-dates!" But let's face it: we live in a feedback culture today. From Amazon.com customer reviews, to eBay seller ratings, to viewer voting on *American Idol*, to TripAdvisor and hotel guest-satisfaction surveys, to automated telephone recordings that warn "This call

> **We live in a feedback culture today . . . [it's] normal in every other part of our lives.**

may be recorded for training purposes," feedback is normal in every other part of our lives. Many women would feel comfortable seeking feedback in a work context (calling back prospective clients to ask why they took their business elsewhere, or calling job recruiters to ask why they hired someone else), yet never in a million years would these same women allow someone to seek feedback from a *date*. It's ironic because dating is perhaps the most important area where feedback can literally change your life.

After ten years of experience with Exit Interviews, please believe me when I tell you that **Exit Interviews are more empowering than embarrassing**. It's proactive, not desperate, to get answers and make improvements—as you probably do every day in your job. And in the dating world, I'm not suggesting you make the calls yourself; you need a third party to get the feedback for you (more on this later). Of course no one *ever* enjoys having an ex-date called on her behalf, but it is a means to an end. Just like getting vaccines is a means to prevent diseases (and no one likes having a needle jabbed in her arm). If you truly want to find the right mate, it can be extremely helpful to bite the bullet and find out what's really going on during and after your dates. Uncovering the gap between your perceptions and his perceptions will enable you to find your mate quickly and efficiently.

Remember, according to my research, 90 percent of women are wrong when they guess why their date didn't call back. You may have a recurring pattern of which you are completely unaware (or perhaps now are a little suspicious about) that is sabotaging your dates and potential relationships. Why wonder needlessly when you can just get the information you need, direct from the source?

The Tower Window

Last May I spent a few days in Chicago. I stayed in a big downtown hotel, and my room was located on the thirty-seventh floor in the tower. I woke up the first morning at 8:00 AM because I had plans to walk around the city sightseeing with a friend. I looked out the window and wondered whether I should bring a jacket with me. I didn't want to lug one around all day if I didn't need it. I couldn't feel the air outside because the windows didn't open in my tower room, but I saw that the sun was shining. I reasoned that if it was sunny, and it was May, I wouldn't need a jacket. When I emerged later from the lobby, I discovered to my chagrin that the air outside was freezing! It wasn't what I expected; I hadn't known about the wind chill. I was already late to meet my friend and didn't have time to go all the way back to my room and grab a jacket. So I pretty much spent the whole day shivering and feeling miserable as we walked around the city.

Looking through a glass window from a tower doesn't give you an accurate perception of what's happening down on the sidewalk. Next time, I'm going to call the hotel concierge directly and simply ask for the weather report. Information is power!

Four Out of Five Dentists Agree

One common objection I hear about getting feedback from dates is that every guy is different: what bothers one person will attract someone else. I touched on this issue under the "Time Out" heading in the chapter 3 section on The Closer, but let's consider another example now. Here are two different perspectives about one incident at a restaurant where a waiter refills a woman's water glass and she doesn't acknowledge his service. In one scenario, a guy might observe the woman's silence to the waiter and think, "She was so rude! She didn't even thank the waiter when he refilled her glass." But in another scenario, a guy might observe the same behavior from the woman and think, "I loved how she was totally focused on me—she didn't even notice when the waiter refilled her glass!"

Sure, there is a lid for every pot . . . but what if four out of five guys saw the same restaurant incident above and thought she was rude? Then one guy is no longer an anomaly—there's a definite "rude" vibe she emits or a Bitch-in-Boots stereotype she reinforces. And that's all you need to find out: are your no-callbacks a pattern or simply a few random situations in which you said "potato" and he heard "zucchini"? If it's a pattern, then you probably want to do something about it.

If you agree to some Exit Interviews, what's the worst that could happen? The way I see it is that you'll find out a few misperceptions men have about you (or accurate perceptions you should address), you'll make some adjustments on your upcoming dates, and suddenly you'll have *too many* guys calling you back for second dates. At that point, you'll need to give men packets of Kleenex to absorb the river of tears they're crying because you're turning down nine out of ten offers. To me, Kleenex is the worst-case scenario.

Remember, you don't have to call your former dates yourself. You are going to ask someone to do it for you because a third person is more likely to get honest feedback. You can select any friend or relative (female or male) who meets the following four criteria: they must be outgoing, bold, perceptive, and able to put people at ease. If no one you know fits the bill, consider connecting with another single woman to "swap calls" or hiring a trained professional. (Check my website at www.whyhedidntcallyouback.com.)

Your Exit Interviewer should call at least three to six men who either never called (or never e-mailed) you after a first date or broke things off with a glib excuse (e.g., "We didn't have enough in common"). They should be men whom you would have liked to hear from again, expected to hear from again, or at least felt weren't ogres. Ideally these are men you've dated in the last two years, and they represent a variety of personalities, situations, and sourcing (i.e., online and offline introductions).

Coaching Your Interviewer

Exit Interviewing is not exactly a skill you'll find on most people's résumés. Thus, if you don't hire a trained professional, it's vital to spend time coaching your interviewer on what to do. Emphasize these three things:

1) She was selected for the job specifically because you are seeking *the truth* about how men perceive you on dates. You don't want anything sugarcoated; she is one of the few people in your life who tells it like it is. You promise not to shoot the messenger.

2) Explain the glib or politically correct reasons that men typically provide in the beginning: "No chemistry," "Wasn't my type," "Busy at work," "Started dating someone else," and "It wasn't her, it was me." Provide her with the probes listed in Sample A (at the end of this chapter) to get past those smoke screens. And tell her that if a guy struggles to come up with helpful answers, she can use this line: "I'll give you a minute to think about it." Then if she stays completely silent for about twenty seconds, she will inevitably get *something* useful out of him. He'll come clean just to break that uncomfortable silence.

3) The guys who help out (and probably 80 percent will) are doing you "a favor." Make sure your interviewer is gracious, solicitous, enthusiastic, and not defensive on your behalf. She should make no excuses, only listen and ask clarifying questions.

Then make a copy of the suggested script in Sample A directly from this book, or create your own script using Sample A as a template. Give it to your interviewer with names and contact information for your ex-dates. Also give your interviewer the voice mail/e-mail script in Sample B to use if she encounters voice mail or prefers to establish via e-mail an advance phone time with your ex-date (this is highly recommended). These scripts are deliberately vague, designed to "hook" the interviewee by piquing his curiosity, thus increasing the odds he will reply.

Remember to have your interviewer write down your guesses up front about why *you think* these men didn't call back, so you can compare them later with the actual responses compiled.

Have some fun with this process too. Since there is no statute of limitations on Exit Interviews, why not take this opportunity to find out why that one guy in high school or college suddenly lost interest? Since you have a willing interviewer lined up, seize the moment! Track down that old flame and have your interviewer ask the question you've wondered about all these years. Maybe you can finally get some closure.

What to Do with Exit Interview Results

Encourage your Exit Interviewer to take notes during her conversations, but have her wait to call you with the feedback until she has aggregated all the data. It will be more helpful if you know whether only one out of five men versus four out of five men made particular comments.

This information is not always easy to handle but will make all the difference in helping you avoid the same mistakes going forward. Be sure to consistently encourage your Exit Interviewer to be completely honest with you and not hold anything back. As she relays the feedback to you, try to keep a neutral demeanor (don't be defensive or give excuses), even if you feel like you've just been kicked in the stomach. Otherwise, your interviewer will instinctively start to edit the feedback.

Realize that this feedback typically isn't about the *real* you, it's more like a *performance review* of the first impression you make. How a date perceives you isn't that different from how a client perceives you at work. For example, when your boss gives you your annual review, she might mention that while you're doing a great job, there's just one thing you could work on. It turns out that during your client presentations you tend to fiddle with a pen while you're speaking. She worries that the fidgeting distracts the clients from your smart marketing ideas. When you left your boss's office, you'd probably think her comment was helpful, be glad someone pointed it out to you, and stop fiddling with your pen in your next presentation.

Negative feedback is never easy to handle in any situation, even if it's superficial. But keep your eyes on the prize, and know that anything you hear is only helping you achieve your goal of finding the right partner. And be sure to ask your interviewer up front to conclude her feedback call to you with some *positive* comments from the men as well.

I want you to listen carefully to any negative feedback and treat it seriously, but use your judgment and always take it with a grain of salt. Of course some men who exited your life will have many problems and issues of their own, and you will not necessarily respect all their opinions. If only one guy said you talked too much about yourself, you should be conscious of that going forward, but don't assume it's a major issue. But if four out of five men said you were too aggressive, you either need to make some adjustments in your behavior or pick different types of guys who would consider that trait as a plus. Brainstorm with your interviewer some solutions and ways to improve.

No pain, no gain . . . remember that as you're going through this process to visualize turning down lots of second dates in the future while you concentrate on getting to know one Mr. Potential you really like.

SAMPLE A
Suggested Dating Exit Interview Script

Hi, this is Susan. I'm calling about Laura Smith. Do you remember meeting her on Match.com about a month ago—she's the lawyer from Boston who just moved to San Diego? I only need five minutes of your time. I'm her _____ [friend/sister/coach] trying to help her better understand her dating patterns. Okay, I know this phone call may seem *unusual* [laugh here!], but she told me you're a thoughtful guy and I'm hoping you can shed some light about why you two never went out again. It's no big deal to her that things didn't work out, but I really care about her and want her to find the right relationship. So I convinced her to let me call five guys she dated to hear what kind of first impression she makes. I think your feedback could *really* help her find more successful relationships in the future.

Most important, I have so many great single friends! If you can help me better understand what you *are* looking for, I might be able to introduce you to someone else fantastic.

She said she values your opinion, so I'd be very grateful if you would spend a few minutes talking openly with me. I'm calling a few other men too, and I will group all the results together so she won't know specifically who said what (unless you tell me it's okay to share some details with her). Just let me know anything that you prefer to stay confidential.

I'd appreciate your candor in answering some questions: [*Interviewer to probe for details after each answer provided*]

1) In your mind, how would you rate the date on a scale of 1 to 10? What could have made it a 10?

2) What was your first impression when you met her?

3) How was she different than you expected?

4) How would you describe her now that you've spent a few hours with her?

5) What were her best qualities?

6) What qualities could she most improve upon?

7) What was the main reason you decided not to pursue her?

8) Were there any other reasons you decided not to pursue her?

9) If you were her straight-talking best friend, what advice would you give her for future dates?

10) Can you describe a date with a different woman that went well?

11) [*Insert questions here about any specific problem areas that concern you about your friend.*]

Thanks so much for your time and honesty! This has been *very* helpful and I know it will really provide some good insights for her. And I am going to give some serious thought about whether any of my other girlfriends might be a good match for you, if you're interested. If you have any other thoughts that you'd like to share with me after we hang up, here is my phone number and my e-mail address:

_____

260 | Rachel Greenwald

SAMPLE B
Suggested Voice Mail/E-mail Script

Hey John!

I'm a friend of Laura Smith. She gave me your contact info because she thought you'd be perfect to answer a few questions I have about single men. She said you're great, and I'd love the chance to pick your brain for five minutes by phone sometime today or tomorrow. Also, I might have someone fabulous you should meet. Here are my numbers—can we set up a time? I *really* appreciate it—I'm sure you're superbusy. I look forward to hearing back from you. Thanks so much!

Susan Jones

 **CHAPTER 9**

Success Stories

This chapter demonstrates how getting dating feedback helped three women meet the right man and fall in love. Among hundreds of success stories I've witnessed from my clients and the women who send e-mails to my website every day, I selected these three very different case studies to demonstrate the power of Exit Interviews. These women did the work and found their happy endings—and so can you.

Julia

As a newly promoted senior editor at a large Manhattan publishing company, Julia's career was taking flight. But at age twenty-eight, her number one goal (when she was really honest with herself) was to be in a serious relationship that could lead to marriage. She was perplexed that she could be so successful at work but not successful in love.

Julia hired me as her dating coach. I was eager to hear why she felt she needed my help, because I quickly assessed her as a 9 out of 10 on a first-impressions scale. She was pretty, smart, and personable. As we discussed her dating history, Julia said that only two of her last seven dates had called her back. This woman should have had a stronger dating retention rate from what I could see, so I set out to discover what was going on. For my Exit Interviews, she (hesitantly) provided me with the names of five men she had dated in the past year who had not called her back. While not all of them were potential Mr. Rights, she had nevertheless assumed those particular five men would ask her out again. In her opinion, those first dates were either "good" or "great."

I quickly learned one cold fact about Julia from the men I called: she fell into the "I wanted to hire her, not date her" trap. The general feedback I received about her was that she was terrific, just the kind of woman the men admired. They described her as assertive, confident, and smart. All five men were professionals in the finance, media, or law industries. Having spoken to them extensively, I can tell you they sounded impressed with—not intimidated by—her. But as one man reluctantly admitted, "I don't see myself coming home to that after a hard day at work." Call it what you will—chauvinistic or old-fashioned—but this is what they told me, their truth (and Julia's reality).

One guy said, "There's a fine line between having a backbone and being a ball buster . . . I don't know her very well, but I think she might be on the wrong side of that line for me." Another ex-date explained it this way: "Work is a battleground, and for me, home is meant for relaxing . . . sort of recharging. It's not that I want a 1950's wife—I'm definitely looking for someone smart and interesting, and I'm sure she'll have a career . . . but I want her personality to be warm . . . you know, not domineering."

One example from Gary seemed best to illustrate Julia's date behavior. On their first date, Gary and Julia attended a music performance at the 92nd Street Y. When they arrived, Julia pointed out one of the singers she knew across the room and said, "Hey, look, there's Rex Carlisle." Gary looked over and said, "Oh, that looks like Rex Carlisle, but actually it's Harry James. I just met him last weekend at a party." Julia replied, "No, that's Rex Carlisle. I saw his picture in the newspaper yesterday. I'm positive." They debated the man's identity, both convinced they were correct. According to Gary, Julia became increasingly insistent, capping off the debate with "Let's make a bet right now! Ten bucks says that's Rex Carlisle. I'll go over right now and talk to him." He said that he wished she had "a softer approach to the disagreement—maybe something like 'Well, they look similar, I'm pretty sure it's Rex Carlisle, but it's not important. Let's enjoy the concert . . .' and then changed the subject." But Gary told me that it no longer mattered whether it was Harry or Rex: after that brief exchange, combined with two other issues he had already observed since he had picked her up (she assertively tried to hail the taxi instead of letting him do it, and she had argued about something with the coatcheck attendant), he had decided he wouldn't be asking Julia out again. He said he glimpsed the future with her and it looked "exhausting."

Unfair? Maybe Gary's too demanding or Julia's too bossy. Maybe they just aren't a match—sure, it happens. Yet before dismissing their potential, consider whether Julia could have presented her soft side first. And she *does* have a soft side. In my exchanges with her, she seems caring and sensitive. At work she's used to (and rewarded for) being a "tiger," but most single men I speak to are more charmed initially by women who are warm and compassionate. Later the tiger can come out—and it's usually an intriguing dimension to keep things interesting over the long run. But again, he can't get to know all of you if he doesn't want a second date.

It's hard to switch aspects of your personality off and on, yet Julia is the first to admit she has many faces and moods. Of course we all do. When I asked Julia in advance of the Exit Interviews what she predicted Gary would say, she had guessed he wasn't over his ex-girlfriend. He had mentioned a recent, devastating breakup and still seemed hurt. When I debriefed her (with Gary's permission), she barely remembered the concert performer debate. And she explained that she'd tried to hail a taxi because Gary wasn't being aggressive enough to snag one during rush hour . . . she didn't want to be late for the concert. And she said the coat-check attendant was rude to her. But she never thought any of those "trivial" things could be date-breakers.

Fortunately, Julia took her feedback to heart. She acted on what she needed to do to succeed in the dating game (versus the career game). On dates, she toned down her assertive argument style and consciously tried to maintain a sense of playfulness instead of debate. She kept the conversation away from her work projects (where she found herself most likely to get riled up), and focused on discussing her other interests, such as travel and music. She also took the edge off her workday with a couple sips of wine at home before she met someone for a date, which helped her relax and transition from work mode to social mode. And she let the guys hail taxis on first dates even if it took longer.

By tweaking her dating behavior, Julia quickly increased her callbacks. Following the Exit Interviews, she received invitations for second dates from three out of the next four men she met. Julia was only interested in one of those three men, so she graciously declined two offers (which she now had the option to do since the ball was in her court) and started dating Peter. A year and a half has passed, and Peter has come to know and love the "real Julia" (both tiger and kitten). The update? They are now living together and Julia says, "We are on the path to marriage."

Madison

A few years ago I was at the Canyon Ranch Spa in Arizona giving a dating lecture. During that weekend, I met a fabulous thirty-three-year-old woman from Santa Barbara, CA, named Madison. We found ourselves huffing and puffing side by side one morning on a hike (okay, I was the one huffing and puffing; Madison was in great shape and slowed down to chat with me). We discovered we had some mutual friends and hit it off immediately: she's one of those friendly, warm, genuine women who immediately becomes your new best friend. As we exchanged background information, I learned she'd graduated from an impressive college, had gone to Japan as a Fulbright Scholar in her early twenties, and currently worked as a management consultant. Her passion was biking, so she spent most of her free time mountain biking and attending cycling camps. She was attractive and single, and it wasn't long before our conversation turned to dating.

During our three-hour hike, Madison told me about numerous fix-ups and online dates that hadn't panned out for her. She was meeting a fair number of men, but she couldn't seem to move beyond the early dating stages. A few guys she liked had asked her out again but then stopped calling. She said her friends encouraged her to keep trying, saying it was only a matter of time before the right guy came along. But she was sick of dating and wanted to find love. When she asked my opinion about her situation, you can probably guess by now what I told her: "There's only one way to find out what's really going on here . . ."

Madison was basically horrified by my offer to conduct Exit Interviews with her ex-dates but thanked me for the "entertaining suggestion." Don't worry, I get that a lot; I wasn't offended. We parted ways after the weekend, kept in touch occasionally for two years, and then one day I received this short e-mail from her right after her thirty-fifth birthday: "I'm ready to find out. Will you make the calls for me?"

Madison sent me contact information for six of her ex-dates (including a few with whom she was still friends) and I diligently called each of them. Five were willing to talk to me, but I had a perplexing experience. All five men—those who hadn't called her back for second or third dates—*raved* about Madison. My phone calls were one praisefest after the next. And because I knew her personally, I obviously agreed with their comments: she was "really cool," "easy to talk to," "impressively fit," and "smart, outgoing, bubbly." No matter how long I stayed on the phone with them, no matter how many clever probes I used to pry constructive criticism from them, I couldn't figure out why they didn't want to date her.

Finally I saw the light during my last interview, with Carl, when I asked him, "What did you talk about with her during your first date?" He told me they spoke a lot about their mutual interest in biking. Madison shared her experience at a cycling camp she had attended in Colorado Springs, where she was coached by Lance Armstrong's trainer. She talked about her fitness training for an upcoming century ride, and how excited she was about placing second in the Danskin Women's Triathlon in Hawaii. He was certainly impressed—he didn't meet a lot of girls who were performance-level athletes. Carl said their second date was a twenty-mile bike ride along the Pacific Coast near her town house in Santa Barbara, and they'd had a great time even though he could barely keep up with her. He didn't sound intimidated by her though. "I just don't get it," I sighed. "Then *why* didn't you want to see her again?" His response was, "Oh, I'd love to *see* her again . . . I guess I just wasn't interested in *dating* her."

Carl went on to explain that Madison had everything he wanted, except when he looked at her, he "didn't want to ravish her." I was finally on to something that might help Madison, so I called back the other four men for follow-up conversations. This time around, I asked questions such as, "Do you remember what she wore on your date?" and "Can you give me three adjectives which best describe her?" and "What types of girls are you usually attracted to?" Here's what they said:

> "Our first date was a fifty-mile bike ride . . . She's in great shape . . . a real athlete . . . she wore bike shorts and a North Face tank top . . . she has really strong shoulders."

> "I'd love to keep in touch with her; she could really help me train for this Elephant Rock charity ride I'm doing in Colorado this summer . . . [the adjectives I'd use] to describe her would be 'fit,' 'healthy,' 'fun.'"

"She was just the type of person I'd want as my partner on *The Amazing Race* . . . but I wasn't feeling the physical chemistry."

"I usually go for someone more fashionable, more feminine . . . I like a girl who leads an active lifestyle, but nothing extreme. Maybe calves without sinewy muscles would be good?"

I heard more feedback from one of the guys whom Madison had met on a group adventure trip biking in Patagonia. While he wasn't technically a "former date," she had put him on my interview list. They had spent seven intense days together and she'd developed a crush on him. While the two of them were inseparable on the trip, he never even tried to kiss her. Now they were each back home in towns only forty-five minutes apart, and his e-mails remained platonic. She was brave to allow me to call this guy, especially since he didn't know she was romantically interested in him. He told me, "Look, I wish I was attracted to her—she's really a great girl and we have lots in common—but she falls into a buddy category for me."

This type of praise evoked The Blahs stereotype. Women can be perceived as great but something holds the man back. It's critical to discover what's really going on. In Madison's case, it turned out she had a unique form of The Blahs: The *Sensual* Blahs. And this was not something her female friends, including me, had picked up on when trying to guess why guys weren't calling her back. Everyone liked her, but when guys thought about her naked, they had images of a strong (maybe more masculine) body rather than a sexy, curvy woman. Men who had a "solid" first date with her weren't hopping off their indecision fence to pursue her romantically. Some of them had asked her out one or two more times because she's *such a great girl*, but nothing sparked.

When I relayed this feedback to Madison, she was hurt. Of course she would be. The fact that guys aren't lusting after her but would be happy to hang out with her isn't exactly what every woman wants to hear. Certainly there were other guys who had had romantic feelings for her in the past: she'd had two or three long-term boyfriends during and after college, as well as one guy she'd dated seriously in her early thirties. So her diagnosis was by no means unanimous. But if she could make some simple adjustments going forward, I was sure she could ignite romantic interest in the men she wanted. In the long run, I think most men want and appreciate a sporty girl—they just have to lust after her first.

Based on our subsequent tactical discussions, Madison made a number of changes. First, she wore skirts on dates, even for casual coffee dates. She bought some new outfits that were casual yet chic. Depending on the weather, she wore strappy sandals or stylish boots with a little heel, and a few pieces of small-scale jewelry. She wore nothing flashy, but her new clothes were more on the flirty side than her standard "bohemian" style.

Next, she changed some of the photos on her online dating profile; instead of three photos of her in various athletic/outdoor situations, she posted four new photos: one new head shot that I'd encouraged her to get from a professional photographer (it was stunning!), one wearing a dress at a formal party, one wearing jeans while sightseeing in Japan, and one wearing bike shorts at a cycling event. The photos were not misleading: they simply reflected a better ratio of her total personality and revealed the girly side of her first. Men who eventually met her in person would be predisposed to see her as more well-rounded than 100 percent sporty.

She steered the bulk of her conversation topics away from biking. While she absolutely shared *some* of her passion for biking—it was a big part of who she was—she was careful to monitor the bike talk so it didn't dominate more than a small part of the first or second date. And Madison would be the first to acknowledge that cycling isn't her entire life. She has many interests and dimensions and was happy to chat about other things.

She avoided bike rides as the venue for early-stage dates, steering men instead toward evening dinners where the setting was more cozy and where a cocktail could prompt a flirty mood. And finally she became more conscious of her sensuality. She traded in her sporty nylon bra for a lacy bra with more support. She did *not* start wearing low-cut shirts (that would send the wrong signal), but her new bra simply gave her a better shape and made her feel sexy. She relaxed into new conversation topics and still felt true to herself.

Madison turned around her date energy and had a serious boyfriend three months later. A great girl like her didn't need any more help than that. When I saw her recently in Los Angeles at a mutual friend's fortieth birthday party, she was glowing. She showed me an engagement ring. The serious boyfriend had proposed and she asked me to be a bridesmaid at her wedding.

Catherine

Catherine is a fifty-one-year-old single working mom from Morristown, NJ, who had two great dates with Bob. She was eager to see him again when he suddenly e-mailed to cancel their next date without explanation. She never heard from him again, despite her three attempts to follow up via e-mail and phone. She was extremely disappointed and perplexed.

I conducted an Exit Interview with Bob six weeks later. He was reluctant to speak with me at first, but our conversation eventually revealed a "fatal incident." He had phoned her a few days prior to their scheduled date to say hello. He told me, "Catherine answered the phone and sounded very flustered. She told me she had a crazy day at work and her live-in, elderly father was sick, so she needed to take his temperature. She also was trying to start dinner for her thirteen-year-old daughter. She said she'd call me back later, but by the time she called it was ten PM and I was asleep. We spoke the next day and had a nice chat, but I realized that I would never be a top priority in Catherine's busy life, so I decided not to pursue a relationship."

When I gave Catherine this feedback, she was very surprised that one little phone call had sabotaged her budding relationship with someone she really liked. She clearly had a different interpretation of the same phone call: Bob had called at a bad moment—she had just walked in the door from work and had ten things going on. She thought it would be best to speak when everything settled down, so she simply asked to call him back later.

Understanding Bob's perception of this phone call made Catherine wonder if he was too needy for attention and thus not the right fit for her anyway. But after I conducted Exit Interviews with four other men whom she'd dated briefly in the past year, I heard similar Busy Bee feedback from three of them. One man noted, "I'm a single parent too—it's hard to balance kids and dating. I actually wouldn't even *like* her if she put me before her daughter." When I asked him how he coped with similar challenges, he said, "I try to finesse my comments so that a woman doesn't feel as though she'll *never* come first. I say, 'This other [issue] isn't more important, but it feels more urgent.'"

Catherine realized that even though she is extremely busy, she needs to remember to make a man feel important in her life too. Especially early on while first impressions are being formed. She could have simply said to Bob on the phone that night, "I'm so glad to hear from you! I'm in the middle of making dinner right now, but can I call you back around ten PM tonight?"

Catherine not only started to edit her phone manner when she spoke to her future dates, but, for example, when a man asked her out for Thursday night and she was busy, she didn't say, "Sorry, that's the night I take my dad to physical therapy, and I can't do Monday night or Wednesday night either because that's when my daughter has soccer practice, and next weekend I have a work conference in Florida, but how about two weeks from Sunday?" Instead, she simply replied, "I'm so sorry, I can't make it Thursday night, but I'd love to go out with you. Let me rearrange some things . . . how about Monday?"

The insight gained from these Exit Interviews helped Catherine retain the right man when he came along four months later. She met a single dad named Steve on YahooPersonals.com, built a strong relationship with him, and I attended their beautiful wedding last summer.

And They Lived Happily Ever After?

These case studies aren't meant to imply that Exit Interviews guarantee an instant wedding. But I *can* guarantee you that Exit Interviews will help you retain the men you want so you can really get to know each other.

CHAPTER 10

So, What Now?

Rachel, help! I have a first date tomorrow with this guy I'm really excited about. We're meeting for coffee at Starbucks, and I need your advice urgently! Since you have all that research from your Exit Interviews, I need to know what I should wear? (Please include detailed shoe information: heels or flats? If heels, one inch or two?) And is it okay to order my usual grande half-caf vanilla latte, no whip/no foam, extra hot? Or better to stick with a simpler drink to appear low-maintenance? What about adding a food item to my order: yes, no, or only something that doesn't crumble? Is it right or wrong to call the server by name? What about leaving a few coins in the tip jar—good or bad? When we get to the condiments bar, should I use the sugar first, or offer it to him? Should I use sugar at all, or select a sugar substitute? AND WHO PAYS? Maybe I should be seated with my drink before he arrives to avoid the payment, ordering, tip, and sugar issues entirely? Please reply ASAP!

This is an actual e-mail I received from a client. I call it The Starbucks Chronicles. The moral of the story: take a deep breath and relax. The goal is to be prepared, not paranoid.

I recently saw an old episode of *Seinfeld*. Elaine had a new boyfriend, and she said, "Dating him is like trying to catch a squirrel—*don't make any sudden movements!*" After reading hundreds of confessions from men about why they didn't call women back, anybody would feel like Elaine. You might be afraid that if you sneeze, blink your eyes "too loudly," glance around for the waiter, or wear a sweater tied around your waist, you will be mistaken for somebody unhygienic, noisy, demanding, or fat.

In the business world, this fear of action is called "analysis paralysis." If you overanalyze every element of a situation, you can be paralyzed with too much information. You literally become unable to make decisions and move forward.

The trick here is just to figure out what your key issues are and be aware of them. You will continue to gauge men's reactions as you keep dating, and you'll adapt along the way.

One Strike Doesn't Mean You're Out

As you consider the impact of this research on your future dates, there is one thing I want to emphasize: despite all the little things that men said rubbed them the wrong way, what they described to me was usually not "one strike and you're out." Remember that stuff built up. A woman said or did one thing that raised a question about her in his mind. Then that question turned into a hypothesis about a negative stereotype (such as The Boss Lady) in his mind, which he set out to prove or disprove. Then he started looking for new pieces of evidence one way or the other.

Sure, a few men reported immediate date-breakers—like Asher with his menu pet peeve about women ordering the same thing he did. Fortunately guys like Asher were the minority in my research (and I doubt you'd want to date them anyway). So it's not when you ask a guy, "Do you have a one- or two-bedroom apartment in

Manhattan?" that he dubs you The Park Avenue Princess. It happens after you ask him three or four or seventeen similar questions, all the while twirling one of your blinding, three-karat diamond stud earrings.

And remember the quote from Dean in Raleigh, NC, in chapter 6? He fell in love with his future wife *despite* the fact that she tripped down the stairs, stepped in dog poop, and ordered three plates of Parmesan cheese, all on their first date.

Seeing the Forest and the Trees

Deciphering date-breakers does not mean getting obsessed with minutiae (like The Starbucks Chronicles). What you need to focus on is identifying which stereotype you most resemble (either mistakenly or deservedly so) in this book. In general, do you think some of your first dates don't lead to second dates because you tend to come across as The Closer? Could that cute guy you had coffee with, but who brushed you off with a "no chemistry" line, secretly have thought you were The Bitch-in-Boots? Do you think the guy you met at that party recently walked away without asking for your number because he thought you were The One-Way Street?

What if you've read through all the anecdotes in this book and honestly answered all the "Sound Familiar?" questions, but you're still not certain which stereotype you most resemble? You'd like to see the forest, but you're stuck in the trees. Then you have two paths: take the Easy Way or the Better Way.

The Easy Way is simply to enlist the help of a few insightful friends and family to guide you. Target anyone who has been with you at a party, in a singles group, or on a double date, and review the stereotypes in this book with them. Ask them about their own observations and interactions with you to determine your predominant stereotype. It may be a little embarrassing, but those who know you best are usually good sounding boards. Make sure to let them know you want the truth, even if it is uncomfortable to hear. Collect their opinions until you have a majority view that "feels right." Remember to be open to the possibility that your stereotype may be something you'll be surprised about.

The Better Way gives you the most accurate picture of what's happening on your dates. Take the plunge and initiate your own personalized Exit Interviews, as described in chapter 8. By enlisting a friend (or a trained professional listed on my website) to call a few of your ex-dates, you can be 100 percent certain which stereotype men are labeling you as. I've seen this enlightening feedback lead to successful dating results again and again. And again.

After verifying the major (and maybe a few minor) stereotypes you might fall under, think about how to minimize that perception of you with the next guy you date. Follow the advice I've listed in your section of the book. The key here is to get rid of any "extremes" that may stereotype you. For example, if you find yourself in The Park Avenue Princess section, here's a basic road map for your next Starbucks date:

→ Wear something casual you feel comfortable in. But avoid too many designer labels and flashy accessories.
→ Use a down-to-earth tone with the server and order a relatively simple drink.
→ Offer to pay with a five-dollar bill, not your gold card. When he chivalrously declines your offer, thank him graciously.
→ If you chip a nail reaching for the sugar, don't start crying.
→ While sipping your beverages, ask genuine "why" questions rather than fact-seeking questions: "Why did you decide to move to Chicago?" instead of "Is your apartment near the Gold Coast?"

And the rest shouldn't really matter. If you follow the above road map but you happen to mention buying your dad a Rolex watch for his birthday, your date will probably consider that a one-off remark (rather than using it as a clue to brand you The Park Avenue Princess) and will call you back for a second date. Then *you* can decide if you want one!

Information is power, whether you're in a business meeting or staring at a handsome stranger over a candlelit dinner. The research in this book should be used as a general guideline, not as a play-by-play instruction manual. Realize that while the first date is a test, it's more like a college essay exam than a true-or-false exam. It helps to be familiar with the issues, but you can't memorize the right answers.

The New Rules

Like it or not, early-stage dating has, and always will be, a game. And in recent years, the game has become more difficult to win, in part because daters are more sophisticated (influenced by more and deeper previous relationships) and because there are infinite players (courtesy of the online dating and social networking frenzy). Sophisticated singles with too many choices are playing with the strategy that someone "more perfect" might be only a mouse-click away. The new rules of this game are to rule out, not rule in. So the object of *your* game should be to pass "Go," collect $200, and land where you can accept or decline the offers you want.

The strategic fumble I see most women make is going out on one first date after the next, sending the same signals over and over again, without learning what went wrong if the last date didn't work out.

This doesn't mean that you need to change your personality. You do not need to highlight your hair, stop succeeding at work, freeze your eggs, alter your core opinions, or find new friends. That's like a joke LA-based comedian Steven Wright tells: "My watch is broken. It's three hours fast. So I think I'll just move to New York." The solution here is to make a simple adjustment, not change your whole life. You need to set the watch, not move to a different time zone. Adjust certain comments and behaviors on your first dates; don't repeat the same ones with different guys. Ultimately, you will be spending more of your valuable time on second dates with the men you want, rather than spending more time on first dates with men you don't want.

The Good Guys Are Out There
(and I Know Because I've Interviewed Them)

It's a bit strange to tuck my three young children into bed at night, to leave my patient husband of sixteen years to fend for himself as the babysitter, and then drive across town with my researcher's notepad to another speed-dating event "for singles twenty-five to thirty-five" (I'm forty-four, by the way). Welcome to my world.

When I was working as a dating coach and writing my first book, not a day went by when I didn't hear women tell me how hard it was to find the right guy. Actually, forget about finding the right guy; they said there were no good men left. The men I heard about were jerks, liars, weirdos, commitment-phobes, or overly eager puppy dogs. I assumed my clients' views were accurate: this was Dating 911! The tactics I advised in my first book were tough tips for the emergency situations women described. And when I decided to write this new book based on interviewing *a thousand single men*, I shuddered. Yeah, I'd get invaluable male perspectives, but could I survive all those hours talking to jerks?

The thing is, something changed for me as I conducted all these Exit Interviews. My pessimistic view changed. Instead of talking to single women every day who told me there were no good men left, I started talking to single men every day who were great. Obviously not *all* of them were great—yes, some were downright horrible, and I've pointed that out a few times in this book—but hundreds and hundreds of wonderful men talked my ear off about all the misfires that were happening on their dates. I talked to so many smart, interesting, warm men who were trying hard to find the right person and be the right person, even through their own past failures. Granted, a phone interview is a different vantage point from being at the table with them on a date like you are, but I was taken aback by their willingness to open up and share their disappointments and hopes.

I truly believe it's not that good guys don't exist, but rather that simple (mis)perceptions—which can be easily fixed—are standing in Cupid's way. It's time to stop accidentally blocking those arrows and reach the fun part: really getting to know someone and creating a fulfilling relationship.

Over the last decade, I have taken the pulse of good single men; they are alive and well! In fact, I even did the math for you: after one thousand interviews, I am 100 percent certain there are a million great men out there wanting to get to know you better on that *second* date.

Notes: A Thousand Splendid Sons

Research Methods and Data Details

For those of you who want to feel my pain, I can tell you that it took me ten years and over three thousand (wo)man-hours to collect, code, and write about the one thousand interviews in this book. Here are the highlights of the research.

TIME FRAME

I conducted my first Exit Interview in 1998. For the next ten years as a dating coach, I offered this service to my private clients (and occasionally to a few friends). My client list multiplied after my first book was published (*Find a Husband After 35: Using What I Learned at Harvard Business School*), and I was able to reach out to more male subjects, one phone call at a time. As the idea for *Why He Didn't Call You Back* came together, I hired three research assistants (two female and one male) and together we revved up our outreach. Approximately 80 percent of the data was collected in 2007 and 2008.

THE SAMPLE GROUP

Though I was trained in statistics and research when studying for my psychology and MBA degrees, I fully acknowledge that this research study is not perfectly scientific. Using the training I have in data collection, limited financial resources, and plain old common sense, I did my best to interview a quantity and range of educated men in a variety of interesting professions (from teaching to investment banking) whom my clients, friends, and readers might be interested in dating. But full disclosure: this data does not include a statistically significant sampling from every male subgroup in the world. So if you're wondering, "Did she interview left-handed lion-tamers from Charleston?" that would be a no. However, here's what I did do:

→ My researchers and I initially contacted over 1,090 single men. Approximately 20% declined to speak to us for various reasons, or didn't return e-mail requests or phone messages. Responses from 19 men were discarded.[1] Ultimately I used interview data from 878 men and then added responses from 122 online interviews to reach my goal of 1,000 men with completed interviews.

→ In total, these 1,000 men discussed 2,374 "no-callback" women, providing 4,152 reasons[2] why they didn't ask for a second date (or in some cases, a third or fourth date). Each man therefore gave an average of 1.7 "primary" reasons per no-callback woman. See Exhibit A for data distribution of all the reasons mentioned in chapters 3 and 4.

→ The men were coded by these details for further analysis:

Age group (21–35: 35%; 36–49: 42%; 50+: 23%)

Geography[3] (East Coast: 32%; West Coast: 26%, West/ Midwest: 26%, South: 14%; International: 2%)

Ethnicity (Caucasian: 76%; African-American: 12%; Hispanic: 8%; Asian: 3%; Other: 1%)

---

[1]Data from 19 interview subjects was discarded because we deemed the men "undesirable." This was a subjective judgment when a man's comments were excessively crude or his behavior was inappropriate during the interview.

[2]"Reason" is defined as why men stated they didn't want another date with one woman. The reason is summarized after a man cites a few specific examples.

[3]Geography was coded using personal judgment (i.e., if someone told me he grew up in Detroit, lived in LA for three years, then moved to New Jersey six years ago, he was coded "East Coast").

Marital Status (Never married: 67%; Divorced: 22%; Separated: 6%; Widowed: 5%)

Marriage-minded[4] (Yes: 78%; No: 12%; No answer/not polled: 10%)

RANGE OF DATA COLLECTION METHODS

I contacted single men in a variety of settings and found them through random intercepts and known contacts (both ex-dates of former clients and single men referred through friends of friends).

→ The majority of the 878 single men interviewed "live" were questioned via telephone. Other venues included speed-dating events, random intercepts (at airport lounges, Starbucks, bookstores, etc.), and other professional matchmakers who interviewed a sampling of their clients on my behalf. Of the telephone interviews, 357 were "proper" Exit Interviews (as described in chapter 8) in which I called three to six men whom *one* woman had dated, looking for individual patterns about why different men didn't call back the same woman. The 521 remaining interviews consisted of asking men to describe one woman (or more) of their choice whom they had not called back for a second date.

→ I used the answers from the first 122 single men who responded via e-mail to postings on Craigslist, where I solicited volunteers for an online dating survey. The ad was posted in early 2008 in four cities (Philadelphia, Austin, Seattle, Minneapolis). The survey was designed to probe specific questions that had surfaced throughout my research. Some of the questions included "What is the ideal job that a woman would have when you are looking for a future mate?"; "What would you like to see a woman wear on a first date, if she's someone with

---

[4]Marriage-minded men were defined as agreeing with the statement "If I met the right woman, I am interested in a committed relationship now."

long-term potential?"; and "How do you prefer women to handle the first-date dinner check?"

PRIVACY

→ Most names and a few identifying personal details have been
changed in this book to protect the privacy of the interview
subjects and my clients.

EXHIBIT A

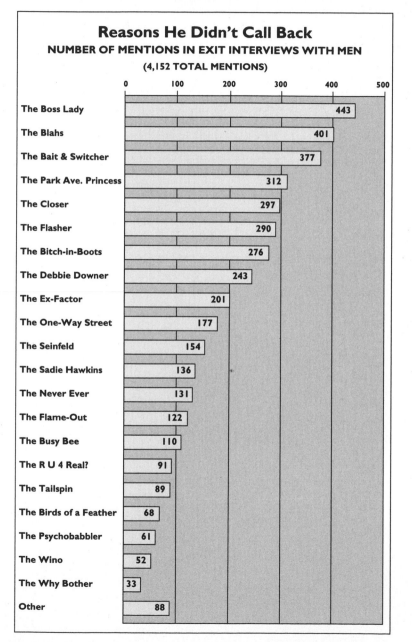

Reasons He Didn't Call Back
NUMBER OF MENTIONS IN EXIT INTERVIEWS WITH MEN
(4,152 TOTAL MENTIONS)

	Mentions
The Boss Lady	443
The Blahs	401
The Bait & Switcher	377
The Park Ave. Princess	312
The Closer	297
The Flasher	290
The Bitch-in-Boots	276
The Debbie Downer	243
The Ex-Factor	201
The One-Way Street	177
The Seinfeld	154
The Sadie Hawkins	136
The Never Ever	131
The Flame-Out	122
The Busy Bee	110
The R U 4 Real?	91
The Tailspin	89
The Birds of a Feather	68
The Psychobabbler	61
The Wino	52
The Why Bother	33
Other	88

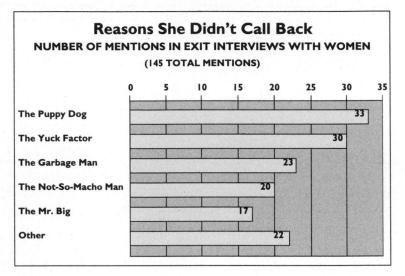

Reasons She Didn't Call Back
NUMBER OF MENTIONS IN EXIT INTERVIEWS WITH WOMEN
(145 TOTAL MENTIONS)

	0	5	10	15	20	25	30	35

The Puppy Dog — 33

The Yuck Factor — 30

The Garbage Man — 23

The Not-So-Macho Man — 20

The Mr. Big — 17

Other — 22

Acknowledgments

A research and writing project spanning ten years involves a lot of people. First and foremost, my ICM literary agent Andrea Barzvi is phenomenal! She believed in the proposal for this book immediately and gave it her all. She went above and beyond at every stage, professionally and personally. Andy is someone every author would want in her corner, and I am one of the extremely lucky people with that privilege. Thanks also at ICM to the eminent Binky Urban, who played a key role in the genesis of this book proposal, and to Josie Freedman, my amazing and über-talented film agent.

A big thank-you to my superstar team at Crown: Suzanne O'Neill (my incredibly supportive and esteemed editor), Lindsey Moore, Tina Constable, Jenny Frost, Heather Proulx, Jill Flaxman, Campbell Wharton, Annsley Rosner, Christine Aronson, Patty Berg, Mary Choteborsky, Tricia Wygal, Alisha Burns, Jacob Bronstein, and Kyle Kolker. And especially to Aja Pollock, my copy editor, an unsung hero, who was meticulous and supersmart.

My research assistants, Shannon, Jonathan, and Ellie, were invaluable, insightful, and tireless in their interview efforts. They were creative in locating a demographically diverse range of single men and dug beneath the surface with their questions.

Sandra Bark, freelance book editor and consultant, was crucial to every aspect of this book: from honing the original proposal, to reorganizing the text, to brainstorming book jacket ideas, to contributing brilliant insights both big and small. She has the whole editorial package: smart, strategic, creative, detail oriented, and funny. I can't imagine ever writing another book without her help.

Everyone should have her own "humor consultant"—both in life and in writing a book. Mine was the witty, sarcastic genius Stephen Abrams. He's sort of a Jerry Seinfeld–meets–Stephen Colbert–meets–Jon Stewart. I can't thank him enough for all his comments and his generosity with his time.

Josh Greenwald, my brother-in-law, deserves all the credit for inventing the "Exit Interview" concept for me so many years ago. He and my sister-in-law, Holly Greenwald, graciously devoted their time to read this manuscript and contribute creative and clever ideas.

Other manuscript readers who generously gave their time and insights include Andrea Bloom, Michelle Burford, Shannon Chafin, Sandy Dugoff, Emma Lewis, Joy Mendez, Stacy Preblud Robinson, Hillary Schubach, and Melanie Sturm. Each one of you added a dimension that made the text richer and more accurate. I am so appreciative!

Several male friends went out of their way to help me with key components of this book, from answering my nosy questions, to playing devil's advocate, to connecting me to intriguing single guys for interviews, to providing feedback on this book jacket or simply by devoting a lot of time to me on the telephone. My sincerest thanks to Kevin Harrang, Bruce Kershenbaum, Howard Levy, Jimmy Lynn, Rob Mintz, Jon Nassif, Larry Pidgeon, Eldar Shafir, and Irwin Shorr.

Several female friends provided unique insights, referrals to single guys, or moral support, for which I am very grateful: Shawn Chereskin, Sue Cooper, Alison Dinn, Marea Evans, Eileen Kershenbaum, Laura Lauder, Wanda Lockwood, Laurie Nassif, Karen Onderko, Jennifer Risher, Emily Sinclair, Beth Vagle, and Elena Weschler.

Colleagues in the dating business lent a helping hand in providing access to or opinions from their single male clients: Lisa Ronis Personal Matchmaking, Kris Kenny Connections, Julie Ferman at Cupid's Coach, and Adele Testani from Hurry Date. A big, big thank-you!

To all the single men and women who generously shared their time, trust, and insights with me: this research wouldn't exist without you. While I may be credited as the author, you are definitely the spirit and the substance of this book.

A sincere thank-you to all the single women who write to my website with questions and who tell their friends about my book. I love hearing from you!

To Starbucks stores from Denver to Barcelona: where else can you sit with your laptop computer and nurse a two-dollar cup of tea for eight uninterrupted hours of writing?

During every step of the publishing process, my mother, Eleanor Hoffman, was my biggest cheerleader, tireless editor, and creative idea generator, while my father, Murray Hoffman, served triple duty as a wise reader, encouraging parent, and devoted family medical consultant.

My children, Max, Gracie, and Oliver: thank you for being so patient with me while I was focused on this book. More than simply being "understanding" all those times I was distracted with this project, you were encouraging and interested in what I was doing. And for that I am most grateful and extremely proud.

To Brad, my wonderful, amazing, and eternally supportive husband: I'm so lucky you called me back!

If you would like information about:

➔ What to do when men don't call back (more tips!)

➔ Resources to conduct your own Exit Interviews

➔ How to submit your personal stories about why **you** didn't call **him** back

➔ How to receive Rachel's free online newsletter

➔ How to arrange for Rachel to speak to your private group

➔ Private dating coaching and matchmaking services

➔ Rachel's story about how she met her husband

. . . please visit www.WhyHeDidntCallYouBack.com